Complexity in Classroom Foreign Language Learning Motivation

SECOND LANGUAGE ACQUISITION

Series Editors: Professor David Singleton, *University of Pannonia, Hungary* and Fellow Emeritus, *Trinity College, Dublin, Ireland* and Dr Simone E. Pfenninger, *University of Zurich, Switzerland*

This series brings together titles dealing with a variety of aspects of language acquisition and processing in situations where a language or languages other than the native language is involved. Second language is thus interpreted in its broadest possible sense. The volumes included in the series all offer in their different ways, on the one hand, exposition and discussion of empirical findings and, on the other, some degree of theoretical reflection. In this latter connection, no particular theoretical stance is privileged in the series; nor is any relevant perspective – sociolinguistic, psycholinguistic, neurolinguistic, etc. – deemed out of place. The intended readership of the series includes final-year undergraduates working on second language acquisition projects, postgraduate students involved in second language acquisition research, and researchers, teachers and policy-makers in general whose interests include a second language acquisition component.

Full details of all the books in this series and of all our other publications can be found on http://www.multilingual-matters.com, or by writing to Multilingual Matters, St Nicholas House, 31–34 High Street, Bristol BS1 2AW, UK.

SECOND LANGUAGE ACQUISITION: 101

Complexity in Classroom Foreign Language Learning Motivation

A Practitioner Perspective from Japan

Richard J. Sampson

MULTILINGUAL MATTERS
Bristol • Buffalo • Toronto

Library of Congress Cataloging in Publication Data
Names: Sampson, Richard J., author.
Title: Complexity in Classroom Foreign Language Learning Motivation: A Practitioner Perspective from Japan/Richard J. Sampson.
Description: Bristol; Buffalo: Multilingual Matters, [2016] |
Series: Second Language Acquisition: 101 | Includes bibliographical references and index.
Identifiers: LCCN 2016004828| ISBN 9781783095889 (hbk : alk. paper) | ISBN 9781783095902 (epub) | ISBN 9781783095919 (kindle)
Subjects: LCSH: Language and languages—Study and teaching—Japanese speakers. | Languages, Modern—Study and teaching—Japan. | Second language acquisition—Japan. | Motivation (Psychology)—Japan. | Teacher-student relationships—Japan. | Japan—Classroom managment.
Classification: LCC P57.J3 S26 2016 | DDC 418.0071/052—dc23 LC record available at https://lccn.loc.gov/2016004828

British Library Cataloguing in Publication Data
A catalogue entry for this book is available from the British Library.

ISBN-13: 978-1-78309-588-9 (hbk)

Multilingual Matters
UK: St Nicholas House, 31-34 High Street, Bristol BS1 2AW, UK.
USA: UTP, 2250 Military Road, Tonawanda, NY 14150, USA.
Canada: UTP, 5201 Dufferin Street, North York, Ontario M3H 5T8, Canada.

Website: www.multilingual-matters.com
Twitter: Multi_Ling_Mat
Facebook: https://www.facebook.com/multilingualmatters
Blog: www.channelviewpublications.wordpress.com

Copyright © 2016 Richard J. Sampson.

All rights reserved. No part of this work may be reproduced in any form or by any means without permission in writing from the publisher.

The policy of Multilingual Matters/Channel View Publications is to use papers that are natural, renewable and recyclable products, made from wood grown in sustainable forests. In the manufacturing process of our books, and to further support our policy, preference is given to printers that have FSC and PEFC Chain of Custody certification. The FSC and/or PEFC logos will appear on those books where full certification has been granted to the printer concerned.

Typeset by Nova Techset Private Limited, Bengaluru & Chennai, India.

Contents

Tables and Figures		ix
Acknowledgements		xi

1	Introduction	1
	Setting the Scene: Misplaced Expectations	2
	'What Have I Been Doing for the Last Five Years?'	3
	For Learners and Teacher: Introducing Research	4
	Complexity in the Classroom	5
	Giving Voice to Motivation	7
	How to Read this Book	9

Part 1: Growth: A Research Narrative

2	Groundings from Foreign Language Learning Motivation Research in Japan	13
	Japanese EFL Learning and (De)motivation	14
	The Influence of Recognition of Relevance and Interest	16
	The Influence of Understandings of an 'English-using Self'	19
	The Influence of Perceptions of Competence	21
	The Influence of Classroom Language Lessons	23
	Moving on	25

3	A Move to Socio-dynamic Motivation	26
	The Theory of Possible Selves	27
	The L2 Motivational Self System	28
	Applications of Possible-self Theory	33
	Moving on	35

4	Research Design	37
	Action Research	38
	Initial Philosophical Considerations	39
	Philosophical Underpinnings of Complex Systems Theory	40
	Action Research and a Complex Systems Philosophy	42

	Design and Context of the Study	45
	Data Collection Methods: Introspective Tools	48
	Data Analysis During the Action Research	50
5	Action Research Narrative	52
	Cycle 1. Sowing Seeds: April	53
	Cycle 2. Tentative Beginnings: April–May	55
	Cycle 3. A Puzzling Outcome: June–September	57
	Cycle 4. Delving Deeper: September–November	61
	Cycle 5. New Directions: December–February	64
	Moving on	68

Part 2: Re-viewing

6	Revisiting Complex Systems Theory	73
	Features of Complex Systems	73
	Approaching Education from a Complex Systems Perspective	77
	Complex Systems Theory in Language Learning	79
	Moving on	82
7	Class Group as Open System	83
	Past Experiences and Initial Ideas of an Ideal Self	86
	Transportable Identities	89
	Absorbed Expectations	96
	Prosaic Contextual Influences	100
	Reflecting on Openness	102
8	Co-adaptation Between Self and Environment	104
	Nested Motivational States Related to English Use	105
	Nested Motivational States Related to Interaction	111
	Nested Motivational States Related to Realisations	116
	Reflecting on Co-adaptation in State Space	123
9	Motivational Phase-shifts and Self-organisation Across the Class Group	126
	Phase-shifts Related to Transitions	126
	Self-organisation: Fostering Communication	133
	Reflecting on Functional Pattern-building: The Self-organising Whole and Parts	137
10	Novel Motivational Emergence in the Class Group	141
	An Emergent Motivational Outcome	143
	Identifying Interactions in the Context of Emergence	145
	Reflecting on Conditions of Emergence During this Project	151

Part 3: Reciprocity

11 The Landscape of Classroom Motivation 157
    Individualised, Dynamic English-using Self Ideas 157
    Complex Systems Theory and the Importance of Interactions
        in Classroom Motivation 164

12 Conclusion and Iteration 170
    What Do Students Gain from EFL Lessons? 170
    Intervening in the Possible-selves of Students 173
    Reflecting on Action Research 177
    Representing Research as Voiced Experience 180
    Future Directions 182
    Iteration 185

Appendix A: Overview of English Course 186
Appendix B: Learning Journal Instructions 187
Appendix C: Outline of Sessions in Action Research Cycles 188
Appendix D: Change-action in Cycle 1 190
Appendix E: Change-action in Cycle 3 192
Appendix F: Change-action in Cycle 4 198
Appendix G: Change-action in Cycle 5 200
Appendix H: Outline of Final Infomercial Project 206

Glossary 208
References 210
Index 225

Tables and Figures

Tables

Table 4.1	Links between different foci of action research (AR) and philosophical underpinnings	40
Table 4.2	Data sources and volume (in A4 pages)	49
Table 5.1	Questionnaire data about other-comparison	59
Table 5.2	Questionnaire data about future English-using self image	60
Table 5.3	Questionnaire data about future English-using self image and connection to present	66
Table 5.4	Questionnaire data about social elements of motivation	67
Table 11.1	Common general qualities of L2-related self ideas of students	159

Figures

Figure 2.1	A visualisation of the use of English at companies where kosen graduates find employment	18
Figure 4.1	Cyclical model of action research	38
Figure 7.1	A *partial* abstraction of open systems related to a classroom learner	84
Figure 7.2	Summary of qualities of students' past experiences of English lessons and initial ideas of a best-possible English self	86

Figure 7.3	An abstraction of the multiple 'external' systems revealed through analysis to be interacting with students' motivation in the classroom	103
Figure 8.1	State space of the L2 Motivational Self System in this class group	106
Figure 8.2	Graph showing the evolution of nested motivational states involving co-adaptation between opportunities for language use and self-ideas	123
Figure 8.3	Graph showing the evolution of nested motivational states involving co-adaptation between opportunities for interaction and self-ideas	124
Figure 8.4	Graph showing the evolution of nested motivational states involving co-adaptation between opportunities for realisations and self-ideas	124
Figure 9.1	Graph showing increase in number of student references to fostering communication in the English classroom	138
Figure 9.2	Multiple threading (Davis & Sumara, 2006) representation of the self-organisation of motivation in the class group towards fostering communication	139
Figure 11.1	A summary of understandings emergent from the current research and their connections to the properties of complex systems	165

Acknowledgements

I would like to express my appreciation to the following people for their assistance and support in the preparation of this book: Kerry Taylor-Leech, Rod Gardner, Mark Freiermuth, Yoshiaki Hachitori, Ema Ushioda, Lourdes Ortega, Elizabeth Stevens, Richard Pinner, Laura Longworth and Steve McGuire. Communication at various points in time had a disproportionately large impact on my motivation in pressing forward with this project.

I would naturally like to note my gratitude towards the student participants with whom I worked over the course of the research reported herein. There would have been nothing to describe without your action and reflection. I wish you all the very best with your future life trajectories.

My deep thanks are due to my family – Junko, Rich Taishi and Lucas Jun. Rather than missing time with you over this research and writing process, all of our constant interactions (including and especially the monster *gokko!*) provided valuable stimulation to think and rethink, and continue writing.

Finally, I wish to extend my gratitude to certain organisations that gave their permission to re-use text from earlier versions of sections of this book appearing in the following articles: 'Complexity theory, action research, and the study of EFL learner motivation' (2011) *OnCUE Journal*, 5 (1), pp. 24–36 (with kind permission of *OnCUE Journal*); 'Tracing motivational emergence in a classroom language learning project' (2015) *System*, 50, pp. 10–20 (with kind permission of Elsevier Science); 'Absorbed expectations about English study of adolescent Japanese students: Insights to the ought-to L2 self' (2015) *The Language Teacher*, 39 (5), pp. 3–8 (with kind permission of JALT Publications).

Richard J. Sampson

1 Introduction

> *Leaving the classroom, I felt uneasy. Puzzled. As a foreign language teacher, there was something nagging me. That said, the students had not given me any overt cause for concern. It was not that they paid little attention. They had not slept, or walked out of the classroom, as I had experienced in extreme cases in the past. We were working through the material on time and on target. Each lesson they participated in the activities I had planned. Yet there was a lack of engagement, a sense of little passion. What was driving, or rather not driving, my students' motivation in the classroom each lesson?*

Classroom foreign language teachers work day in and day out to foster more effective learning environments with students. Part of this quest involves striving to gain a greater understanding of what motivates learners in the classroom. While different theoretical constructs abound, the essence of motivation is that it refers to the direction and magnitude of human behaviour, that is, why, how long, and how hard people try to do something (Dörnyei, 2001: 7). It is a *want* towards future action. My own interest in classroom motivation has emerged from a range of experiences teaching English as a foreign language (EFL) in Japan over the past 17 years. In some settings, students have professed a wish to study 'authentic', communicative oral English for travel or business. Yet while they seem to have a clear-cut purpose to their studies and are active during our time together, individual students' drive to conduct additional study outside lessons has varied greatly. In other situations, students have had very little in the way of opportunities to use English in their everyday lives. Nevertheless, students (and teachers) have together enriched the class atmosphere, the class motivation, with their enthusiasm in using basic English to carry out tasks and interactive activities.

This book presents my own journey in working to conceptualise the complex and dynamic interactions that influence the evolution of the motivation of a language class group. It describes the processes of action research through which I came to understand classroom language learning motivation as emerging from constantly changing relations between elements of the classroom system and the experiences and perceptions of class members, and why this matters. Following the work of such scholars as Miyahara (2015) and Takahashi (2013), the book also aims to lend support to a more narrative-based and situated approach to representing the insights gained through listening to the voices of those involved in additional language learning.

Setting the Scene: Misplaced Expectations

Just before commencing the research project that forms the basis of this book, I had gained full-time employment at a *kosen*, a Japanese National College of Technology. These colleges combine the traditional three years of senior-high school in Japan with the first two years of university. Students range from around 15 to 20 years old. The institutions specialise in producing young technologists who are ready to apply their knowledge and skills on graduation. English studies are part of a compulsory set of subjects. One of my primary motivations for seeking employment at a kosen had been my belief that the style of education would be very practical, with students learning by doing. I predicted that the clear focus of the kosen system on future outcomes – producing practical, work-ready technologists – would encourage students and teachers to be cognisant of how graduates might use English in the future in a variety of engineering fields.

My expectations turned out to be overly simplistic. Many of the students I was teaching seemed disinterested and lacking direction in their English studies. Such a decrease in motivation – termed *demotivation* – is something not uncommon in Japanese classrooms (e.g. Carpenter *et al.*, 2009; Kikuchi & Sakai, 2009; see also Chapter 2). The students' apparent aimlessness reminded me of research I had conducted previously at a women's university (Sampson, 2012). While in that case the English-major learners had been engaged during lessons, conversations with them revealed very little about how they imagined themselves using English after the completion of their studies. An apparent lack of purpose and ownership of their learning puzzled me as I worked with them each lesson. I therefore decided to introduce a range of classroom activities designed to encourage them to think about their future using English. The study found students to be motivated by activities which: (a) assisted them in thinking about steps they could take towards an ideal self using English; (b) allowed them to add detail to this ideal or a feared self; and (c) had a social component encouraging them to share reflections about their (future) self ideas.

Influenced by my experiences at the women's university, my perceptions of demotivation in kosen classrooms prompted me to ask learners to reflect on their English studies. I decided to encourage students in five of my classes (18- to 19-year-old students) to write freely about why they believed they were currently studying English, and in what ways they envisioned themselves using English in the future. My concerns deepened. Responses to the first question were ultimately rather vague: words like 'globalisation', 'world language' and 'international language' were recurrently representative. Furthermore, students expressed no clear purpose for the activities they might undertake using English in the future, giving responses such as:

- 'Read something in English' (Japanese response)
- 'Listen a news' (English response)
- 'Do conversation' (Japanese response)
- 'I don't know' (Japanese response)

Although these students had been studying for a number of years at this college, their reactions indicated a disturbing lack of understanding of the purpose of their English studies in the classroom. A conversation with one of these students further motivated me in the research project that is the focus of this book.

'What Have I Been Doing for the Last Five Years?'

Nineteen-year-old *Hiroki* (a pseudonym) had just returned from an overseas exchange trip, his first visit to a country where English is spoken. Arriving unexpectedly at my office, he talked enthusiastically about how much he had enjoyed his experience abroad and how it had given him a new perspective on English. Yet at one point in our discussion his expression changed; he stared into the middle distance and seemed to be struggling with his emotions. 'You seem upset', I offered. 'Is there a problem?' Hiroki leaned forward and spoke intently:

> 'At first I thought I would be hopeless', he told me, 'but then I just thought I'd give it a try. I said something in English to another student. He understood me! And not only that, he told me his ideas. And I *understood*!' Hiroki's surprise and pleasure at this successful encounter were almost equally balanced by his sense of frustration: 'Here at school', he confided urgently, 'I just sat in English lessons, but I didn't *realise* ... I didn't know how I could use English ... if only I'd studied more ... if only I'd *known* before ... there was so much more I wanted to say, so much more I wanted to understand ... *what have I been doing for the last five years?*'

What had started as an interesting, though not unprecedented, exchange about a student's first experiences abroad turned into a deeply moving interaction that pushed me to reconsider my own actions as a classroom teacher. Hiroki's remarks clearly revealed a lack of practice in using English communicatively in his experiences in formal education; his initial expectations of his near-future were that he 'would be hopeless' in trying to communicate. However, when he at last had such an opportunity – provided not in his regular college environment but as part of a study-abroad programme – he was able to experience success and realised that English might be useful as a communication tool. His words and posture gave a sense of his motivation soaring at this newfound realisation. Yet I could also sense all too clearly his bitter disappointment as he reflected on his perception of lost opportunities in his past classroom English learning. Devastatingly, from Hiroki's perspective, his realisations about using English and resultant motivation came five years too late. He could not get back those five years in the classroom.

Hiroki's experience is perhaps not all that unusual for many around the world, for whom foreign language learning first and foremost involves study in the formal education system. While learners might ideally elect to study a particular foreign language, in many cases study is part of an additional language requirement. Yet Hiroki again reminded me that without any clear idea of how time spent in the classroom studying language connects to the possibility of *using* the language, learners may well 'just sit in lessons'. After all, what is the point? For learners like Hiroki, not majoring in English yet studying it as a required classroom subject in an environment in which it is not the main language, English might at times seem quite irrelevant to both their current and their future lives. The specific purposes for which policy makers, administrators and teachers assume that learners are studying English may indeed not be all that visible to the students themselves.

For Learners and Teacher: Introducing Research

Starting from such considerations, this book focuses on a research project that aimed to gain a deeper picture of the lived experience of the classroom motivation of adolescent language learners studying EFL as a compulsory subject. As a teacher-researcher, I wanted to work to create more purposeful English lessons with my students while at the same time endeavouring to understand their motivation in the classroom. The trigger for the research was my puzzlement at a gap between the fact that my students were highly likely to need English in their future careers (*Koseneigo kenkyuuiinkai*, 2008; see Chapter 2), and what I perceived as a common lack of interest and direction in their English studies in the classroom. Simply put, I faced some perennial pedagogical problems. Why were many of my students apparently demotivated in the classroom? What relevance was there in their learning of English? What were their ideas of themselves as future users of English? Indeed, had anyone ever asked them? How could I engage my students more actively in the classroom in envisioning themselves as future English users and investing more fully in their long-term English learning?

These and similar questions provided my own motivation for embarking on an investigation of the motivational development of students who had just entered the college. My experiences with older students at the college as well as my conversation with Hiroki gave me the impression that there could be a great opportunity in catching students at an earlier stage and encouraging them to reflect on the meaning of their English studies. At 15–16 years of age, these young adolescents transition from junior-high school at a time of life when they are developing numerous new self-descriptions and motivations based on different perceived roles, relationships with peers and a growing capacity for reflection on the function of their learning tasks (Harter, 2003; Wentzel, 2005; Wigfield & Wagner, 2005). I was scheduled to be both a homeroom teacher for one class of first-grade students – meeting once a week as an advisor for their studies and conveyor of administrative information from the college – as well as their English teacher for one of three weekly English lessons. These roles presented an ideal opportunity to undertake classroom research that could enhance the students' understanding about language learning and self at this pivotal stage in their educational journey, with the added bonus of bringing interest to lessons and furthering my own understandings of my students and what drove their motivation for learning English.

Based on these foundations, the project had three aims: (i) to gain a clearer picture of the ways in which self-concept affects language learner motivation; (ii) to explore the ways in which teacher-instigated change-action might affect students' motivation; and (iii) to generate a more complex, holistic understanding of dynamic motivation in the class group. Considering my interest in self-concept and motivation, I found Dörnyei's (2009a) L2 Motivational Self System to offer a useful starting point to conceptualise the motivation of my learners (see also Chapter 3). Moreover, with my intention to introduce activities encouraging students to reflect on their understandings of self and motivation related to English learning and their future, I applied an action research design in order to pursue the development of new knowledge and change in my classroom (Dick, 2000). The action research involved five cycles, focusing on students' experiences in their weekly English lessons as well as additional homeroom sessions over the year that we were together as a group. I develop these ideas further in Chapters 4 and 5.

Complexity in the Classroom

To jump ahead slightly, this book draws on my experiences and the understandings that evolved during this research project to illustrate how the motivation of classroom foreign language learners might be profitably conceptualised through the images, metaphoric tools and theoretical underpinnings that complex systems theory offers. My work comes at a time when complex systems theory and related approaches such as dynamic systems theory are beginning to gain increasing attention in the field of language learning motivation (e.g. Dörnyei *et al.*, 2015a) and applied linguistics in general (e.g. Larsen-Freeman & Cameron, 2008a). I did not, however, set out to understand classroom motivation from a complex systems perspective. Over the course of the research I became increasingly aware of the usefulness of this theory in making sense of my experiences. As such, I will introduce complex systems theory in more detail in later chapters. Nevertheless, I feel it necessary at this point to give the reader some idea of what complex systems involve.

In the scientific field there are considered to be three types of systems – simple, complicated and complex. *Simple systems* involve a small number of similar components which are connected and interact with each other in a predictable and unchanging fashion (Weaver, 1948). Systems of this type include trajectories and collisions. *Complicated systems* are used with statistical and probability mathematics. Complicated systems may involve thousands or millions of components, but again the components and interactions between components do not change. Complicated systems are considered to be predictable because 'the system as a whole possesses certain orderly and analysable *average* properties' (Weaver, 1948: 538; emphasis added). Examples of this type of system include molecular interactions or astronomical phenomena. Both simple and complicated systems share a mechanical construction; they can be dismantled and put together again with the same function.

However, the third kind of system, a *complex system*, cannot be dismantled and reconstructed in such a way. In Mitchell's (2009: 13) definition, a complex system is one 'in which large networks of components with no central control and simple rules of operation give rise to complex collective behaviour, sophisticated information processing, and adaptation via learning or evolution'. Although it is understood that at times such systems involve fewer components than a complicated system, they reveal what Weaver (1948: 539) terms 'organised complexity'. The interactions between components in these systems are not orderly and the components themselves change through mutual co-adaptation, whereby the components make adaptations based on the actions of other components. The system becomes an organised whole because of these interactions, and attempting to dismantle it would remove co-specifying elements that produce the organic whole. The study of such systems, known as complex systems theory, attempts to 'account for how the interacting parts of a complex system give rise to the system's collective behaviour and how such a system simultaneously interacts with its environment' (Larsen-Freeman & Cameron, 2008a: 1). Examples of this kind of system include ecologies, cities or economies.

While this may sound rather far removed from the context of this book, let us return to considering the classroom. A class group is made up of individual teachers and learners. These members bring their own dynamic understandings of the relevance, purpose and form of study to the foreign language classroom. Moreover, these learners and their teachers bring with them their own personal histories and experiences, influences from those around them and in society, and indeed influences from what happens before or will happen after the lesson. Some of these influences may relate directly to language learning, such as a past encounter with a user of the language. Others may appear to have little connection with their study. These individuals come together at set points in time in a particular location to form a group focused around a specific learning domain, but they are not bounded purely by the temporal, physical or psychic constraints of the classroom (van Lier, 2004: 194). They are *real* human beings in dynamic interrelation with other *real* human beings and the social context of which they are a part.

In the classroom, these individuals interact together to co-form the language learning class group. That is, members and their interactions form the social context of the classroom. This jointly created social context feeds back iteratively to influence the forms of behaviour and understanding of the individuals making up the group. While teachers may endeavour to create opportunities for learning, the direction and quality of learning is ultimately co-formed with and between all the members of the class group. It is also influenced by interactions between members' pasts, presents and futures. Students' motivation to engage in learning emerges and dynamically ebbs and flows, as a confluence of these elements comes together across different timescales in the classroom. I would like to argue that these are the kinds of experiences to which many involved with foreign language classrooms can relate. Such ideas have also been proposed in the theoretical literature about classroom language learning (see, in particular, the work of Ushioda). My intention in this book is to work to show how some of the key complex systems theory constructs can be located and applied usefully to understanding the dynamic life and motivation of (the members of) a language learning class group.

Giving Voice to Motivation

While motivation has frequently been recognised as a key aspect of additional language learning, there has been a preponderance of large-scale quantitative research conducted. Much work has centred on the development of general theories of motivation rather than exploring practical approaches to motivation in the classroom (Lasagabaster *et al.*, 2014). Through this book I aim to show that investigations of classroom motivation can gain a lot from allowing human members to relate their own dynamic perceptions of motivation in these spaces. Complex systems theory posits a vital interaction between the learner and the environment that makes accounts in specific contexts crucial to gaining insights into the development of motivation. In Ushioda's (2015: 48) words, 'learners are not simply located in particular contexts, but inseparably constitute part of these contexts' such that they 'shape and are shaped by context'. How do students negotiate and alter their forms of behaviour through transitions to new learning environments and work groups? What colours of the life experiences of an individual suddenly spur a student into life from some trigger in the classroom? How do students perceive and act on comparisons with others in the learning group? How do the future self-concepts of learners dynamically develop as they interact in the classroom? And, importantly, in what ways do these perceptions and actions shape the trajectory of motivation in the whole class group? I believe that the voices of the members that come together in a classroom can lend a vital richness to descriptions of the experience of formal foreign language learning.

While the primary focus of the book is on the motivation of the student participants in a language learning class group, complex systems theory would also urge that the observer (in this case myself as teacher/researcher/author) should be very much part of the system being studied. In representing this research project and the understandings at which I arrived, I have struggled with two conflicting constraints on its presentation. On the one hand, a research monograph needs to provide stand-alone chapters to which the reader can come, 'dip in', and find something useful without having to read from page one. In many senses, it presents a 'tidied up' version of events written by the researcher-as-accomplished-expert, emphasising findings over process. On the other hand, there is a need for descriptions of classroom-based, practitioner-led studies. Such literature might encourage teachers to become more agentic (rather than passive recipients) in the development of educational theories of classroom practice and learning (Burns, 2005; Dörnyei, 2007). My experience in this research process was emergent and highly contextually contingent. I worked together with students to challenge existing understandings and move towards outcomes considered more beneficial by those in the classroom. It was an additional part of my constant attempt as a practitioner to make sense of experiences in the classroom and to develop as a teacher. All too often the researcher is 'written out' of representations of research. As will become apparent, through my interactions with the class group in the particular context of the research project reported in this book, the emergent possibilities of the group were altered. Such a mutual dependence between the observer and the observed is reflected in a complexity philosophy. As Davis and Sumara argue:

> Complexity thinking compels researchers to consider how they are implicated in the phenomena that they study – and, more broadly, to acknowledge that their descriptions of the world exist in complex (i.e. nested, co-implicated, ambiguously bounded, dynamic, etc.) relationship with the world. (Davis & Sumara, 2006: 15)

In the pages that follow I therefore aim to provide a detailed account of not only the understandings at which I arrived, but also a narrative of the lived experience through which these understandings evolved. This work reflects a growing call in the field of second language acquisition (SLA) for renderings of research as a *situated process* from the point of view of those in the classroom (Ushioda, 2013a).

In the study presented in this book, I focus on the specific context of one language learning class, including myself as part of this group. The themes that emerge are based on my experiences from an emic perspective as one of the participants in this class group. As such, they are limited to being the subjective understandings and interpretations of one teacher-researcher. From a complex systems perspective, while we may be able to uncover tendencies or patterns for specific systems, these understandings are applicable only to the particular system and timescales observed (Larsen-Freeman & Cameron, 2008a). We cannot claim universal generalisability, nor the related prediction of similar outcomes for other systems. However, classroom foreign language learning is an experience shared by many, as both student and in some cases teacher or researcher. Indeed, such is the spread of EFL study as a core part of educational curricula in various contexts worldwide that some contend that it is becoming a fundamental educational skill much like literacy and numeracy (Graddol, 2006). By endeavouring to give sufficient detail about the context and nature of the research introduced, and providing a rich and detailed representation of the development of motivation in this context, I attempt to ensure that readers involved in other classroom foreign language learning situations may find the insights useful in their particular circumstances (Edge & Richards, 1998; Lincoln & Guba, 1985).

How to Read this Book

Reflecting my stance that it is vital to push for representations of research detailing both outcomes and process, this book is broadly split into three interconnected parts. Part 1 (成長 – *seichou* – growth) involves a narrative account of the groundings for the research (Chapters 2 and 3) and my decision making in setting up and carrying out the action research study (Chapters 4 and 5). Part 2 (再見 – *saiken* – re-view) builds on these groundings to introduce complex systems theory (Chapter 6) and explicate how this framework threw new light on my understandings (Chapters 7–10). Finally, Part 3 (相互 – *sougo* – reciprocity) offers a set of possibilities for theorising motivation emergent from the study (Chapter 11) and concludes with implications for classroom pedagogical practice and research methodology (Chapter 12). Through the narrative of my experiences I hope to show not only that this research came from somewhere, but also that it is connected with, grounded in and affects a wider network of knowledge.

In delineating these three parts, I aim to allow readers to adopt different pathways through the book. Some readers may wish to follow the narrative thread of my experiences by reading the three parts sequentially. Others may choose to progress more selectively, for example by reading the summary of the study in this Introduction and then jumping to Part 2, or finding those chapters in which they are especially interested.

Part 1
成長
Growth: A Research Narrative

2 Groundings from Foreign Language Learning Motivation Research in Japan

Like it or not, the majority of schooling involves the study of subjects chosen not by students themselves, but dictated by what a particular society deems to be necessary. In classrooms in which learners are studying such required subject areas, the selection of content and tasks presented may be far removed from activities on which students actually wish to spend their time. Although some argue that children are naturally imbued with a curiosity and motivation to learn about the world around them (e.g. Kohn, 1993), students can experience increasing discord as they move upwards through the grades of schooling, as required study loses its self-apparent relevance to the day-to-day world they see around them. Yet, as the content is *required*, learners somehow need to gain the motivation to engage with it and develop their knowledge or skills in line with society's expectations.

As introduced in Chapter 1, in Dörnyei's (2001: 7) well-known definition, *motivation* relates to the direction and magnitude of human behaviour, that is, why, how long, and how hard people try to do something. Dörnyei (2009b: 209) adds that 'motivation refers to a cumulative arousal, or want, that we are aware of'. In general, this book will apply the definition of motivation as a 'want' towards action. Borrowing from Brophy's (1998) concept of 'motivation to learn', motivation in the classroom therefore entails the volition to act and develop one's capacities through the content and activities presented. My understanding of classroom motivation also draws on that of Ushioda (2001: 96), who argues that 'as a qualitative variable ... motivation may be defined not in terms of observable and measurable activity, but rather in terms of what patterns of thinking and belief underlie such activity and shape students' engagement in the learning process'. Chapter 3 will expand on the specific framework of motivation utilised in the empirical study reported later. The current chapter focuses on some of the pivotal literature from Japan that influenced the selection of this motivational framework and the trajectory of my study. The chapter aims to provide a contextualised overview of classroom EFL motivation in Japan. However, readers will no doubt find issues of relevance across different contexts of formal foreign language learning. The chapter begins with a brief discussion of EFL learning in Japanese schools, before providing an extended examination of the past research literature about situated influences on motivation and engagement in the EFL classroom that informed my research.

Japanese EFL Learning and (De)motivation

In Japan, despite a range of other languages spoken and the study of EFL in schools, the Japanese language is given special prominence, as evidenced in the use of 国語 (*kokugo* – national language) for its denotation. As Gottlieb (2005: 18) remarks, Japanese 'has never faced the struggle for dominance against the language of a colonizing power we find in other parts of Asia … there has been no other contender for the status of national language'. Against this backdrop, when Japanese education was essentially reborn in the Meiji period (from around 1870) to compete in an industrialising world, English classes were introduced for the practical purpose of developing human resources able to absorb textual information from abroad (Butler & Iino, 2005). By the early 2000s, foreign language education, almost invariably English, had become a required subject at junior- and senior-high school (MEXT, 2003).

At first glance, it may well appear that Japan has a fascination with the idea of 'English' that might seem to suggest motivated learners of the language (McVeigh, 2002). Scholars in various fields show that 'English, in some form or at some symbolic level has … become a significant part of everyday life in Japan' (Seargeant, 2011a: 3): English-language advertising signs are visible wherever one moves (Backhaus, 2007; Seargeant, 2011b); English loanwords are increasing in the Japanese lexicon (Stanlaw, 2004; Yano, 2011); and J-Pop (Japanese Pop) music frequently incorporates English lyrics into the Japanese. In the formal education system, Japanese learners study English in one form or another from elementary school through to the last grade of high school. If students wish to attend university, they then take entrance examinations which include, in almost all cases, an English component. These young people then continue to study English for the first two years of university, regardless of their specialisation (Aspinall, 2003).

Despite the strong presence of English in the linguistic landscape of Japan which might suggest otherwise, studies of the motivation of Japanese EFL learners frequently note a disturbing decrease in engagement after students commence formal English studies from junior-high school. Students' drive towards English study in many cases appears to gradually decelerate across their years of adolescence. Such decreases in existing motivation are termed *demotivation* – defined here as 'various negative influences that cancel out existing motivation' (Dörnyei & Ushioda, 2011: 138). A related yet qualitatively different concept is that of *amotivation*, a state of no motivation or intention to act. Amotivated people either do not act in the domain in question (such as language learning), or act passively and 'go through the motions with no intention to do what they are doing' (Ryan & Deci, 2002: 17).

A number of studies have found demotivation among secondary and tertiary EFL students in Japan to be particularly widespread (e.g. Carpenter *et al.*, 2009; Falout & Maruyama, 2004; Hasegawa, 2004; Kikuchi & Sakai, 2009; Kimura *et al.*, 2001). For instance, the study by Hasegawa (2004) used a questionnaire to examine the time span and degree of this demotivation by asking 223 students at junior- and senior-high schools about their English lessons. The study found that 71% of the junior-high and 77% of senior-high school students reported EFL demotivation. The trend is further reflected in studies at the tertiary level. In one example, Falout and Maruyama (2004) conducted a survey with 164 non-EFL major university students, asking about their secondary school English study. Results revealed that over 70% of both students with high and low English proficiency reported having been demotivated in their past English studies, with Kikuchi and Sakai (2009) finding that even university students majoring in courses related to English reported demotivation during their secondary years.

Taking into account the context of the research reported in this book, a longitudinal study by Kunishige *et al.* (2011) also shows a broad pattern of demotivation towards EFL learning for many students over their time at colleges of technology in Japan. Kunishige *et al.* (2011) followed two cohorts of students from first grade to fourth grade, asking learners to respond to questionnaires about their motivation and attitudes towards English learning. There was a sharp drop in the number of students who studied English outside lessons in the second grade; by the fourth grade the number who studied English outside class was about equal to the number who stated they did not study English at all of their own accord (Kunishige *et al.*, 2011: 18).

Clearly, adolescent Japanese students lacking a sense of direction in their English learning is far from an unusual phenomenon. Research studies overall identify an evident lack of engagement and enthusiasm for English learning for many Japanese students. Indeed, the extent of the literature regarding demotivation in this context leads Dörnyei and Ushioda (2011: 150) to suggest that 'in Japan ... demotivation among learners of English seems to be a major educational concern'. So what affects the development of this perplexing state of affairs? What are some of the critical influences on the motivation and demotivation of learners in this context?

The Influence of Recognition of Relevance and Interest

During adolescence, there are a number of important changes that occur both developmentally and contextually that mean the perceived relevance of learning may impact on motivation in the classroom. At this time of life, adolescents are attempting to create a coherent sense of self that involves in part the exploration of life aspirations in education and occupation (Wigfield & Wagner, 2005). However, as mentioned in the introduction to this chapter, transitions in the schooling context often engender more de-personalised learning and a focus on increasingly abstract educational content. At this stage of education, rationales for learning take on additional importance. Through communicating why effort on classroom activities would be a worthwhile investment for learners, rationales have been found to significantly facilitate engagement and motivation by increasing students' sense of the personal relevance of study (Jang, 2008; Reeve & Jang, 2006; Reeve et al., 2002).

A learner-internal recognition of the relevance of study has also frequently been included as an influential factor in Japanese students' interest in learning. Indeed, the importance of this connection can be observed in a definition of *interest* by Renninger et al. (2008: 463), in which they state that: 'Interest is identified based on a learner's feelings, principled knowledge, and *value for particular domain content* [relevance], and evolves over time through interaction with the others and objects/activities in the environment' (emphasis added).

Research shows a clear link between demotivation and lack of interest in EFL study across a range of schooling contexts in Japan. For example, in the senior-high school setting, Sakai and Kikuchi (2009) used a questionnaire with 656 Japanese students, finding that very low motivation was strongly linked to not understanding the purpose of studying English and having little interest in the subject. These results are supported in research by Carpenter et al. (2009: 263), who invited 285 university students studying a variety of majors to reflect on what demotivated them in their EFL studies. The results of analysis of the questionnaire found that 7% of their respondents linked lack of interest in and relevance of EFL study to demotivation during their years in both junior- and senior-high school.

In this area, however, two studies reveal vital insights into the effects of relevance of English study on students' motivation and actions in the classroom. Responses to a questionnaire by Agawa et al. (2011: 13) in a university setting uncovered amotivation, in which the participants noted 'no interest in foreign languages, cultures or people' and 'not understanding for what purpose English is being studied' (my translation). The crucial finding was that this amotivation moreover correlated with an aversion to making an effort, resistance to vocabulary and grammar study, and anxiety about using English (Agawa *et al.*, 2011: 11). These insights led the authors to urge that 'for English learners who have lost all motivation, it is strongly desirable to include teaching about how students can connect English lessons to learning for themselves' (Agawa *et al.*, 2011: 14; my translation). Although the study by Agawa and associates groups together interest and the relevance of learning, a questionnaire study conducted by Yashima (2000: 131) with 372 first-year university students who were not majoring in English more explicitly revealed that a factor labelled as a 'vague sense of necessity' to learn English had no correlation with motivation or English proficiency. As Yashima (2000: 131) observed:

> For many students English is an academic subject which they have been encouraged to study without having a clear objective. They feel it will become a necessity to use English in the 'internationalized' society, but they do not have a clear idea of how they are going to use it.

The literature suggests the perceived relevance of English study to be an integral influence on the motivation of Japanese students. Sitting in classrooms week in and week out as part of a set of compulsory subjects, many learners may have only a vague idea of the purpose of their EFL studies and be uncertain as to how they might use English in the future. This research begs a simple but challenging question related to the relevance of EFL study in this context: the question of whether Japanese students really need English.

Is there a need for English in Japan?

As I remarked in Chapter 1, in an era of globalisation, international data suggest English to be increasingly considered a basic educational skill much like literacy and numeracy (Graddol, 2006). Indeed, a range of actions by various educational institutions seems to imply a similar conclusion that for the majority of the Japanese population English is a fundamental skill. For instance, the Japanese Ministry of Education, Culture, Sports, Science and Technology (MEXT) pushes schools to foster the development of young Japanese people who can practically communicate in English (MEXT, 2002, 2003). In parallel, there exist myriad private English conversation schools known as *eikaiwagakkou* (英会話学校) which promote 'real' English communication through 'authentic interaction' with non-Japanese (in most cases Western) English speakers. Moreover, universities in Japan are increasingly creating courses advertised as preparing students to use communicative English, drawing on a mindset of 'globalisation-as-opportunity' (Yamagami & Tollefson, 2011). However, for the average Japanese person there is little to no use of English in day-to-day life in Japan. For some, this stated need and consequent policy formation is seen as having been overemphasised by the demands of industry and corporations (Mizuno, 2008). Indeed, Kubota's (2011; see also Kubota & McKay, 2009) research suggests there is little evidence for the exclusive need for English in occupational settings in Japan in general. Kubota (2011: 106) concludes that there is 'a gap between the discourse that elevates English as an essential language and the actual demands'.

Considering the particular educational context of the research reported in this book, however, investigations from the science and technology setting of kosen suggest that it is also too strong to claim that *no* need exists. Rather, the requirement for English abilities may depend on the occupational sector in which learners hope to gain employment. In two nationwide studies conducted by a kosen-based group (*Koseneigo kenkyuuiinkai*, 2001, 2008), the researchers used surveys to gain a picture of expectations about English recognised by a variety of kosen stakeholders. On the one hand, the results revealed that English teachers at these colleges of technology and teachers at universities place more emphasis on reading, vocabulary and grammar than on other English skills (*Koseneigo kenkyuuiinkai*, 2008: 16, 38). The focus on these skills may reflect a need for kosen graduates continuing on to university to read English literature related to their research specialisation. On the other hand, managers at 273 companies at which kosen graduates find employment also noted various practical, communicative needs for English depending on the size of the company. In smaller companies English was not

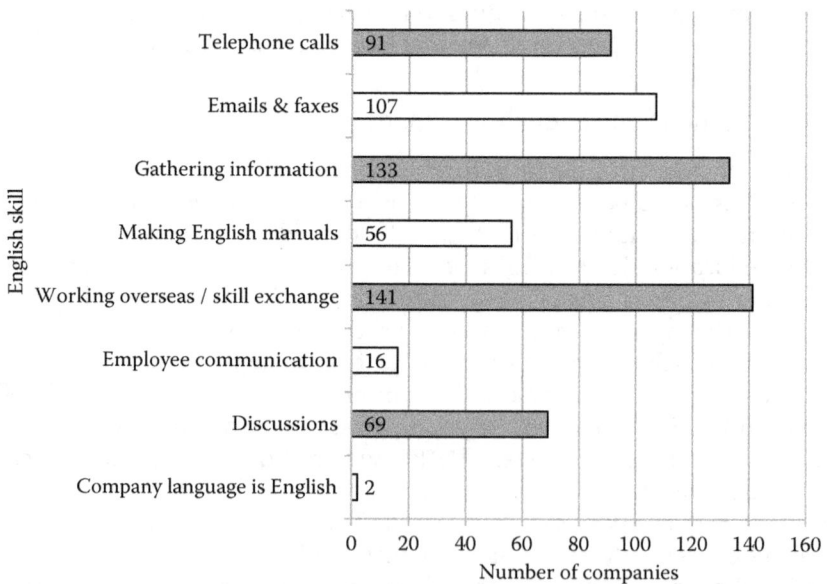

Figure 2.1 A visualisation of the use of English at companies where kosen graduates find employment
Source: Adapted by the author from *Koseneigo kenkyuuiinkai* (2008: 29).

considered important. However, there was a gradual increase in the need for English in companies of between 51 to over 500 employees (*Koseneigo kenkyuuiinkai*, 2008: 28). This necessity was furthermore dependent on the particular section of a company to which an employee was attached (*Koseneigo kenkyuuiinkai*, 2008: 27). The domains in which English is used, according to these managers, are displayed in Figure 2.1.

These findings from the kosen setting revealing the academic and occupational needs for English use are both informative yet also puzzling. As there is a need for English in the future of kosen graduates, the results certainly indicate the relevance of English study. However, one major limitation of the *Koseneigo kenkyuuiinkai* (2008) study is that it only illustrates the understandings of kosen teachers, university academics and company managers. One essential missing group of stakeholders is the learners themselves. In Chapter 1 I introduced my perceptions of learners in my kosen classrooms. There seems to be a glaring gap between the recognition by teachers and company managers of a need for English, and what my initial enquiries with students revealed of their understandings of a future 'English-using self'.

The Influence of Understandings of an 'English-using Self'

As introduced in the previous section, for learners, adolescence is a time of vital reflection on ideas of self and identity. As many writers attest, although it is difficult to arrive at a definition of 'self' upon which all will agree, the self is in some form or other involved in 'people's experience of themselves ... their perceptions, thoughts, and feelings about themselves ... and their deliberate efforts to regulate their own behaviour' (Leary & Tangney, 2003: 8). The self is our reflexive conceptualisation of the person that we are, including out past and future ideas. It makes sense then that such a concept fundamental to the experience of being human would play a part in motivation towards additional language learning.

The work of Yashima (2000, 2002, 2009) has been integral to revealing the importance of learner understandings of an English-using self for motivation in the Japanese context. Yashima's (2000) early research uncovered the idea that some learners identified instrumental reasons, such as studying abroad or the benefits of English for a future career, as most important for their English learning. These factors moreover strongly correlated with motivation. Yashima's results were further confirmed in a later study (Yashima, 2002), in which she examined the relationships between willingness to communicate and motivation, using a questionnaire with 297 Japanese university students. The analysis augmented her previous findings by showing that the largest influence on motivation was a factor that she termed 'international posture' (Yashima, 2002: 61). Yashima (2009: 146) later defined this concept as 'a tendency to see oneself as connected to the international community, have concerns for international affairs and possess a readiness to interact with people other than Japanese'. That is, students' ideas or images of a self, connected to and interacting internationally, affected their motivation.

A study by Ryan (2009a) supports Yashima's assertion that the way in which Japanese EFL learners 'see themselves' using English in their future influences motivation. Ryan examined this area of self-concept with 2397 students from secondary and tertiary institutions, collecting a questionnaire about motivation and demotivation. Ryan's results are truly insightful as they add additional detail to the qualities of an imagined English-using community for Japanese learners, finding that:

> Learners of English in Japan regard the notion of an English-speaking community freed from the ties of nationality and locality to be a more powerful motivating factor ... because it presents to learners the possibility of legitimate, full membership of that community. (Ryan, 2009a: 131)

A retrospective study by Miura (2010) also hints at the importance of future ideas of self for EFL study. He asked 196 university students about the dynamics of their motivation towards English learning. Miura (2010) found a difference in the ways in which learners with different English proficiencies focused their motivation: while students with lower English proficiency targeted short-term goals such as passing an upcoming test or earning a credit, those with higher English proficiency focused on longer term goals such as their future career. These findings led Miura (2010: 49) to argue that 'having distant future goals that go beyond passing a university entrance examination is important for sustaining the long-term learning motivation that leads to higher levels of foreign language proficiency'.

Moving on to the context of the research presented later in this book, Otani's (2001: 203) findings from a college of technology again suggest the influence of ideas of a future self, with 54% of students from the five grades connecting the importance of English study with their future career. However, Otani's research is critical in that it also revealed a vital discrepancy through the analysis of qualitative data from an open-ended section of the questionnaire. Although the students recognised English as important for their future occupations, the content of their goals for study was extremely vague. Otani (2001: 201–202) concluded that many of these students had what he termed 'big motivation' involving 'non-concrete aspirations and vague, second-hand acceptance of gossip from society about the need for English' (my translation), but were unclear about 'small motivation' involving concrete steps towards their larger hopes.

Taken in combination, these results suggest the influence of learner-internal images of an 'English-using self' for Japanese EFL students. The literature implies that in Japan, learner images of a self using English, perhaps vocationally, as part of an international community of English speakers that is not geographically or culturally defined, may allow students to perceive relevance in their English studies. These findings also align with insights from my own past research showing that undergraduate English major students were motivated by reflecting on and developing their ideas of a future self using English (Sampson, 2012). However, in the main research reviewed in this section is limited by its quantitative nature in its description of what detail Japanese students actually envision for their future English-using selves. Moreover, Otani's (2001) insightful findings imply a need to examine how students might link concrete actions and experiences in classrooms in the present to their ideas of a future English-using self. In considering a qualitative dimension to these ideas, what influence might students' own perceptions of their competence have on their motivation? Further, how might classroom teaching engage students to develop images of themselves competently using English in their future?

The Influence of Perceptions of Competence

Simply put, some of the vital questions we ask when setting out to undertake activities and persisting with tasks involve ideas of competence: What is success in this task? Can I succeed? Am I improving? What degree of capability have I obtained? These are all questions concerned with moving towards mastery of some kind – to 'develop, to attain, or to demonstrate' mastery (Urdan & Turner, 2007: 297). While at times feedback about progress towards competence comes from sources external to the learner – such as a score on a test or remarks on an essay – this feedback is mediated by the perceptions of the individual (Bandura, 1986). Rather than competence being purely an objective notion, the actions that people take are influenced also by 'the beliefs they hold about their capabilities' and not only 'by what they are actually capable of accomplishing' (Schunk & Pajares, 2007: 86). The potential influence of competence beliefs on classroom language learning motivation gains increasing importance when we consider the consistent finding that the transition to early adolescence coincides with a sharp decline in perceptions of competence (Wigfield & Wagner, 2005).

Indeed, in the Japanese context various studies strongly suggest that the motivation of Japanese EFL students is linked to their perceptions of competence, and demotivation to perceived lack of competence (e.g. Carpenter et al., 2009; Falout & Maruyama, 2004; Hiromori, 2003; Tanaka, 2009; Tanaka & Hiromori, 2007). In a study of the learning histories of 285 Japanese university students, Carpenter et al. (2009: 262) found that 'feelings of inadequacy may lead a learner to defensively dismiss the whole subject as irrelevant'. The factor emerging from their study that played the strongest role in leading to demotivation was when students experienced a sense of failure through the difficulty of lessons or a lack of comprehension. Similar findings have been reported in Falout and Maruyama (2004: 5), in which both low and high English proficiency students attributed disappointment with their performance to being the strongest influence on demotivation. Conversely, Hiromori (2003: 174) presented findings from the senior-high school context in which 'learners' perceptions of their own self-competence had a strong influence on motivation'.

A series of studies in this area by two Japanese researchers provides valuable teaching suggestions to engage learners and assist them in becoming more motivated to learn by addressing their need for a feeling of competence (Hiromori, 2003; Tanaka, 2009; Tanaka & Hiromori, 2007). Tanaka and Hiromori (2007) used questionnaires in a pre-test/post-test design to determine the effectiveness of a group presentation activity for enhancing the intrinsic motivation of 78 university students. Their results revealed that, while students with lower levels of motivation appeared to benefit most from fostering their sense of competence, students with a medium level of motivation required both support of their need for competence and chances to work autonomously in order to further foster motivation (Tanaka & Hiromori, 2007: 60). In another study, Tanaka (2009) conducted research with 52 university students utilising a series of four open- and closed-ended questionnaires regarding lessons over one 15-week semester. Termed by Tanaka (2009) as an 'intervention', the lessons involved a range of communicative activities that focused in particular on speaking skills, using language connected to the everyday lives of students, and listening skills through watching foreign television drama programmes and films from English-speaking countries. Tanaka's findings in part aligned with those of the previous study. He found that students' need for and perception of competence most affected their motivation in listening activities – they reported higher levels of motivation when they could feel success in understanding (Tanaka, 2009: 244). With regard to speaking activities, however, both perception of competence and relatedness – the 'feeling [of being] connected to others' (Ryan & Deci, 2002: 7) – through interacting in the classroom speaking tasks played a vital role in students' motivation (Tanaka, 2009: 244).

In one way, the studies in this area suggest that students who have negative feelings about their ability to use English or who experience failure, for example through a lack of comprehension, are more likely to become demotivated (Carpenter et al., 2009: 262–263). That is, learner-internal *perceptions* of success or failure link with motivation. However, the studies by Tanaka and Hiromori (2007) and Tanaka (2009) also intimate that if students have opportunities to experience success, they may become more motivated. These opportunities for feeling competent using English in the present might foster students' motivating images of a successful, future English-using self. Perhaps the classroom may play a vital role in its presentation, or lack thereof, of such opportunities for success.

The Influence of Classroom Language Lessons

Government policy documents in Japan from the late 1980s onwards have emphasised the development of students' communicative abilities through their time in the English classroom (Yoshida, 2003). This apparent need for English communicative ability has been linked officially with globalisation:

> With the progress of globalisation in the economy and in society, it is essential that our children acquire communication skills in English, which has become a common international language, in order for living in the 21st century. This has become an extremely important issue both in terms of the future of our children and the further development of Japan as a nation. (MEXT, 2002: para. 1)

A 2003 MEXT document again stressed the intention for a communicative focus to lessons in Japanese schools. This document is insightful as it outlines a clear vision of the style of lesson that one might expect at junior- and senior-high schools in order to foster 'communicative ability':

> Instruction mainly based on grammar and translation or teacher-centred classes are not recommended. Through ... activities making use of English as a means of communication, the learning of vocabulary and grammar should be enhanced, and communication abilities in 'listening,' 'speaking,' 'reading,' and 'writing' should be fostered. ... To carry out such instruction effectively, it is important for teachers to establish many situations where students can communicate with each other in English. (MEXT, 2003: paras 3–4)

However, research by Kikuchi and Browne (2009) suggests that, despite MEXT's (2003) stated intentions, EFL classroom teaching in Japan has not become more communicatively focused. Kikuchi and Browne asked first-year university students to rate how closely pedagogic goals from the 2003 English Course of Study guidelines matched their actual experience in high school. Results revealed that 53% of students *strongly* disagreed with the statement 'I studied how to use English to communicate about everyday topics', and 68% *strongly* disagreed with an item stating 'Our teacher had us discuss and exchange opinions in English about reading and listening activities' (Kikuchi & Browne, 2009: 187).

Students' perceptions about the non-communicative nature of high-school English lessons are evident in a study by Falout *et al.* (2008). In a rare application of qualitative data collection in Japanese EFL learning research, Falout and associates asked university students to write 'advice letters' to their secondary-school English teachers. The results showed that the majority of students 'expressed a desire for more chances and time to practice oral communication skills and less time on grammar ... and less teacher-centred classrooms' (Falout *et al.*, 2008: 18). These results are also highly relevant to the study reported herein, as research into the specific context of kosen classrooms also suggests that EFL learning is focused on grammar translation and teacher-centred lessons rather than communicative activities (Humphries, 2011; *Koseneigo kenkyuuiinkai*, 2008).

A critical issue that emerges from this body of research is the extent of influence on students' motivation of learner-externally determined lesson style. Questionnaire studies by Kikuchi (2009) and Kikuchi and Sakai (2009), in which university students reflected on their past EFL studies, reveal a wide variety of elements from Japanese EFL classrooms that reduce motivation in students. From these studies, three demotivating factors emerge: pedagogical materials, a focus on tests and entrance examinations, and a lesson style involving non-communicative methods such as grammar-translation with a memorisation focus. These results, although elicited through quantitative means, nevertheless align with Falout *et al.*'s (2008) study in which students called for more interactive, student-centred lessons.

A mixed-method study by Carpenter *et al.* (2009) is particularly revealing of the potentially negative effects of lessons on students' motivation. Carpenter and colleagues invited 285 Japanese university students studying a range of specialisations to draw timelines of their English language learning motivation; they were also asked to write language-learning histories and complete a questionnaire. Carpenter *et al.* found that students who had negative experiences early on in their formal English studies (from junior-high school) developed progressively lower motivational trajectories, while those students with positive experiences of an initial learning environment related much higher levels of subsequent motivation (Carpenter *et al.*, 2009: 263).

Taken together, the findings from these studies suggest that learner-external factors from lessons that are perceived negatively by students, such as classrooms involving passive learning, an examination focus or uninteresting materials, strongly affect motivational outcomes for learners. Of these factors, there is a large literature in Japan concerning the washback effects of high-stakes examinations on learning activities in the classroom (e.g. Gorsuch, 2001; Kikuchi & Browne, 2009; Miura, 2010). However, such research did not have a marked influence on the study reported in this book, as the most prominent exams in Japanese schooling – entrance exams for the next level of education – are not relevant for kosen students for the first few years after their initial entry to the college. Nevertheless, the literature does imply that the ways in which students *perceive* English lessons in their previous schooling prior to transitioning to a new learning environment may continue to affect their motivational trajectories.

Moving on

In summary, the literature about classroom EFL study in Japan reveals both *internal* factors that affect the dynamics of students' EFL (de)motivation – those stemming from within and potentially controllable by learners – and *external* factors – those imposed from without and not directly under the control of learners. What is, however, striking is that few studies overtly consider the *interplay* between these factors. One possible explanation is that the overwhelming majority of research into motivation in the Japanese EFL classroom has used large-scale, quantitative methods, including surveys and retrospective investigation of motivational states at fixed points. In asking learners to respond to preset statements, such instruments may not sufficiently allow participants to explore *their own* understandings of their motivation. Moreover, and rather surprisingly, although the research is focused on learner motivation in Japanese EFL classrooms, very few of these studies actually take place *in the classroom*.

The foreign language motivation literature from Japan suggests the need to apply a framework of motivation incorporating both learner-internal and learner-external factors. In order to understand the ebb and flow of students' motivation in the classroom, such a motivational framework must also take into account the dynamic influences of students' experiences in these learning spaces. Chapter 3 turns its attention to one such framework.

3 A Move to Socio-dynamic Motivation

It is evident from the discussion in the previous chapter that additional language learning motivation has attracted considerable attention from researchers, not least in Japan. The early work of Gardner and Lambert is fundamental to research in this field (e.g. Gardner, 1985, 2001; Gardner & Lambert, 1959, 1972). This research was principally located and focused on the very specific situation of bilingual second language learning in Canada. From these beginnings, Gardner's evolving yet influential model of motivation in SLA revolved strongly around the notion of integrativeness, which was defined as a desire to assimilate into the target language community or to 'come closer to the other language community' (Gardner, 2001: 5).

However, recent years have seen a number of reconceptualisations of the phenomenon of language learning motivation. In particular, the spread of languages used as lingua franca across national and cultural boundaries has engendered a rethinking of the notion of integrativeness as a (or *the*) driving influence on motivation. The use of languages in such ways is clearly fundamentally different from the very specific setting in which the concept was initially conceived. With regard to English, when it is perceived as a tool by a wide variety of different communities, there appears to be no one 'other language community' to which learners might try to draw closer. As Ushioda and Dörnyei (2009: 2–3) ask, 'does it make sense to talk about integrative attitudes when ownership of English does not rest with a specific community of speakers?'

In light of such concerns, and especially considering the literature in the previous chapter indicating that Japanese learners are more motivated by the idea of an English-speaking community independent of nationality (Ryan, 2009a; Yashima, 2002), I believe that the concept of integrativeness offers little to the understanding of classroom language learning motivation in this context. Similarly dissatisfied with the concept of integrativeness, Dörnyei (2005, 2009a) drew on the idea of possible selves elaborated earlier in the field of social psychology by scholars such as Higgins (1987) and Markus and Nurius (1986). Basing his work on a longitudinal study reported in Dörnyei *et al.* (2006), Dörnyei reconceptualised the integrative motive in language learning. Rather than attempting to draw closer to an external community, Dörnyei proposed that learners attempt to draw closer to their idea of a possible self.

The Theory of Possible Selves

The concept of possible selves appeared in its current form in the literature in two key articles: Markus and Nurius (1986) and Higgins (1987). Markus and Nurius (1986: 954) proposed that 'possible selves are the ideal selves that we would very much like to become; they are also the selves we could become, and the selves we are afraid of becoming'. In Markus and Nurius' view, possible selves are images of ourselves and actions in possible future situations, some of which we might wish for, while others we may want to avoid. Possible selves differ from goals in that they are more holistic, involving combinations of cognition, emotion and vision into an experiential *image* (Dörnyei, 2009a).

Whereas Markus and Nurius (1986) provided numerous examples of possible selves, Higgins (1987) more precisely defined two aspects: on the one hand, the *ideal self* is a representation of attributes one would ideally like to possess. Dweck *et al.* (2003: 241) summarise that 'strong ideal self-guides result in an overall *promotion focus*, creating goals that concern aspirations, advancement, and accomplishments or, more generally, the presence or absence of positive outcomes' (emphasis in original). Motivation considered from a possible-self perspective is also deeply intertwined with emotions. As such, the ideal self engenders 'eager' engagement in working to approach positive outcomes (Idson *et al.*, 2000). On the other hand, the *ought-to self* is a representation of obligations, felt expectations or responsibilities. The ought-to self is believed to entail a prevention focus, in which people are more concerned with safety and security and the existence of negative outcomes (Dweck *et al.*, 2003). Affectively, the ought-to self fosters 'vigilant' efforts in working to avoid negative outcomes (Idson *et al.*, 2000). In line with this theorising, in 1996 Higgins also expanded the definition of the ought-to self to include the person you do not want to be, echoing Markus and Nurius' reference to a possible self that we want to avoid. Although it is argued that people hold both ideal and ought-to self ideas, the degree to which these play a guiding role in motivation differs between individuals (Dweck *et al.*, 2003).

Considering the notable ebb and flow – particularly in a negative direction – of motivation evident in research from Japan, a definition by Erikson (2007) adds clarity to the dynamic processes involved with possible selves. Erikson drew on research over the 20 years since the original propositions to contend that:

> Possible selves are conceptions of our selves in the future, including, at least to some degree, an experience of being an agent in a future situation.

> Possible selves get vital parts of their meaning in interplay with the self-concept, which they in turn moderate, as well as from their social and cultural context. (Erikson, 2007: 356)

Erikson's definition includes the concept of imagined experience playing an agentive role, involving a sense of narrative in which we imagine how the situation would feel 'from the inside'. Moreover, there are dynamic interactions between self-concept and the environment, such as influences from social and cultural contexts in possible-self construction. Such an assertion finds agreement with the writing of Markus (2006: xii), who contends that 'the social world, particularly peoples' relations with others, is very often the source of the materials for the creation of possible selves, and has a large hand in what, if anything, is done with them'.

I believe that the way in which internally held possible-self images are theorised to be constructed in interaction with the environment holds considerable potential for understanding the fluctuating EFL motivation that has been identified in Japan, especially considering the importance of the learner-internal and -external influences on motivation detailed previously.

The L2 Motivational Self System

Drawing on the theory of possible selves, Dörnyei (2009a) reformulated language learning motivation as the L2 Motivational Self System. The system is composed of three elements: First, the *Ideal L2 Self* is the image of who we wish to become. It is our idea about our 'best' possible self in the second language domain. Secondly, the *Ought-to L2 Self* is what one believes about external influences, the 'attributes that one believes one *ought to* possess to meet expectations and to *avoid* possible negative outcomes' (Dörnyei, 2009a: 29; italics in original). These external influences are largely socially constructed, often by the explicit or perceived expectations of significant others. Lastly, the *L2 Learning Experience* concerns the motives generated through the learning environment – elements such as the teacher, curriculum, lesson style, and so on. A range of published studies has claimed to validate the three elements and structure of the L2 Motivational Self System in different contexts (e.g. Al-Shehri, 2009; Csizér & Kormos, 2009; Csizér & Lukács, 2010; Ryan, 2009a; Taguchi *et al.*, 2009).

In order to outline the motivational processes of possible selves, Dörnyei (2009a) incorporated the work of Higgins and associates concerning 'self-discrepancy theory' (Higgins, 1987). This theory describes a process in which 'we are motivated to reach a condition where our self-concept matches our personally relevant self-guides' (Higgins, 1987: 321). It is the attempt to decrease the gap between our present self in context and future possible selves that provides motivation in additional-language learning (Dörnyei, 2009a). That is, when we perceive a gap between our current, actual self and our conception of a best possible self (the ideal self) or a self that we believe may be expected of us (the ought-to self), motivation is forthcoming as we attempt to decrease this discrepancy.

Dörnyei (2009a) and Dörnyei and Ushioda (2011) categorise a variety of conditions for the L2 Motivational Self System to foster the development of motivation. These conditions have been derived from studies in settings other than second language learning (e.g. Hock *et al.*, 2006; Oyserman & Markus, 1990; Oyserman *et al.*, 2002, 2006; Sheldon & Lyubomirsky, 2006). However, in connection with these categories a variety of studies also draw attention to the significant role that individual variation and differing contexts play in the potential for motivation based on possible selves.

Detailed future-self images, regularly activated

Adolescence is a time of creating, 'trying on', developing or discarding visions of future possible selves in different domains (Oyserman & Fryberg, 2006). First, then, there is general agreement that, in order to be motivating, future-self images must exist and be sufficiently detailed in a particular life area (Dörnyei, 2009a; Dörnyei & Ushioda, 2011; Markus & Ruvolo, 1989). As Markus and Ruvolo (1989: 219) argue, 'the more elaborated the possible self in terms of semantic, imaginal, or enactive representations, the more motivationally effective it can be expected to be'. Such a proposal is in line with research into the use of visualisation techniques for motivation. Particularly in the area of athlete training, research into the imagination of future action has revealed its assistance in areas such as performance enhancement, arousal regulation and the control of affective states (Gould *et al.*, 2002; Jones & Stuth, 1997).

In addition to the requirement for detailed possible-self images to exist, research by Norman and Aron (2003) contributes a further, related condition for motivation – the need to regularly activate these possible selves. In a study with American undergraduate students, results suggested possible selves that were *available* (the ease with which the possible-self detail could be envisioned) and *accessible* (how easily they could be brought into awareness) had greater motivational potential (Norman & Aron, 2003: 505). In straightforward terms, the more often possible selves are instantiated into the working self-concept, the more they are likely to be accessible and affect action.

However, research has also indicated that the content and likelihood of activation through reflection on future possible selves varies by gender and culture (Knox, 2006; Oyserman & Fryberg, 2006; Unemori *et al.*, 2004). For example, Unemori *et al.* (2004: 333) found that Japanese participants in their research generated twice as many career- and education-related possible selves as participants from other cultures. Furthermore, Knox (2006) found both differences in the content of possible selves by gender and a trend for adolescent females to reflect on possible selves more than adolescent males. Considering the classroom, such literature implies limitations to expecting all learners to hold possible-self images for a particular educational domain, such as language learning. What this literature moreover suggests is that to investigate language students' motivation from a possible-selves perspective, one would first need to obtain a picture of their initial ideas of future self in this domain. The literature also prompts consideration of what motivational benefits there might be in introducing activities that allow students to develop and explore these English-using selves in the classroom.

Plausible discrepancy between present- and future-self images

A future self must be plausibly yet sufficiently different from the current self (Dörnyei & Ushioda, 2011). On the one hand, this means that one must feel that the power to attain a possible self is within one's own capabilities. Each individual has their own specific cognitive representations of what is indeed possible for themselves in their own particular circumstances (Ruvolo & Markus, 1992). In addition to the necessity for detailed, readily accessible possible-self images, research by Norman and Aron (2003: 505) revealed that 'if an individual believes she or he has control over attaining (or avoiding) a particular possible self, motivation relevant to this possible self will be greater'.

On the other hand, however, there must also be a sufficient gap perceived between the present and future self. The motivational power of possible selves is affected by perceptions of their likelihood of attainability in an inverse 'U-shaped' function (Oyserman & James, 2009). If the possible self is perceived as not overly different from the present self and seems attainable with minimal increase in current effort, it is unlikely to provide much motivation. That is, the perceived certainty of achievement of the possible self may lead one to feel comfortable entrenched in a present state, believing that the possible self is only a hands-grasp away. These insights imply that the degree to which learners perceive 'closeness' to a future self – that is, both whether it is plausibly possible and/or a foregone conclusion – is a valuable gauge of the motivational potential of these constructs.

Understanding of strategies to move towards future-self images

While the existence and plausibility of future-self images are of import, for motivation to be translated into action in the present there is also a necessity for cognisance of concrete strategies that might move one towards the possible-self (Dörnyei & Ushioda, 2011; MacIntyre *et al.*, 2009; Oyserman *et al.*, 2004; Taylor *et al.*, 1998).

Research by Oyserman and her associates (2004) with 160 American middle-school students provides informative insights into individual variation related to this proposed link. Students in Oyserman *et al.*'s study were asked to write about their personal expectations and concerns for the following year, and the strategies they planned to use to move towards or away from these possible selves. Although the study revealed that the majority of participants held visions of possible selves focusing on wanting to do well in school, there was again variation in their individual ability to link these images with action plans to attain them. Of critical importance, only those with a range of simple, concrete strategies to work towards their future self showed significant improvement in measures of academic achievement such as grade point average (GPA) and observation of attitudes by teachers (Oyserman *et al.*, 2004: 144).

This area of possible-self research strongly recalls findings in the previous chapter from the kosen context in Japan (Otani, 2001). While Otani's students held what he termed 'big motivation' – ideas of the necessity of English for a future career – through a qualitative element of his research he also found that most students were unable to write about concrete actions in the present that might move them towards this possible English-using self (Otani, 2001: 202). The notion of a connection between present actions and strategies and a more distal possible self would therefore seem to offer an invaluable tool for investigating the motivation of classroom language learners, because 'it is [the] system of specific proximal subgoals that distinguishes reality-based future goals from empty dreams and fantasies' (Miller & Brickman, 2004: 16).

Congruence between future-self images

Dörnyei and Ushioda (2011) assert that ideal and ought-to selves might foster motivation to a greater extent when they are congruent. Their claim resonates with other research findings. Of significance to educational settings, adolescence is a period marked by increased efforts to fit in with peer norms and behaviour, which might not always run in parallel with individually held possible-self ideas (Bukowski *et al.*, 2011; Kiesner *et al.*, 2002). Research by Pizzolato (2006) with university students in late adolescence offers a perceptive glimpse into the potential influence of those people in the surrounding context on students' possible selves. The participants in Pizzolato's (2006) study were in fact able to discuss procedural schemas involving strategies to move towards their possible selves, suggesting the potential for motivation. However, they also frequently reflected on conflicts between their own possible-self goals and the influences of relationships with important others such as peers or family members (Pizzolato, 2006: 65). Pizzolato concluded that a lack of congruence between one's own ideal-self ideas and perceived expectations or group norms making up ought-to-self ideas may negatively affect motivation.

Other studies point to individual differences in the influence of social comparisons on possible selves during adolescence (Kemmelmeier & Oyserman, 2001a, 2001b). Moreover, research also reveals the tendency to socially compare as linked to contextual perceptions of the task at hand. A range of researchers have found that inclination towards an ought-to self or ideal self can be momentarily induced in reaction to particular situations or activities (e.g. Higgins *et al.*, 2001; Shah & Higgins, 1997; Shah *et al.*, 1998). As a result, although Dörnyei and Ushioda (2011) assert the motivational benefits of ideal and ought-to possible selves being congruent, research findings may leave the classroom practitioner wondering how such congruency might come about, especially considering the individual differences in learners making up any class group.

Counterbalance between positive and negative future-self images

As previously mentioned, Dörnyei (2009a) conceives of the motivational processes involved in the L2 Motivational Self System as following Higgins' (1987) self-discrepancy theory. This theory proposes that people are motivated to reach a state where their present or actual self matches their ideal self. There is general agreement that balance in positive and negative possible selves provides an additive form of motivation to work towards this state, and that this balance has a greater and more varied effect on behaviour than either a positive or negative self-image alone (Hoyle & Sherrill, 2006; Oyserman & Markus, 1990; Oyserman *et al.*, 2006). A balance between positive and negative future-self images fosters an ideal-self image to provide a 'pull' while a feared-self image provides a 'push' (Dörnyei & Ushioda, 2011).

Oyserman and Markus's (1990) research into delinquent youth makes a vital contribution in this area. They concluded that without the pulling influence of a positive possible self, one may be more susceptible to despondency through focusing purely on a feared self. In addition, they claim that individuals with various positive possible selves might have difficulty in focusing on one specific possible self, in which case a matched feared self can foster persistence in the pursuit of the positive possible self in the same domain (Oyserman & Markus, 1990: 123).

However, it has also been found that degree of balance and action resultant from matching positive and feared possible selves varies with culture (Lee *et al.*, 2000; Unemori *et al.*, 2004). For instance, research by Unemori *et al.* (2004: 335) showed that, rather than balanced positive and negative possible selves, Japanese people generated matched possible selves with the *same* thematic content, for example, 'expect to be idle' and 'fear to be idle'. Unemori *et al.* drew on prior research into cultural differences to conclude that this may stem from a tendency for self-criticism and modesty in Japanese culture.

Applications of Possible-self Theory

The conditions for motivation from possible selves provide a useful set of starting points for investigating motivation in the foreign language classroom. However, much of the research on which these categories are based is primarily theoretical and experiment based, rather than founded on practical applications of possible-self theory. Fortunately, in recent years there has been a gradual increase in research into possible-self 'interventions'; examples include minority groups (Destin & Oyserman, 2009; Lee & Oyserman, 2007), academic motivation and outcomes (Hock et al., 2006; Oyserman et al., 2006) and life and career planning (Plimmer & Schmidt, 2007; Ronfeldt & Grossman, 2008). Albeit predominantly from North America, these studies provide convincing evidence of positive outcomes through encouraging reflection on possible selves. In what follows, I look at two studies from general education settings that greatly influenced the empirical study reported later in this book. Both studies suggest ways in which holistic, integrated programmes that introduce a variety of possible-self activities may work to bring about positive change in classroom contexts across individuals.

The possible-selves programme

In line with my own concerns, Hock et al. (2006) noticed a gap between theoretical work regarding the possible-self construct in the field of social psychology and practical application of the theory in real-life situations. They developed a possible-selves intervention in the United States involving junior-high school students and student athletes in the first year of university. In this study, students were assigned to one of two groups: a control group that took part in the usual career-orientation and academic counselling programmes at their institution, or an experimental group that participated in the possible-selves programme.

Hock and associates (2006) describe in valuable detail the activities involved in their programme, which was divided into six stages. In the first two stages, teachers assisted students to identify positive experiences, skills and interests, and then outlined hopes, expectations and fears in particular life areas. Following this, students drew a connected image of expressions from the previous stage as a 'possible-self tree'. The students then discussed their possible-self tree and thought about how learning could support the whole tree. The teachers and students next worked on action plans involving longer term hopes, a short-term goal on the road to the hope, tasks to reach the goal, and finally a timeline to complete the particular tasks, focusing on areas from the possible-self tree. In the final stage, students revised and reviewed their goals, action plans, hopes, expectations and fears and connected them to current learning.

Hock et al. (2006) found that participation in the possible-selves programme produced very positive effects. The participants identified more specific life goals across a broader range than participants in the control group. There was also a higher rate of retention and graduation among the students who participated in the possible-selves programme and a higher average GPA than students in the control group. As a result, Hock et al. (2006: 216) concluded that their programme might serve an important educational function, in that 'once students begin to see the relevance of academic skills, knowledge, and effort as the means to attain what they have identified as important hopes for the future, commitment to learning may follow'.

Although the review of past research in the previous section reveals variation in the ability to construct and reflect on possible selves between individuals, the possible-self tree activity from Hock et al.'s (2006) study is particularly notable. Not only did the programme apparently foster positive motivational outcomes, but the detail that the researchers provide in describing activities related to this possible-self tree might allow teachers to visualise a concrete way of assisting students to develop elaborate, individualised possible-self images. Further, the study also reveals the potential to foster a clear connection between present and future selves through the use of such activities in combination with an exploration of strategies that students could use to support their possible selves.

The school-to-jobs intervention

Cognitively, adolescence witnesses the development of more sophisticated information-processing strategies and the ability to consider problems from a variety of angles, enabling a greater capacity to manage and regulate actions (Wigfield & Wagner, 2005). Studies by Oyserman and associates (e.g. Oyserman et al., 2002, 2006) specifically focus on links between possible selves and such self-regulatory behaviour in academic settings. In particular, the research reported in Oyserman et al. (2006) fostered positive academic behavioural change, and once again provides a detailed account of the programme that was developed. What is especially illuminating in this study is the potential it suggests for bringing individuals together in a shared context to work cooperatively in order to foster congruence between ideal-self ideas and social identities.

The programme that these researchers developed consisted of 11 sessions. In the first two sessions, students discussed skills or abilities that would assist them to study for that year, and selected photographs as images of their adult, successful possible selves. In sessions three and four, students drew positive role models and negative forces, as well as timelines into the future considering divergent paths and the obstacles they may face. The next three sessions involved students using poster boards to link specific strategies to move towards or away from next-year expected or feared possible selves.

In sessions eight, nine and ten, students worked in small groups on collaboratively solving social, academic and everyday problems. In the last stage, students reflected on the sessions to help them make their ideas and experiences over the sessions more concrete.

Oyserman et al. (2006) conducted a two-year intervention with 264 American students from low-income households moving from junior- to senior-high school. Results revealed that the possible-self images of students in the programme altered markedly, which in turn affected their behaviour. Participants' school attendance improved, as did their participation in lessons and time spent on homework, further leading to higher GPA (Oyserman et al., 2006: 201).

Of key significance for the study reported later, Oyserman et al. (2006: 200) argue that in their school-based intervention 'structured group activities evoked academically focused possible-selves [and] made clear that academic possible-selves were held by peers (and therefore something that "we" aspire to)'. As a potential starting-point to fostering congruency between ideal and ought-to possible selves, these ideas illustrate the possibilities for developing a classroom atmosphere with students in which not only are individual possible-self ideas fostered, but also one in which peers are supportive of each other's ideal-self images.

Moving on

The literature detailed in this chapter suggests that theoretically the L2 Motivational Self System (Dörnyei, 2009a) holds great promise for exploring classroom language learning motivation. The three elements of this framework – the ideal and ought-to selves, and the language learning experience – provide a good fit with the literature reviewed in the previous chapter, which indicates learner-internal and -external influences on the motivation of EFL students in Japan. However, as I argued at the end of Chapter 2, a major limitation of the existing EFL motivation research in Japan to date has been its failure to consider in any depth the interplay between these learner-internal and -external influences.

In fact, Dörnyei (2009a: 29) identifies a clear gap in the research when he introduces the *language learning experience* element of the L2 Motivational Self System, writing that 'this component is conceptualised at a different level from the two self-guides and future research will hopefully elaborate on the self-aspects of this bottom-up *process*' (emphasis added). Although a number of quantitative validation studies have been conducted investigating the elements and structure of the L2 Motivational Self System, these studies do not describe adequately the subjective understandings of the dynamic processes involved in language learning motivation. The review of necessary conditions for motivation from the L2 Motivational Self System reveals a range of research showing variation between individuals that might challenge the usefulness of these categories. However, the literature also strongly points to the importance of interaction between the individual and their environment for motivation from possible selves, through contextualised activation, ideas of what is plausibly possible in one's life situation, and the influences of particular tasks or peer relations on possible-self congruence. Indeed, the research literature indicates that interventions and applications of possible-self activities might have beneficial effects on learners and help enhance their motivation for language learning. What may provide outstanding hope to language educators (myself included, considering the background presented in Chapter 1) is the potential for holistic possible-self interventions to foster positive learning outcomes for students.

The next chapter therefore presents a description of my decision making in implementing research in order to longitudinally investigate the motivation situated in one foreign language learning class group while introducing a variety of possible-self activities.

4 Research Design

As outlined in Chapter 1, my role as a homeroom and classroom teacher for first-grade learners at the educational institution in which I was employed in Japan provided a unique opportunity to explore the language learning motivation of newly arrived students while also working to make their EFL studies more relevant. While the literature confirms that low motivation is a widespread problem in Japan, it also helps to establish the need for studies that investigate motivation in context in the language learning classroom. The review of the literature further served to inform the design of a research study that explored my students' motivation and views of a future English self from their own perspectives.

Considering the interactive, dynamic nature of motivation proposed in the last two chapters, a research approach based on positivist understandings that tested hypotheses about fixed variables would not provide the texture of subjective experience in which I was interested. Moreover, through uncovering an overwhelming majority of quantitative research in Japan, the review of the literature firmed up my conviction that a qualitative study could add much to situated understandings of language learning motivation in this context. Although conducted in different educational settings, the possible-self interventions (Hock et al., 2006; Oyserman et al., 2006) suggested the possibility of very positive outcomes for the participants. My review of the strategic implications of the L2 Motivational Self System (Dörnyei & Ushioda, 2011) inspired me to consider ways of introducing change-action to the classroom to foster similar positive outcomes and deepen my understanding of the motivation of my own students.

I developed three research questions at the beginning of the study: (1) How do the participants express their ideas of an English-using self at the commencement of the study? (2) What ideas of an English-using self emerge among the participants from experience of the classroom? (3) In what ways do shared understandings of an English-using self appear to affect the participants' motivation to learn English? These research questions pointed to the adoption of a flexible approach through which activities exploring the self-ideas of students could be introduced to the classroom, and which would allow investigation over time. One method which has been held up as particularly useful in allowing multiple perspectives from participants in a

38 Part 1: 成長 Growth: A Research Narrative

group situation of change is that of action research (Cohen *et al.*, 2011). This chapter therefore provides an introduction to action research and considerations of my philosophical stance in undertaking this research, before moving on to a description of the design of the study.

Action Research

Action research first gained its current form through the social experiments of Lewin in the 1940s, in which he worked with community groups in the United States on the resolution of social problems. Lewin developed an approach based on the idea that knowledge ought to spring from problem solving in concrete situations, rather than abstract experiments (Herr & Anderson, 2005). Currently, action research is used in a wide range of forms in order to understand change in human social settings. In many cases it seeks to 'bring together action and reflection, theory and practice, in participation with others, in the pursuit of practical solutions to issues of pressing concern to people' (Reason & Bradbury, 2006: 1).

A fundamental methodological process in action research is a series of research *cycles* (Lewin, 1948). Initially, the researcher or a group of participants recognises a problem or challenging issue in their particular social context. Change-action is developed by those inside this social group in order to explore the problem and move towards outcomes that these participants perceive as beneficial. That is, action research employs intentional and strategic intervention through the introduction of such change-action to encourage the development of meaningful change for those involved in a particular setting (Burns, 2011). The actual outcomes are then reflected on through analysis of data elicited from participants concerning the implemented change-action. The understandings of this change and the emergent outcomes are then used to create further change-action in a following cycle. These processes are visualised in Figure 4.1.

Action research is concerned with contributing to new practices through action, and new knowledge and theory, through research into this action (McNiff & Whitehead, 2011). In other words, action research focuses on concrete issues and the move towards better practice and the sharing of

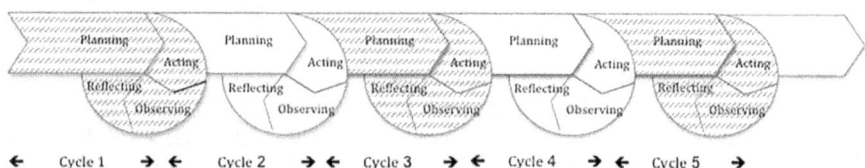

Figure 4.1 Cyclical model of action research
Source: Adapted from Burns (2010: 9).

understandings gained from exploration of these issues. It is intended to reduce the distance between research and practice, bringing those involved in organisations into the research process (Somekh, 1995). In educational settings this means that action research is an attempt to understand and interpret professional action from the inside, conducted by practitioners on experience of the classroom or other educational context by participants – for example, students, teachers or administrators.

Initial Philosophical Considerations

Although offering a practical process for investigating change in social systems, the positioning of action research paradigmatically is not straightforward. Due to its focus on exploring the perspectives of humans involved in particular contexts, there is a tendency in the literature to position action research within a qualitative paradigm (Cohen *et al.*, 2011; Lincoln & Guba, 2005). This positioning is largely founded on the understanding that the *interpretation* of a particular setting in action research places it in opposition to an objective, positivist philosophy. One useful way of exploring the philosophical underpinnings of action research is to consider the 'arena of human action' being studied (Newton & Burgess, 2008: 21). Researchers recognise distinctions between action research that focuses on: (a) technical knowledge building and improvement; (b) practical exploration of (personal/group) action; and (c) critical-emancipatory-participatory studies (Burns, 2005; Cohen *et al.*, 2011; Masters, 1995; Newton & Burgess, 2008; Noffke, 1997). The paradigmatic underpinnings vary between such differently focused action research (see Table 4.1).

Although these different foci of action research allow various philosophical stances, there have been criticisms regarding action research in practice by teacher-researchers in education settings. The debate centres around whether teacher-researchers are equipped with the training to fully develop knowledge claims from their research that are based on sound philosophical foundations and methods of data collection appropriate to the research problem (Jarvis, 2001; Newton & Burgess, 2008). Particularly in the field of language teaching, emphasis has been placed on classroom problem solving and improvement of practice (Burns, 2011). As Lytle (2000: 694) argues, there has been increasing 'debate about whether [such] teacher research is a new *paradigm*, a new *genre* of research that is part of a wider social and political movement, or even qualifies, epistemologically and methodologically, as *research* at all' (emphasis in original).

In light of these criticisms of action research in education settings, as a teacher-researcher I wanted to provide a philosophical grounding to my study that was as sound as possible. I was not convinced that the existing literature from the action research field provided a base that matched my

Table 4.1 Links between different foci of action research (AR) and philosophical underpinnings

AR Focus	Technical AR	Practical AR	Critical AR
Philosophical base	Natural sciences	Hermeneutics	Critical theory
Ontology (nature of reality)	Single; measurable	Multiple, constructed, holistic	Interrelated with social/political power structures
Research problem	Defined in advance (problem posing)	Defined in context (problem solving)	Defined in context based on values clarification (problematising)
Epistemology (understandings of knowledge)	Separate, deductive/predictive, causes and effects	Inductive, descriptive based on interaction of external context and individual thinking, theory producing	Inductive, emancipatory, theory producing, embedded in society
Research purpose	To discover 'laws' of underlying reality	To understand what occurs and the meaning people make of experiences	To uncover and understand what impedes equal practices
Change outcomes	Short-lived	Potentially longer lasting, dependent on participants	Social change, emancipation

Source: Adapted from Burns (2005), Masters (1995), Newton and Burgess (2008) and Noffke (1997).

own personal philosophies. When considering the implementation of this study, I had been reading about ideas of complex systems theory applied to language learning (e.g. Dörnyei, 2009b; Larsen-Freeman & Cameron, 2008a). The importance that this theory places on dynamic, co-influencing interactions seemed to mesh well with the interplay between the learner-internal and -external elements revealed in the Japanese EFL motivation research. I therefore turned to the literature regarding complex systems theory to assess what it might offer as a potential philosophical foundation to my action research study.

Philosophical Underpinnings of Complex Systems Theory

The spread of complex systems theory began relatively recently in the fields of mathematics, physics and biology through explorations of neural network theories, cybernetics, artificial intelligence, non-linear dynamics such as dissipative structures and fractal theories, evolutionary biology and economics. Perhaps as a result of the variety of input in the emergence of complexity theories, Richardson and Cilliers (2001) discern three different approaches to the study of these complex systems which engender different ontological and epistemological stances.

First, *reductionist complexity science* or *hard complexity science* is aligned with the use of algebraic expressions to reduce complex systems to a set of general principles, and as such is closely related to empirical positivistic thought (Richardson & Cilliers, 2001: 6). Morin (2006: 6) argues that this approach to 'restricted complexity' recognises complexity yet remains fundamentally philosophically bound to classical science through its methods of 'decomplexifying' systems. Hard complexity science turns a blind eye to the uniqueness of the complexity being studied and instead seeks theoretical models claiming universal laws.

A second stance has been termed *soft complexity science*. This approach draws on metaphors from complexity theories to understand or explain phenomena (e.g. Eoyang, 2004, applying complex systems images to human organisational practice). This approach has also, however, been attacked due to its primary use of metaphors to 'visualise' organisations without basing these constructions on rigorous and sound research processes (Phelan, 2001; Richardson & Cilliers, 2001). An additional area of concern regards the real degree to which such approaches have truly taken on board the fundamental implications of a complexity philosophy. Merely borrowing language or images from another area may lead to problems because the understandings on which the language is based might not be present (Richardson & Cilliers, 2001).

A final perspective, termed *complexity thinking*, draws more on the philosophical consequences of complexity understandings. Building on a complex ideation of human systems, social reality is conceived as both external and internal to the individual at the same time and across time dynamically. The individual, as part of innumerable social, cultural or linguistic systems, is influenced in behaviour by these systems. However, at the same time the individual acts within these systems, changing the form of the systems with every action or utterance.

In adopting a complexity thinking ontology, due to constant interactions between systems at innumerable levels, it is understood that there is co-adaptation as the individual both shapes reality through interaction, while at the same time being shaped by reality. It is in such a sense that Kuhn (2007: 173) argues in complex systems theory, 'not only are the knower and the known dynamic, self-organizing and emerging, the relationship of the knower to the known is likewise dynamic, self-organizing and emerging'.

Due to this understanding of the co-forming nature of reality, proponents of a complexity thinking epistemology consider that knowing is provisional and limited, and that understandings of phenomena are not explanatory or predictive but interpretive (Alhadeff-Jones, 2008: 77). Such interpretive knowledge exists in interaction with reality:

> Descriptions of the universe are actually part of the universe. Hence, the universe changes as descriptions of the universe change. ... Knowledge in this frame is understood to inhere in interactions – that is, to be embodied or enacted in the ever-unfolding choreography of action with/in the universe. (Davis & Sumara, 2005: 314)

A positivist, reductionist epistemology (also related to so-called 'hard complexity science') would reduce a system to its componential parts and study it objectively in the search for truths considered fixed and absolute (Radford, 2008). In contrast, an epistemology based on complexity thinking favours understanding phenomena as intricately integrated into a fabric of relations (Alhadeff-Jones, 2008: 68).

Scholars of complexity thinking argue that approaches to research and collection of data must vary depending on their appropriateness for the particular circumstances under investigation (Richardson & Cilliers, 2001: 12). In research exploring human social systems, reductionist approaches are insufficient as the behaviour and influence of every component part involved can never be fully known. As Larsen-Freeman and Cameron (2008b: 201) contend in discussing the integration of complex systems approaches with applied linguistics research, 'from a complexity theory perspective, knowing about the parts individually is insufficient because complexity theorists are interested in understanding how the interaction of the parts gives rise to new patterns of behaviour'. Complexity thinking prompts us to understand research as an interpretation of such interactions, an interpretation in dialogue with reality. These interpretations are necessarily partial, and we must take a pragmatic approach towards representations emergent from research. How useful are they? What do they do? What do they involve? What do they foreground and what do they background (Davis & Sumara, 2005)?

Action Research and a Complex Systems Philosophy

In educational action research, teacher-researchers attempt to interpret the complexity of the learning environment. They describe its continuing alteration through the perceptions of participants, while concurrently working cooperatively to produce more effective conditions for all participants. In what follows I detail my understanding of complementarities between complexity thinking and action research which suggest this combination of philosophy and methodology to be particularly applicable to the study of classroom language learning motivation.

Focusing on change

Both action research and complex systems theory posit the critical need to focus on change. Indeed, motivation itself is fundamentally concerned with change, the 'want' that moves us to act. Action research has been held up by Larsen-Freeman and Cameron (2008b: 207) as an effective tool for investigating classroom complex systems as teacher-researchers use longitudinal designs to 'deliberately introduce "noise" into the system' and this 'investigation of the system's response to a perturbation contributes to a deeper understanding of system dynamics'. Moreover, in alignment with a complexity philosophy, action research recognises the subjectivity of the researcher in this overt introduction of change (Davis & Sumara, 2005). In a classroom-based study, the teacher-researcher is part of the change.

Furthermore, complex systems theory offers the suggestion that energy applied at a variety of systemic levels may push systems out of stable states towards change (Mason, 2008), even if we cannot know which particular component brought about the change. The introduction of change-action in action research parallels complex systems theory in that action research 'is more concerned with the processes involved in change and learning and how they might support participants to better adapt to their environment and circumstances' (Phelps & Graham, 2010: 189). In action research, researchers introduce change from a variety of different angles, based on existing and developing understandings of the system under study.

Focusing on a specific level

Van Geert (2008) contends that a complex systems approach to research requires a focus on one specific level of complexity. By examining this one particular level, we can observe the qualitative dynamics of the system. In alignment, the majority of educational action research focuses on change at a particular educational level, whether it be the individual, a group of learners, a class group or an educational institution as a whole. As such, action research on learner motivation might provide a detailed examination of multiple interactions between environmental and learner factors and has the potential to provide insights into both emerging changes in the learner and the classroom environment linked to the introduced change. In refraining from attempting to generalise, action research aligns with a complexity thinking philosophy in recognising that we cannot know all of the influences that make up the system/s under study, as for example with human motivation, but that we can focus on how introduced change affects one particular level of the system under observation.

Being attentive to initial conditions

In complex systems theory, the way a system is set up at the point at which study commences is of great importance (de Bot *et al.*, 2007). The initial state of the system influences the trajectory of future change. This consideration of the initial conditions of the system is in direct parallel with action research, in which a detailed study of problematic or challenging conditions leads to the introduction of some change-action attempting to address this feature. The implementation of change-action is followed by the collection of information about the change taking place and reflection on this information with the potential for further, revised change-action. The change-action that is introduced is heavily dependent on the initial understanding of the system.

Seeking attractor states

In complex systems theory, states that the system 'prefers', in which it shows relative stability over a particular timeframe, are termed 'attractor states' (Thelen & Smith, 1994: 56). Dörnyei and Ushioda (2011: 247) argue that in the study of language learning motivation 'meaningful research ... needs to focus on identifying potential attractors and attractor states, and then describing their scope and relevance'. Motivation involves a directed 'want' towards a given outcome or form of behaviour. In the action research process, change is introduced to the system with the intention of producing better outcomes or environments for participants. In this way, action research focusing on motivation might deliberately seek relatively stable attractor states that parties experience as connected to the 'want' of motivation. In the case of classroom language learning motivation, as we are dealing with humans, action research would describe the *subjective* process of change to perception of motivation in the classroom being studied.

Researching as co-adaptation

While taking as their starting point the initial understanding of challenges, action research studies develop as the understandings of participants develop. As the cycles of research are conducted and new data are elicited, the direction of the study may change as new questions and deeper understandings are facilitated (Burns, 2005; Herr & Anderson, 2005). Action research is responsive to the input gained through ongoing cycles of change-action, data collection, analysis and the reintroduction of new change-action. The process emerges and develops over time as this input evolves and as the participants and researchers involved refine their understandings and skills of enquiry.

Action research parallels complexity thinking in understanding that 'the universe changes as descriptions of the universe change' (Davis & Sumara, 2005: 315). From a complex systems perspective, the action research process itself might be seen as co-adaptation, as various systems involved adapt dynamically with one another over the course of the project. At the later stages of a study, this adaptation may lead to the investigation – through carefully introduced change-action – of dimensions that were not anticipated at the outset of the research project.

Action research is also conscious of itself as research. Many action research studies in educational settings involve a teacher-researcher diary which is included as part of the analysed data (Burns, 2010). Inclusion of the researcher in such a way meshes neatly with complexity thinking, as it recognises that what is happening through the research changes systems at various levels. There can be no objectivity in a purely scientific sense, because human systems are (a) too complex, and (b) co-adapt to each other (Davis & Sumara, 2006; Horn, 2008). In classroom action research on motivation, the teacher-researcher is part of the system under study and will affect different class members and processes in different ways on different days and across a study. Rather than ignoring or trying to minimise the impact of this influence, action research deliberately recognises this co-adaptation.

Design and Context of the Study

Given my understandings of such complementarities between action research and a complexity philosophy, the research reported in this book was designed as a study of EFL learning motivation in one class group. My exploration of the language learning motivation research from Japan discussed in Chapter 2 revealed the importance of investigating the learner-internal and -external interactions affecting motivation. It also uncovered a shortage of studies focusing directly on the classroom. Therefore, through a total of five action research cycles, I introduced change-action in my efforts to understand motivation across this class group.

As explained in Chapter 1, the study was carried out at my regular workplace in Japan. Over the course of the study I was employed at a kosen, a five-year college of technology spanning the traditional range from senior-high school to technical college. I taught one of three weekly 90-minute mandatory first-grade English lessons. These lessons had a focus on using English in practical communication. Although there was variation in language use by lesson and topic, I used English around 90% of the time and Japanese around 10% of the time. All regular lesson materials were written in English. The style of the lessons was based on task-based language teaching following Nunan (2004) and Willis and Willis (2007), in which a primary focus is given to meaningful language use applied to activity on tasks. The textbook used was *Widgets* (Benevides & Valvona, 2008). In the English lessons, students followed this textbook to use English in undertaking tasks while imagining that they were working as trainees at a fictitious international technology company (see Appendix A for a brief overview of the English course). Further to these lessons, I was also the homeroom teacher for the same class group. Homeroom periods consisted of one 45-minute session per week, essentially to be used for administrative purposes and announcements. However, there were also weeks in which there were no administrative duties. At these times the content of the homeroom period was left up to individual homeroom teachers. I was able to take advantage of this fact and make use of these 'free' homeroom periods to introduce possible-self activities.

The study focused longitudinally on homeroom periods and English lessons over one academic year. There were two primary reasons for a longitudinal approach for this one year. First, from the review of language learning motivation literature discussed in Chapter 2, (de)motivation in Japan was revealed as changing over time. I felt that a longitudinal study would foster a deeper understanding of motivation involving the language classroom through examining the ways in which participants perceived the dynamic interaction of self and environment. Secondly, the present study drew on the rationale of van Lier (2004: 194) that classroom research 'should aim to determine the natural time spans of the phenomena under investigation, including the temporal perceptions and constructions of the participants'. A longitudinal study was appropriate because the focus of this research was a group with boundaries defined by the social and educational structure of the college – one class of students and teacher naturally occurring in the environment of study. However, after one year students would be split into new classes with new homeroom teachers, and would become part of new class groups. Furthermore, I was not going to be teaching second-grade English when the students advanced to the second grade. This social reality suggested that the research should be limited to the one year that the sample composed of the original participants was naturally defined.

Student participants

The student participants consisted initially of 41 learners, aged 15–16 years. Two months into the study one student withdrew from the college, leaving a group of 40 students. All students were Japanese, with five female and 36 male students (including the male student who withdrew). As first-grade students, they had just transitioned from a wide variety of junior-high schools in and around the prefecture in which the college is located. In the regular Japanese education system, the learners were the equivalent of first-grade students at senior-high school. As a group, they had not taken any standardised English proficiency tests, but could be placed in the CEFR A1 to A2 basic user level of ability. Although their English proficiency was still at a basic stage of development, the college of technology is well known in the local area as a destination for junior-high school students with quite advanced academic abilities, particularly in science and mathematics. Among the 50-odd colleges that make up the kosen system in Japan, the college in which this study took place is also renowned for students with an interest in continuing on to complete undergraduate education and postgraduate studies.

The group of participants was chosen out of convenience as the only group with which I had both English lessons and homeroom periods. I hoped that having two sessions with students per week would allow sufficient opportunity for possible-self activities to be introduced. Moreover, the purpose of this study was to gain a deeper understanding of *my* students' motivation and self-ideas through the introduction of change-action to a class group of which *I* as the teacher was also part. The group of participants was therefore also chosen for its 'fitness for purpose' (Cohen *et al.*, 2011: 161), as I conceived the class group as being at a particular level of educational complexity in which it might be possible to examine qualitative dynamics.

Adolescents of this age range are developing the capacity for self-reflection through the expansion of cognitive abilities (Keating, 1990) and self-awareness (Damon & Hart, 1988). The ability to articulate through narrative and reflection on life events is also increasing at this stage (McAdams, 2008); indeed, adolescents may be keen to express their ideas about learning and their futures (Mornane, 2009: 227). I anticipated that classroom activities which promoted such metacognitive thinking would have the added bonus of providing the opportunity for a detailed examination of student perceptions of multiple learner-internal and -external interactions and have the potential to render insights into emerging change both in the learners and the classroom environment.

Teacher-researcher positioning

I was also part of the classroom group, and so it is necessary to examine my biases and subjectivity critically (Herr & Anderson, 2005). At the commencement of the study I was 35 years old, a Caucasian Australian national who had been living in Japan for the previous 12 years. I mention my cultural background to make explicit any possible influence this may have had on the students. As Seargeant (2009) notes, in Japan government policies and institutions such as private language schools and universities have promulgated an image of the well-dressed Caucasian male as the embodiment of 'authentic English'. I consider myself fluent in Japanese, having begun my study of the language after my first year in Japan. Near-native like Japanese was one of the requirements for employment in order to cope with homeroom roles that included meetings with caregivers. Although the college has a focus on science, engineering and technology, and the majority of teachers come from these fields, my educational background is in education.

It is further important to recognise the influence my dual roles and position of power as teacher/researcher may have had on the students. My actions within the class group were based on my own values and motives, in many ways a blend of my upbringing and education in Australia with my professional and family life in Japan. Students also had their own values and motives. The values and motives of students and the data that they produced will have been influenced through their perceptions of my various roles (McNiff & Whitehead, 2011). However, I felt that my duties as homeroom teacher allowed me to develop trust through my relationships with students, and acted as a balance to the power that I held as teacher/researcher.

Notwithstanding, I also felt it vital to record in my research journal (see the following section) my perceptions as a participant in the class group. What became clear during the research was that I was very conscious of these dual roles at times – as, for example, on occasions when I became concerned that any chastising of the class group might affect their motivation. However, as the research continued I became more accustomed to my roles. I found myself accepting that such occurrences were a natural part of the complexity of *this* classroom context and that it was important for me to continue to record my perceptions of these interactions and to search the data for any ways in which students noted these influences.

Finally, I wish to address a bias that my background may have fostered through my personal history of research with Japanese students. As introduced in Chapter 1, previous to this study I had conducted research about the 'problematic' nature of Japanese EFL classroom learning and motivation (e.g. Sampson, 2010, 2012). This prior research undoubtedly played a role in my definition of the challenge that I perceived initially and may have channelled my voyage through the literature. In particular, the research reported in Sampson (2012) also focused on the use of possible-self activities for the development of motivation. A number of the activities introduced in the present research drew on this previous study. However, I used my research journal to continually ask myself whether the change-action I was introducing flowed from the data, rather than from expectations built up through prior research experience. In such ways I attempted to maintain a critical view of my actions in the research process.

Data Collection Methods: Introspective Tools

This research aimed to explore the self-ideas, motivational perceptions and understandings of the participants. In order to provide a more detailed account of learners' experiences and conceptualisations in their own words, I employed qualitative, interpretive methods and data-collection instruments in which a theory emerges from the data. As Nunan and Bailey (2009: 307) assert, introspective data collection tools 'take us to a place that no other data collection method can reach – into the mind of the learner'.

Table 4.2 Data sources and volume (in A4 pages)

Data collection tool	Volume
Researcher journal	64 pages
Best possible English self (BPES) activity worksheet	41 pages
Past experience of English lessons (PEEL) activity worksheet	41 pages
Learning journal (total of four collection points)	242 pages
Semester 1 questionnaire (checking of themes)	80 pages
Summer holidays English skill building activity worksheet	40 pages
Semester 1 Learning journal self-reflection activity worksheet	20 pages
English expression lesson goal-review and action-planning worksheet	40 pages
Possible-self tree activity worksheet	40 pages
Expectations activity worksheet	40 pages
Semester 2 questionnaire (checking of themes)	80 pages
Semester 2 reflection activity worksheet	40 pages

Introspective journals were used to afford an insightful yet efficient way of gathering regular data from all the participants about the interaction between the classroom environment and self, without obstructing curriculum content to the disadvantage of students. A *learning journal* was used to provide students with a way of reflecting on their experiences in English lessons and homeroom periods (see Appendix B for instructions to students). My experiences and reflections as teacher and researcher member of the group were recorded in my *research journal*, adding further context to the data collected from students and my own perceptions across the year. This research journal contained perceptions from lessons and homeroom periods as well as the research process itself – in short, I was not one person for the lessons and another for research.

I implemented a set time at the end of each session of around five minutes in which participants wrote. This amount of time did not impose on the constraints of the regular curriculum, yet it allowed participants a routine reflective space in which to write directly following activities in the classroom. In parallel, I tried to enrich the quality of the data by making the learning journal part of students' grade, while also emphasising verbally that this grade was not based on quantity but on quality – thinking deeply about their experiences. Although ideally I had wanted to incorporate the meaningful opportunity for English production that writing the learning journal in English would have facilitated, I predicted from past experience with similar learners at the end of junior-high school that these non-English major students could express themselves more fully, fluently and with less perceived pressure in Japanese. I operate comfortably in English and Japanese. Although in the main I did not experience problems with translation, there were occasions when it was necessary to ask Japanese colleagues to read student handwriting.

In addition to these journals, there was also a range of further data collected over the year such as change-action worksheets. Texts produced by students during class activities were collected on completion of their use. The learning journals were collected based on the students' examination periods, as these were times natural to the context at which to collect data and reflect on introduced change-actions. Table 4.2 displays all of the data collection tools and their volume in terms of the A4 format in which they were collected from participants.

Data Analysis During the Action Research

At data collection points at the end of each action research cycle I conducted macro-analysis by reading student texts and looking for repetitions and regularities, drawing on the idea that participants may repeat or emphasise ideas that hold significance for themselves (Ryan & Bernard, 2003). Looking in particular to deepen my understandings of participants' motivation, I drew on Dörnyei's (2009b: 209) assertion that 'motivation refers to a cumulative arousal, or *want, that we are aware of*' (emphasis added). Therefore, although I also examined other areas of note across data sources, one way in which I investigated students' perceptions of motivation was through searching for such instances of a noted 'want' for future action. Broad themes emergent from a selection of texts were then compared with a further selection (Porto, 2007; Sa, 2002), involving the reading of all participant texts at that data-collection point. In this way, themes were interpreted as either representative or atypical. However, while some themes may have been atypical at that point, I was aware that these anomalous themes might gain importance at a later point in the data collection. Anomalous themes were therefore not discarded but noted so as to help give a fuller picture of variation across the class group (Larsen-Freeman & Cameron, 2008a).

The initial analysis was conducted completely in Japanese. I read through the data of every participant and made notes about recurrent themes. Following this process, I translated the students' writing from Japanese into English. Translation helped me to focus in detail once more on themes in the data. I also attempted to bring structure to the themes by organising them into hierarchical trees. During the action research, this structuring was often founded on my reading on the L2 Motivational Self System and possible-self theory: I brought my own list of conceptions and understandings of classroom motivation from my background and experience with the literature. The initial coding schemes were heavily based on my idea of exploring, deepening or testing these initial conceptions with new data as the action research process was underway.

In the next chapter I describe this action research process as it emerged during the research project. The chapter introduces a narrative of the planning, acting, observing and reflecting on data that guided the implementation of change-action over the five cycles of the study.

5 Action Research Narrative

Practitioner action research is a contextually based process. During this process the teacher-researcher attends to and focuses on possibilities that come to his/her awareness over the course of a study. One implication of such an approach is that the methodologies applied and change-actions introduced evolve as the researcher's insights and the practicalities of the context engender new directions in the research trajectory. Practitioner action researchers 'look out for what might be a useful way forward, and try it out' (McNiff & Whitehead, 2011: 35). The narrative in this chapter reveals ways in which my role as a classroom practitioner allowed me to actively make use of certain opportunities that came along. It will also, however, testify to conflicts I experienced due to the constraining realities of the college context. I acted to work with these constraints towards beneficial outcomes for the students and to develop my own understandings of their motivation to learn in the classroom. I became progressively aware of another implication of an action research approach as the study went on. Particularly if we apply a complexity philosophy, the focus of our investigation is conceived to be in constant interaction with innumerable other 'systems'. It is not sufficient therefore to examine only perceptions surrounding the introduction of change-action. While the inclusion of change-action is a key component of action research that can foster the development of new understandings for all participants, these understandings and potential repercussions will not be limited to the temporal or spatial context of the change-action. Put simply, I was interested in developing my understandings of classroom motivation through all the opportunities I had with these students. The change-actions were only part of the experiences that I shared with this class group in homeroom periods and English lessons. It is also with recognition of action research as a process that the analysis presented in this chapter at each stage of the action research represents those themes that I considered most influential to my understandings and change-action *during* the research process. I do not set forth a 'tidied up' version of events and understandings. I hope that these pages may provide insight into the dynamics of my own struggles to understand motivation in this class group while conducting the five action research cycles.

In this chapter I provide a sequential narrative of the *planning and acting* (including details of sessions which had an explicit focus on possible-self activities), *observing* (themes emergent from the data at the time) and *reflections* that informed planning in the subsequent cycle of action research. Please see Appendix C for an overview of the timing of the action research cycles, English lessons and homeroom sessions. In the discussion that follows, where participants are mentioned by name they have been assigned pseudonyms. For longer extracts and where necessary, the date is given and learning journal abbreviated to 'LJ', research journal to 'RJ'.

Cycle 1. Sowing Seeds: April

As detailed in Chapter 1, my initial interest in conducting this research was founded in part on experiences I had had with older students at the college. Many of these students appeared disengaged in my EFL lessons. When I asked them to write about why they were studying English, student responses suggested that they did not understand how they could use English in their futures. It was these perceptions and the insights gained from the review of L2 motivation literature that prompted the idea of exploring the images of an English-using self that were held by newly enrolled first-grade students in the current study.

Action research begins by 'testing the waters', so to speak, using shorter, more limited cycles in order to define issues and shine light on pre-existing assumptions (Cohen *et al.*, 2011). I hoped that eliciting data about the initial English-using self ideas of students would inform my development of activities in order to make more relevant and motivating lessons (see Appendix D for instructions to students for change-action activities in Cycle 1).

In a homeroom period early in the first semester I introduced two activities to encourage students to think about their future-selves. In the first activity, students wrote ideas about their future-selves in three different life areas – related to a job, English, and their general life – and at two time intervals – five and 15 years later. While students were quite hesitant at first as to what to write, they came alive when I asked them then to mingle and compare these ideas with those of other students. As a teacher I was impressed that these students, who had only recently entered the college, showed great enthusiasm in interacting with their new classmates. Linked to this activity, I then encouraged them to individually write specifically about their best-possible English self (BPES). This activity drew on research published in Sheldon and Lyubomirsky (2006), which asked participants to write *daily* about envisaging their 'best possible self' to explore affective and motivational effects over one month. I, however, aimed to gain an idea of the qualities of students' images of an ideal English-using self at the outset of the study. The activity guided students to write about their lives at any point in the future, imagining that they had worked hard and succeeded in their English studies.

The review of the literature had also suggested the strong influence of learners' past experiences in classroom language learning on their current and potential future motivational trajectories. Therefore, in an English lesson orientation session a couple of days later I asked my students to reflect on their *past* experiences of English lessons (hereafter, PEEL). I encouraged them to write a brief reflection on what they had done in their lessons, how they felt, and their ideas of why they had been studying English in junior-high school. Once again, although the writing proceeded in silence, students were a great deal more active when I asked them to mingle and discover who had written similar or different reflections. It seemed that they were exceedingly curious about comparing past experiences with class members from completely different junior-high schools. Following this activity I also introduced the learning journal, and asked students to write an entry at the end of every session directly related to the study.

Although I was busy adjusting to my new role as a homeroom teacher, I wanted to begin to gain an understanding of the students in my new class group as soon as possible. This curiosity was repaid as I rapidly analysed their initial writing about an English-using self in the past and future. I was instantly surprised by the projections collected in the BPES. Students wrote in a clear and developed way of images of a future self using English. Although some of these images concerned fostering friendships or living overseas, they were most often connected to occupation. The detail with which students wrote was completely at odds with the experiences I had had with older students at the college. In stark contrast, the PEEL activity uncovered very negative reflections on past classroom English studies. Students remarked about being demotivated by teacher-centred lessons in which their comprehension was not facilitated. A significant number of students also seemed to lack an understanding of the purpose of past English learning, reflected in comments such as 'I'm not really sure [why I was studying]'. There were even responses written questioningly: 'Because it's a [school] subject?'

I was eager to gain a holistic understanding of the data to consider the introduction of change-action, yet I knew that I could not focus on all of the areas revealed. I determined to focus on further fostering student ideas of a future English-using self related to occupation. I hoped that such a focus would extend the promising insights from the BPES activity, and also push students to recognise the relevance of their classroom English study. This emphasis tied in neatly with the overall vocational focus of the college. Regarding English lessons, the PEEL analysis also supported my intention to include as much group work as possible, in order to move the focus away from myself as the teacher and encourage students to scaffold each other's comprehension.

Cycle 2. Tentative Beginnings: April–May

The English lessons continued with learners starting on a task-based course. The story-based theme of the textbook I employed, *Widgets* (Benevides & Valvona, 2008), sees students training at an international technology company. They use English to communicate about technology and the development of new products (see Appendix A for an overview of the year-long course). I had to select the textbook four months prior to meeting the students. I therefore cannot claim that the curriculum introduced was based on the data collected in Cycle 1. However, the focus in the textbook on using English for a job matched well with what students had written in the BPES activity. I was aware of a cross-cultural study in which Japanese people expressed more developed possible-self images related to occupation/education (Unemori *et al.*, 2004: 333). I hoped to draw on this trend from past research findings and the initially collected data to develop these images through lessons. I anticipated being able to support these images further by introducing possible-self activities into homeroom periods.

However, during these first weeks of the semester I became frustrated at attempting to incorporate research alongside regular college duties. Administrative tasks absorbed almost all of the time allocated to homeroom periods for these new students. I felt the self-induced pressure of trying to make some substantial contribution to students' learning motivation through my research, yet there was little chance to introduce explicit possible-self activities to homeroom sessions.

As it happened, a key development in this cycle of the action research occurred when an older student I had taught previously wandered into my office midway through April. *Ren* had just arrived back from a three-week internship with a Japanese technology company in Thailand. As we were conversing, I developed the idea of inviting him to talk to my students as a kind of role model. I hoped that such an experience might encourage students in some way to view this older student as their future self, and become motivated to work towards this potential. Ren decided the content of the presentation. He arrived at the classroom early, and we chatted in English as we were setting up the presentation. He then talked to the students in Japanese for around 30 minutes, using computer slides to introduce the overseas internship programme and what he perceived about English and communication through his experiences in Thailand. At times he also addressed me in English.

Much to my dismay at the time, this was the only deliberate possible-self activity in Cycle 2. I noted my vexation in my research journal:

> As things are going, there is just so much time taken with boring surveys or menial information I have to pass on to students. ... Looking at the weeks ahead, it's hard to see when the next chance for a PS [possible-self]

activity might be. And so this makes me frustrated for my research, and for the possibilities of doing something worthwhile with these students. (RJ, 21/5/2011)

My initial excitement from Cycle 1 of the action research rapidly dissipated as I felt I was losing opportunities to introduce change-action that could help students to reflect on their English learning. At this point in the study, I was filled with the idea that it was the change-actions that would drive new understandings about my students' motivation. Without extensive change-action, I was dubious that the data would reveal anything particularly remarkable or insightful. Nevertheless, I collected the learning journals in the final English lesson before midterm exams and hurriedly translated and analysed them in the brief period before lessons recommenced.

As the only change-action, I was naturally drawn to data concerning the role-model session. After the older student's presentation I had initially been worried that the topic might have been too far removed from these students, who had only a couple of months previously transitioned from junior-high school. However, despite these fears, students wrote of changes in their perception of the plausibility of an English-using self:

> When I thought that the English I've been studying since junior-high school is actually useful for my future, I felt like I wanted to try myself to make my English even better ... And sometime, I want to become like today's presenter. (Yusuke, LJ, 11/5/2011)

The role-model presentation also encouraged students to write about becoming aware of a gap between their current English-using self and where they would like to be in the future in an unexpected way. Although I had asked the older student to come and speak *to the class*, many students wrote of ways in which their observation of *interactions in English between the older student and myself* fostered their awareness of a gap between their present- and ideal-selves. Sayaka's reflection is illustrative:

> When I saw him [the older student] speaking fluent English without looking at any paper, I thought that I'd like to be able to become like him, and communicate with people from many other countries. (Sayaka, LJ, 11/5/2011)

It was experiences at this time that reminded me of the value (and indeed necessity) of not only looking for insights through data related to the change-actions. One theme from the lessons that was particularly noticeable was the fluctuation in motivation expressed by students. Writing revealed that their motivation in lessons varied from week to week and also within lessons during different activities. This dynamic nature of their motivation was influenced by their comprehension in lessons and also by elements external to the direct lesson environment, such as experiences in other lessons or fatigue. Moreover, in parallel with comments regarding the role-model session, data concerning lessons also revealed a developing awareness of a gap between a present and possible self as students 'tried on' their English self in activities:

> Even though I could imagine a product inside my head, it was very difficult to try to explain it in English so the other person could understand. That was because I know too few words, so when I tried to explain to another student, everything was too vague. I got to know how difficult it is to explain your ideas in English, so I want to work to try to be able to express myself better. (Taichi, LJ, 24/5/2011)

Reflected in Taichi's writing, experiences in lessons encouraged students to express motivation to improve their English. However, although many students often wrote of setting goals for the next lesson or the future, they frequently used only the Japanese word 頑張る (*ganbaru* – to persist/do one's best). As such, these goals were quite vague and lacked the detail of concrete actions to work towards the goal: 'I want to try hard next time, too', 'I want to do my best to be able to listen to English'.

Reflecting on the data analysis, many students had made a connection between self-images and English study through the role-model presentation. However, although students were noticing a gap between their present ability and what they would like to become, the way in which they wrote of steps to move towards this future self was underdeveloped. I picked up on the themes of 'noticing a gap' and 'vague goal-setting'. I had the intention of introducing change-action to push students to think more concretely about the ways in which they could become agentic in studying to decrease the gap between an ideal self and their current self.

Cycle 3. A Puzzling Outcome: June–September

English lessons recommenced after the first semester mid-term exam break with students continuing to 'work' at the international technology company. As an initial attempt to encourage them to think more concretely about ways in which they might work towards decreasing the gap between their present and ideal English-using selves, I planned an English lesson focusing specifically on student-perceived actions they could take (see Appendix E for instructions to students and examples from change-action activities in this cycle). I first made a short presentation to the students about my own learning experiences with the Japanese language, and the way in which I had used writing in a diary as one strategy to improve my Japanese ability. Students then discussed in groups for around 10 minutes about one of four

English language skills and how they could work on improving that particular skill. They next mingled to hear ideas from other group members for improving different skills. After mingling, the students moved back into their original groups to share what they had heard from others, and then wrote those ideas on their worksheets. Due to the restrictions of the curriculum we were using, at the time I had to leave this activity at this stage of development. I was, however, hopeful that it may have at least raised students' awareness of concrete actions they could take to improve their English skills.

A number of weeks passed with again little opportunity to introduce further change-action. Before I knew it the summer holidays were looming. Although I initially had no intention of setting students a task over this period, they seemed quite focused from their preparation for a poster presentation we had done over the last English lessons before the summer break. I recollected the skill-building activity from a few weeks earlier. In a final homeroom period I distributed a worksheet displaying a number of the English study strategies that students themselves had come up with in the earlier lesson. Students first drew a circle next to those strategies that they felt were *possible* for them to try at that point in time, and then chose one of these strategies to actually carry out over the summer holiday break. I asked them to write about why they chose a particular strategy, to make predictions of its effectiveness, and to note any factors that might hinder their implementation of the strategy.

Following the summer holiday break, students wrote reflections about trying to use their selected strategy and compared their experiences with classmates. I had also analysed the learning journals and constructed a simple questionnaire featuring closed- and open-ended items regarding the themes at that point. I was able to make time in another homeroom period for students to think back over their experiences. I first asked them to read and write a brief reflection on their own learning journal entries from the first semester. After collecting these paragraphs, I also asked students to record their responses to the questionnaire.

I combined my initial understandings of themes emergent from students' learning journals with their own reflections on their learning journals, data from the questionnaires, the summer skill-building activity and my research journal. Considering my gradually expanding understanding of the role of context in complex systems theory, an interesting theme of which I became aware at this point concerned students' writing of comparisons of ability with other students. Often these comparisons were within the groups in which they spent a majority of their time. However, activities also fostered in some students comparisons of ability with students from other groups, and perhaps a sense that they might be doing things differently from how they had been done up to that point. Based on this theme and my reading into the L2 Motivational Self System, I asked students in the questionnaire whether such comparisons encouraged them to *want to* study more (linking

Table 5.1 Questionnaire data about other-comparison

	Agree strongly	Agree	Agree somewhat	Disagree somewhat	Disagree	Disagree strongly
When I'm doing English activities, I look at other students and think, 'I ought to study more'.	15 (37.5%)	16 (40%)	4 (10%)	4 (10%)	1 (2.5%)	0
When I'm doing English activities, I look at other students and think, 'I want to study more'.	4 (10%)	13 (32.5%)	13 (32.5%)	8 (20%)	2 (4%)	0

to an ideal-self), or if they felt they *ought to* study more (connecting to the ought-to self). Although there was not a significant difference, the questionnaire data (see Table 5.1) tended to suggest that students perceived comparisons with others as a kind of pressure.

Students frequently wrote of clear future images of themselves, sometimes directly related to using English and at other times more general images from lessons. The following extract is representative of those that directed me to expand a theme entitled 'future self' at this time:

> Today lots of different phrases for agreeing, disagreeing and disagreeing politely came up. ... There will definitely be times when I have to turn down some annoying person inviting me to a meal, or a superior inviting me. So it was very useful. The next time I meet a foreigner, I want to try on purpose to get them to invite me to do something, just so that I can turn them down! (Tetsuo, LJ, 21/6/2011)

I understood students to be writing regarding the ways in which they could feel the plausibility of a future English-using self through using English successfully in activities and making progress. This progress was frequently linked to a future sense of action. They felt energised to work towards a future English-using self by the successes they were having in the classroom. Analysis also revealed students continuing to write about gaps between their current and future self. Sometimes these gaps involved a quite distal future self, while at others the future self seemed more connected to the classroom. The activities that focused explicitly on concrete English learning strategies were frequently linked to this realisation of a gap. Students also noticed a gap in ability during lessons and made reference to concrete actions to lessen the gap in the short term:

> We did listening again after a long break, but I couldn't catch anything. There were so many words that I didn't know. I thought that if I had

only studied the words from the textbook before the lesson, I would have been able to catch more, so I want to do that from now on. (Tomoe, LJ, 21/6/2011)

However, despite *my* excitement as I uncovered students writing of these future-selves, a truly perplexing result at this point was that the questionnaire data suggested many *students* did not consciously recognise these images. Through the participant checking of themes via the questionnaire and the learning journal reflection some students responded in agreement with items related to future image (see Table 5.2). However, what was perplexing was that around half the class did not recognise such an image and did not agree that their future-self image had become more concrete over the semester.

Although perhaps oversimplifying, at the time I understood the connections between student writing of noticing a gap and making more concrete action plans as stemming from the change-action I had introduced, encouraging them to think explicitly about how they could improve specific English skills. I admit, though, that my primary concern at this point in the study was the confusion I felt at the lack of endorsement by the students of the role of a future English-using self image. In Cycle 1 of the action research students had initially expressed clear images of a future self when they had just entered the college. Were these images fading? Were these images not being connected to lessons in a motivating way? Was my understanding of this 'future English-using self-image' different from the students'? I was also intrigued by participant writing regarding comparisons with other students, and in what ways these comparisons were influencing their motivation and English-using self-images.

I wanted to go back over all the data I had collected and revise my analysis. However, the second semester had already begun. With my teaching load, I became frustrated that I simply did not have the time to go through the data again despite the questions that came up from the analysis. I needed to press on with the change-action that the data suggested to me *now*.

Table 5.2 Questionnaire data about future English-using self image

	Agree strongly	Agree	Agree somewhat	Disagree somewhat	Disagree	Disagree strongly
I have an image of 'myself using English in the future'.	5 (12.5%)	5 (12.5%)	10 (25%)	9 (22.5%)	10 (25%)	1 (2.5%)
Through English activities my image of 'myself using English in the future' has become more concrete.	2 (5%)	8 (20%)	12 (30%)	13 (32.5%)	5 (12.5%)	0

Emergent from the mismatch between my understandings and those of students, I determined to implement change-action concerning students' images of a future English-using self in order that the understandings of these images by all participants might become clearer.

Cycle 4. Delving Deeper: September–November

In an English lesson early in the new semester I introduced change-action that combined a focus on future-self image and a continuation of student-determined goal setting (see Appendix F for instructions from change-action activities in this action research cycle). Late one night I had come across a Japanese television programme with the title 'Don't give up on English' (my translation). The 30-minute programme introduced a number of case studies of young Japanese employees at technology companies in Japan being suddenly confronted with the need to use English because of company-internal transfer. It showed various imaginative ways in which these employees worked to improve their English. I decided that viewing this programme might well be beneficial for my students. I gave the students a viewing task of deciding the most important point from the programme. Following viewing, the students talked in groups and wrote on the whiteboard what they considered to be the vital points, which we then discussed. A further activity drew a parallel with the strategies that technology workers had been shown using. Students wrote what goals they held for themselves over the next half-year of English lessons. I encouraged them to think and write in their learning journals about two points: (i) what do you want to be able to do by the end of this semester? and (ii) how will you reach your goal?

A few weeks into the second semester I was able to find an additional opportunity to encourage students to become more cognisant of their images of a future English-using self. In a homeroom session, I first introduced a stress-management technique in which students could experience a physical effect of creating images. I then went through a guided-imagery activity entitled 'two minutes into the future' (adapted from Arnold et al., 2007). This activity asked students to close their eyes and follow my voice as I helped them to envision a future self using English fluently and effectively in social and occupational settings. I was particularly struck by the way in which students all participated in the stress management activity by moving their bodies as directed, and regarding the English-self activity I noted in my research journal that 'students stayed with their image for quite some time even after I'd stopped talking' (RJ, 12/10/2011). Directly after the activity, I instructed students to write down their feelings about their images of a future English-using self. In the following English lesson I further reminded students of these activities, and encouraged them to try to be conscious of their image of a future English-using self during lessons.

I once again collected students' learning journals before the mid-semester exam break and intended to quickly analyse them during this period. This said, there were only the 10 days before lessons recommenced, and I once again had to invigilate a number of 100-minute exams, conduct English presentation skills lessons for older students at the college and deal with regular administrative duties for my homeroom class. In the middle of data analysis I recorded in my research journal: 'A brief reflection: AR [action research] is really rushed!' (RJ, 10/11/2011). In the end, although I analysed the majority of the data during the exam period and was able to return the learning journals to the students, the analysis continued over a number of weeks.

Across the data at this analysis point it appeared that the environment had encouraged students to write more on the development of their images of future self. First, the linking of the guided-imagery activity with English lessons had fostered reflection on a future English-using self. As one student wrote in the homeroom and then in the following English lesson:

I want to become that me of years in the future that I could see in the distance. (Yusuke, LJ, 12/10/2011; homeroom period)

I thought that every little bit of English I try to speak or use now at some point in my future I'll be able to use it. Even if it's little by little, I want to try my hardest to become able to use English normally. There's no harm in doing English. (Yusuke, LJ, 13/10/2011; English lesson)

However, there was also diversity in these reflections and the influence that they had on perceptions by students. Although some were aware of a strongly emotional response during the guided-imagery activity, they nevertheless found it difficult to translate this into action in the English classroom.

Particularly prominent in this cycle was the way in which students described their perceptions of interactions with other students during activities. Classroom interaction allowed a recognition of the value of cooperation with others as well as opportunities to use and build practical English ability. While at times students noted the difficulties of working with others, they also reflected on the capacity of cooperation to extend individual ability:

All the members of the group were throwing their opinions out in a very lively way, we got a little off track, but in the end we were able to pull together the way of using the product that we all agreed upon. Putting how to use something into English that we don't usually use was difficult. But amid that, from the four of us we could make it into one shape, so I was glad. (Eiji, 20/10/2011)

Once again, students continued to write of comparisons with others. They compared their ability and reflected on their ideas or actions in comparison with those of other students. Some students also wrote of pressures that they felt from making comparisons with others: 'I feel something like I can't keep up with the conversation of the others in my team, so I thought I want to do it properly next time.' These perceived contributions to the group varied by lesson, as is evident in the following two entries by Shun:

> Today's lesson was really difficult and there were many things that I didn't understand, so I was helped a lot by the members in my group. I want to also be useful for other members in my team, so by at least looking up words, I want to be a useful person. (Shun, LJ, 29/9/2011)
>
> It was even more difficult than I imagined to make questions. ... But the people in my team are really excellent students, so it worked out somehow in the end. This time, I feel like I was somewhat useful. (Shun, LJ, 10/11/2011)

In this cycle of the action research, through the introduction of activities focusing explicitly on future-self images, some students made connections between their activities in the present and future possibility. This development was exciting for me, and seemed to affirm Ushioda's (2009: 225) observation that 'future self representations or possible selves are entirely continuous with language learners' current selves'. On the other hand, there were students who did not make such connections. Due to my gradually evolving understandings of complex systems theory, I did not want to draw simplistic linear cause-effect conclusions. I became increasingly aware of the need to examine in more depth the dynamics and diversity of students' recognition of these connections by looking further at data from previous cycles. However, at this point in the study I simply did not have time to go back and review my analysis:

> It really is not feasible at the moment. Trying to do this coding [analysis] while teaching lessons, invigilating exams, doing grading and whatnot is just enough already. ... I really feel this is a shortcoming of this kind of research. (RJ, 21/11/2011)

In spite of my growing recognition of the potential value of re-exploring the data, the constraints of the context meant that I could not implement this revision at this point in time. Writing by students about the ways they were being influenced by comparisons with other students was especially intriguing. In Dörnyei's (2009a: 29) description of the L2 Motivational Self System there is mention of the peer group as part of the 'L2 learning experience'. Student writing of other-comparison indicated that the other might act as an ideal self, something to aspire to, or an ought-to self, 'the attributes that one believes one *ought to* possess to meet expectations and *avoid* possible negative outcomes' (Dörnyei, 2009a: 29; italics in original). Students also continued to notice gaps in ability through interaction and comparison with others. However, despite the introduced activities in which they delineated clear goals for the second semester and how they would work towards them, further mention of these goals was not apparent in the data. What the analysis suggested to me was the need to find ways of stressing to students the connection between present action and their possible future, while also explicitly exploring students' ideas of perceptions of motivational influences from others.

Cycle 5. New Directions: December–February

During the final cycle of action research, homeroom periods allowed far more freedom of content. The academic year was winding down through the winter break, and my administrative duties were reduced. I introduced a number of activities with an explicit link to possible-self theory and the L2 Motivational Self System (see Appendix G for instructions and examples of change-action activities in this action research cycle). However, I was also cautious of overburdening the students. As I wrote in my research journal, 'Is it all too onerous on them? Aren't they getting sick of Sampson with his "motivation"?' (RJ, 21/11/2011).

As an initial change-action in this cycle I introduced an activity specifically revising students' self-determined goals for studying English. In an English lesson, students reread their learning journal entry on their goals for the second semester, and then wrote reflections about the actions they had taken to reach those goals. They then wrote revised goals. Following this, students mingled and shared their responses to their goal review. After this opportunity to compare reflections, I drew attention to the whiteboard, on which I had written an outline of the activities we would do in that lesson. I asked the students to look at the tasks and their overall goal for the end of the semester, and to write down the steps they would take in that lesson to work towards their goal. At the end of the lesson, students then judged whether they had achieved, partially achieved, or not achieved their mini-goal. This action planning was repeated over the remaining lessons.

Across two homeroom sessions I also introduced an adaptation of the possible-self tree activity (Hock *et al.*, 2006) which had so impressed me during my initial review of the literature. I began by showing a short presentation of photographs of my past, and the hopes for a possible-future that I had held. I next passed out a worksheet asking students to think and write about their hopes and fears in different life areas, and their current actions, abilities or elements of personality that might affect these hopes or fears.

I asked them to bring this sheet again to the following week's homeroom period. In the second session I gave instructions for drawing a possible-self tree: with the trunk as self; with three branches with hopes for themselves as an English learner, a worker and in general; with poison, lightning and termites as expressions of fear for the same future areas; and finally with healthy and rotten roots representing aspects of the present self, supportive or detrimental to obtaining the ideal self. I recorded in my research journal my pleasure and relief at how students engaged with the activity as they were working individually on their own pictures: 'What I was ... surprised about (pleasantly) was how the students got down to just doing it. I mean, it's kind of a strange thing, your teacher asking you to draw a *tree* in the homeroom period' (RJ, 14/12/2011).

After this very specific focus on connecting the present self to the future self, I also developed an activity in order to further explore students' perceptions of influences from people around them. In a homeroom session, I asked learners to describe what expectations they felt from their family, companies and teachers relating to English and as future college graduates. After they had written their own ideas, I then encouraged them to mingle and compare their ideas of expectations with other students, writing the ideas of others alongside their own. Connected to this activity, in the following English lesson I asked participants to collaboratively order a list of ways in which they predicted that English would be used professionally by graduates of colleges of technology. I then showed them the actual results from the *Koseneigo kenkyuuiinkai* (2008) report, as well as results regarding the English skills that kosen teachers and university academics believe necessary for technology students.

Shortly after the introduction of this change-action I had another opportunity to invite an older student to give a role-model speech to the class. In the summer holidays, *Sho* had studied in Canada for a month, and had begun to regularly visit my office. During our discussions he talked about his experiences abroad as well as reflections on studying English over his time at the college. I thought that his insights might make valuable listening for my students, and he readily volunteered to speak before them. During his 30-minute presentation he showed a variety of photographs of his time overseas, talking in Japanese about things that he had found different between Canada and Japan, and introducing the study-abroad system and facilities. I also prompted him to talk about realisations regarding English that he had made over his time outside Japan.

As the academic year drew to a close, I collected the learning journals and rapidly analysed them. I combined this analysis with that from the previous cycle to draw up a questionnaire and checked the themes with the students in a penultimate homeroom session. I also wanted to ask them to reflect on their own learning journals again and describe what they had perceived over the year. On a final worksheet, I encouraged students to individually reflect on how they perceived their motivation towards English study as changing over the year, any specific events that they recognised as connected with their motivation, and how their ideas of an English-using self had changed. I further wanted to allow them to share their ideas with others in the class and form a sense of closure to the research, yet also feel that their participation would not end abruptly with this final session. As a result, I asked them to discuss and present advice to their classmates about continuing to study English, and for those students who would enter the college in the following year.

I combined these student reflections and questionnaire data with the learning journals, change-action activity worksheets and my research journal. Regarding students' images, the questionnaire revealed images of a future English-using self to be more fully endorsed than at mid-study, and an item focusing on the connection between the consciousness of such an image and motivation was relatively well endorsed (see Table 5.3). However, as was also apparent in Table 5.3, students agreed a lot more with the item concerning future-self image becoming more concrete than at the end of Cycle 3. Students also strongly concurred with an item asking whether their perceived motivation increased when English study connected to their present self.

These results seemed rewarding considering that my intention in the action research was to foster in students more recognition of the relevance of English study through encouraging them to reflect on an English-using

Table 5.3 Questionnaire data about future English-using self image and connection to present

	Agree strongly	Agree	Agree somewhat	Disagree somewhat	Disagree	Disagree strongly
I have an image of 'myself using English in the future'.	5 (12.5%)	7 (17.5%)	18 (45%)	4 (10%)	6 (15%)	0
My motivation goes up when I study being conscious of the image of 'myself using English in the future'.	6 (15%)	11 (27.5%)	13 (32.5%)	8 (20%)	2 (5%)	0
Through English activities my image of 'myself using English in the future' has become more concrete.	5 (12.5%)	13 (32.5%)	16 (40%)	6 (15%)	0	0
When I'm studying English, my motivation goes up when I feel 'this study has a connection to myself now'.	10 (25%)	14 (35%)	16 (40%)	0	0	0

self. Comparisons and interactions with other students also continued to be a strong theme. A key new insight in this area was that English lessons encouraged them to write about showing consideration to other students in the ways that they interacted in activities. Activities in which students could interact and compare their thinking with other students provided an impetus for reflections on their own understandings. Students' increased motivation from interactions and comparisons with others was also evident in the questionnaire. Social comparison in lessons and listening to others talking about English study (such as the role-model speakers, or the teacher) was more strongly linked to feelings of 'ought to study English' than an ideal 'want to study English'. Students also in the main concurred with a questionnaire item about motivation being dynamically linked to others, such as classmates or teachers (see Table 5.4).

A notable new theme of which I became aware was that the classroom environments in this cycle also appeared to encourage students to articulate their worries and fears about their English studies. Students wrote of connections they were making between their current actions and a future feared self in response to the possible-self tree activities. In the English lessons, the

Table 5.4 Questionnaire data about social elements of motivation

	Agree strongly	Agree	Agree somewhat	Disagree somewhat	Disagree	Disagree strongly
When I'm doing English activities, I look at other students and think 'I ought-to study more'.	19 (47.5%)	14 (35%)	7 (17.5%)	0	0	0
When I'm doing English activities, I look at other students and think 'I want to study more'.	7 (17.5%)	12 (30%)	13 (32.5%)	6 (15%)	2 (5%)	0
When I hear other people (students, teachers) talking about studying English I think 'I ought-to study more'.	19 (47.5%)	16 (40%)	4 (10%)	1 (2.5%)	0	0
When I hear other people (students, teachers) talking about studying English I think 'I want to study more'.	8 (20%)	13 (32.5%)	10 (25%)	6 (15%)	3 (7.5%)	0
My own 'motivation to study English' is influenced by the motivation of other people (students, teachers) on that day.	7 (17.5%)	14 (35%)	11 (27.5%)	6 (15%)	1 (2.5%)	1 (2.5%)

activities fostered reflection on current abilities and worries that these abilities would not improve. Teru's writing is representative:

> The thing that I thought today was, why, when I try to speak English, am I embarrassed? I don't know whether that's because of the poorness of my English, or because this is Japan, but I thought that it'd be good if my embarrassment went away. (Teru, LJ, 12/1/2012)

Finally, another newly emergent understanding was that students wrote of their experiences as 'opportunities' for reflection on their self-concepts now and in the future. These opportunities or chances were mentioned in connection with the regular English lessons as well as with sessions in which possible-self change-action was introduced. Student writing often referred to an interactive connection between these opportunities and the project of revising the self:

> Today in the homeroom I received a chance to look at myself. Recently, before I go to sleep I've been thinking about myself, so it was really good. Recently I've been strongly feeling that I lack kindness towards other people. If I hadn't realised, I'd still be doing it when I'm an adult. That's really scary. (Haruki, LJ, 7/12/2011)

Moving on

I had arrived at the end of the action research cycles, yet there were many themes which emerged this time that had not appeared earlier in the study. Although I had initially planned to analyse data only during the action research cycles, the rich and voluminous data took on a life of their own. The students' writing became more explanatory and vivid in their depictions of interactions between self and the classroom environments. The themes in Cycles 4 and 5 set off my thinking, and my understandings that had been gaining volume and shape as the data accumulated began to settle into a new pattern of questions and potential understandings. One vital question was whether students had been writing about 'chances' and 'opportunities' from the beginning of the year. Or was this a perception I had developed over the year? Did students only write of opportunities for realisations, or might their writing also suggest this to be a useful way of conceptualising the ways in which students wrote of interactions being motivating? Had fears been a feature of student writing previously but I had somehow missed these references? Had students' ideas about acting to be considerate of others during interactions developed over the year? And how did these actions interact with the motivation of other students?

I planned this research to be longitudinal because I wanted to introduce change that might be beneficial for students. I planned this research to be longitudinal also in order to look at the *dynamics* of student self in the classroom and connections to motivation. One reason for my application of action research was that it seemed particularly appropriate to study such dynamics (Phelps & Hase, 2002). Yet, as had been nagging me throughout the study, I realised that the action research process itself did not allow me to look at change longitudinally. In the context of the college in which I undertook this study, the *tool* of change, that is, the action research process with its rushed nature, hindered my ability to look at the longitudinal dynamics in the data. The process highlighted a major limitation of action research: the combination of teacher with researcher roles in this context did not allow sufficient time for data analysis and reflection. I also was not the same person with the same thinking as at earlier stages in the research process. My own understandings had developed through my experiences over the year. To deepen these understandings, I needed to go back through the data as a whole.

As I revisited and became more deeply engaged with the data, the interactions between the emergent themes became increasingly noticeable. A key methodological advance at this stage was that I now had the time to conduct Boolean searches through all of the data sources in order to uncover changing relationships between themes and evolution in motivation and self of participants over the course of the study. I compared these new understandings with ideas from the literature. This process might be likened to 'theoretical comparison', a tool with which 'properties and dimensions that are derived from the "outside" ... give us ideas of what to look for in the data, making us sensitive to things we might have overlooked before' (Corbin & Strauss, 2008: 76). I had drawn on a complexity philosophy to underpin my action research (see Chapter 4). As my revised analysis progressed, the features of complex systems moreover seemed to fit well with my developing understanding of the data. The dynamism seemed highly congruent with complex systems theory, and began to take my explorations into new directions, as I sought for a more integrated representation of motivation in the class group.

Experiences during the action research and the evolution of my thinking through this theoretical comparison also engendered a reconceptualisation of my research questions to deepen my understandings of motivation from a complex systems perspective. The first two research questions remained untouched. To recall:

(1) How do participants express their ideas of an English-using self at the commencement of the study?
(2) What ideas of an English-using self emerge among the participants from the experience of introduced change in the classroom?

However, when I returned to the data, I considered the third research question as I had proposed it at the start of the study too narrow (see Chapter 4). It implied a direct, linear path between an English-using self and motivation. In order to reflect my revised understandings, I re-formed Question 3. The new phrasing of the question sought to reflect my interest in investigating the classroom space from a *holistic* perspective, exploring interaction between introduced change in the form of possible-self activities and English lessons, learner self-concept and classroom language learning motivation, asking:

(3) What shared understandings about the emergent spaces appear to affect the participants' motivation in learning English?

Furthermore, a review of literature from applied linguistics and general education revealed an evident gap that could be filled by studying the language learning class group holistically and conceptualising it as a complex system (see the next chapter). The desire to create 'genuinely new insights' (Zuber-Skerritt, 1996: 17) from the action research, and to conduct a deeper, interpretive analysis of the data that might still be transferable to other contexts led me to develop a fourth research question. Question 4 aimed to explore the applicability of using complex systems theory to the investigate motivation in other similar settings, asking:

(4) How well does complex systems theory enable a deeper understanding of motivation and demotivation in Japanese EFL learning?

Part 2
再見
Re-viewing

6 Revisiting Complex Systems Theory

A complex systems approach offers an enticingly fresh yet phenomenologically grounded perspective on the dynamic process of motivation to learn in the foreign language classroom. To recall from Chapter 1, Mitchell (2009: 13) defines complex systems as those 'in which large networks of components with no central control and simple rules of operation give rise to complex collective behaviour, sophisticated information processing, and adaptation via learning or evolution'. In order to provide a glimpse into the potential of complex systems theory, this chapter is split into two broad sections: an overview of the commonly noted features of complex systems, and an examination of theoretical and empirical work exploring education and language learning from a complex systems perspective. While the chapter is predominantly theory based, it also forms a bridge between the description of the action research cycles in the previous chapters and revised analysis grounded in complex systems theory. It serves as a foundation for the presentation of results of my study in the chapters that follow.

Features of Complex Systems

In light of the multiple and dynamic influences on the development of EFL learner motivation in the classroom, the following sections draw on a range of literature to offer a synthesis of the common features and terminology in complex systems theory. Besides offering a useful vocabulary, these features also suggest new angles from which to interpret motivational change in the classroom.

Multiple agents

An important feature in complex systems is that they are thought to be made up of *multiple agents*. These agents are defined by the level at which we choose to look at a system. Proteins, organs, individual animals or species might all be taken as agents depending on the level of the complex system under study. Focusing on motivation in a language learning class group, we can consider learners and teachers as agents in the classroom system. The agents are not cognisant of the overall behaviour of the system as a whole – they react only to information directed through them at the local level (Cilliers, 1998). That is to say, a complex system has *distributed control* across agents rather than being centrally controlled (Davis & Sumara, 2005).

Among these agents there is usually considerable *diversity* and *redundancy*. Page (2011: 20–24) broadly discusses *diversity* as meaning that agents of the same kind may have variations in some characteristic, there may be difference in kinds of agents, or there may be diversity in the composition of groups of agents. The diversity among agents allows various forms of behaviour and novel responses to the environment by the agents in the system. On the other hand, *redundancy* concerns similarities across agents in the system. This feature allows one agent to take the place of another when there is a breakdown of one of the agents or interconnections with an agent. Redundancy also plays a vital role in facilitating interactions among agents – they must be heterogeneous enough to be able to exchange energy in the form of information or behaviour (Davis & Sumara, 2010).

Open interacting systems

Reflecting the notion of motivation involving interaction between self and environment, complex systems can be said to be *open* in the sense that they interact with other systems to both receive and offer energy in interaction with their *environment* – the here-and-now *context* in which the system is evolving (Larsen-Freeman & Cameron, 2008a: 34). The open nature of complex systems implies that, to some degree, any definition of *boundaries* is arbitrary, with the range of the system being instead determined by the purpose of description of the observer (Cilliers, 1998).

Complex systems *interact* dynamically with systems at other levels. Change at any level affects all other levels in some way because there is complete interconnectedness between the elements in the system. Systems depend on both their internal resources through interactions – between agents that may be made up of further complex systems – and external resources through interactions with other systems (de Bot & Larsen-Freeman, 2011). These processes of communication and collaboration between systemic levels are an integral part of complex systems theory, to the extent that one system cannot be considered without also considering the other systems with which it is connected. As a result, we cannot focus only on agents or only on context, but must more appropriately focus on agents-with/in-context (Davis & Sumara, 2006).

Due to the interacting nature of elements, both the agents themselves and the ways in which they interact with one another are constantly changing, such that the same energy introduced to the system at different points in time or through a different area of the system may have very different effects (Radford, 2008). That is, cause-effect relationships are considered to be *non-linear* and *relational*.

Co-adaptive learning systems

Another essential feature of complex systems is said to be their *co-adaptation*, a 'kind of mutual causality, in which change in one system leads to change in another system connected to it, and this mutual influencing continues over time' (Larsen-Freeman & Cameron, 2008a: 233). Co-adaptation means that although agents may be thought to be acting independently their behaviour alters the system as a whole. In this way, complex systems are the embodiment of their histories. Complex systems learn because 'their past is co-responsible for their present behaviour' (Cilliers, 1998: 4).

One way in which systems evolve through co-adaptive processes is via *positive and negative feedback* loops. An agent may attempt a form of behaviour in an environment but perceive *negative feedback* that this behaviour is inappropriate for the circumstances, reducing the likelihood of the adoption of a similar behaviour in the future. On the other hand, *positive feedback* occurs when an agent attempts a form of behaviour and perceives a response from the environment that this behaviour is appropriate. The behaviour is reinforced (Byrne, 1998), and may lead to an increased likelihood of its adoption in the future. These concepts have strongly behaviourist overtones. However, they differ from behaviourist views in the sense that in co-adaptation, any form of behaviour alters the environment at the same time as it alters the agent (Larsen-Freeman & Cameron, 2008a). As a result, both the agent and the environment 'learn', and the system changes dynamically. Such co-adaptive learning processes suggest that in an educational setting it is important to examine instances of positive and negative feedback through which members of a class group co-influence each other's motivation and the motivation of the class system as a whole.

Constant dynamic change

In a complex systems view, the interaction between systems at various levels and indeed the scope and makeup of systems themselves is constantly *changing* and evolving across time as there is internal reorganisation and interaction with the environment. Complex systems develop across different *timescales*: while some change may occur suddenly over a relatively shorter span of time, other change takes place at a slower rate over longer spans of time. As de Bot (2015: 32) notes, complex systems theory holds that 'development on one scale is influenced by what happens on smaller and larger scales'. For instance, while classroom activity may involve a timescale of change in terms of minutes, a lesson or homeroom period entails a timescale of hours. What is moreover important from a complex systems perspective is that these timescales interact with each other, such that perceptions of motivation at a longer timescale are an emergent outcome of experiences at shorter timescales. Lemke (2000: 280) also argues that there is an iterative process of heterochrony in complex systems, whereby 'a long timescale process produces an effect in a much shorter timescale activity'. For example, students' ideas of competence in a particular learning domain that have built up over years of experiences may affect their decision to engage in action in the classroom. The long-term process influences *in situ* motivation.

One analytical tool from complex systems theory that may be facilitative in examining change is that of a *state space*, a representation of all the possibilities for the states of a system at a point in time. A useful image of a state space depicts it as a three-dimensional landscape of hills and valleys made up of intersecting lines representing possible states of the system at the time of observation. System interactions may fall into more stable states known in complex systems theory as *attractor states* (Thelen & Smith, 1994). In an image of a state space, attractor states would be positioned somewhere in one of the 'valleys'. On the other hand, *repeller states* are very *un*stable. In our visual representation these states might be imagined as more mountainous areas. However, even within what we may envisage as the more stable attractor states, systems are still in constant flux (Nowak *et al.*, 2005).

Sharp phase-shifts

Change in complex systems is both gradual and at times sudden, as the system may undergo a *phase-shift*, a sharp alteration in its state and future possibilities as a whole due to the accretion of change at different levels. Byrne describes these processes of 'bifurcation' particularly aptly, while also recalling the non-linearity of change in complex systems:

> Transformations are not really about states or steady conditions. Rather they are about trajectories, about the dynamic development of systems. The connection is the idea of *bifurcation* which describes the development of very different system trajectories in consequence of very small variations in the values of initial conditions. (Byrne, 1998: 170)

As Byrne intimates, a phase-shift involves a systemic-level change in trajectory or 'transformation' in the system as it assumes a very different form. These sudden shifts have also been termed 'tipping points' (e.g. Gladwell, 2000), a vivid metaphor which in the human realm we might imagine as an accumulation of experiences, eventually tipping the system into a new trajectory at a certain point. Dynamic self-organisation of the system into new states is vital to complex systems – stagnation implies the death of the system (Morrison, 2006).

Gradual self-organisation and emergence: Functionality and novelty

Two pertinent processes in complex systems are the different ways in which they are said to react and adapt to changing environments. De Wolf and Holvoet (2005) suggest that complex systems gradually organise themselves in two qualitatively different ways, referred to as *self-organisation* and *emergence*. *Self-organisation* is understood as 'a property of complex systems which enables them to develop or change internal structure spontaneously and adaptively in order to cope with or manipulate their environment' (Cilliers, 1998: 90). That is to say, complex systems self-organise to form patterns through their interactions without any predetermined plan or central governing agent. A central feature of self-organisation that distinguishes it from emergence is its *functionality* – complex systems self-organise into patterns that are more capable of responding to/with their environment (de Wolf & Holvoet, 2005).

Emergence is similar to self-organisation in that it involves the evolution of a complex system through its interactions to display a certain form of behaviour or structure as a whole. However, while self-organisation emphasises functionality, emergence involves the evolution of new, *novel* properties of the whole. These properties are novel because they would have been difficult to predict and are not reducible to the properties of the agents in the system (de Wolf & Holvoet, 2005). Although receiving divergent naming, self-organisation and emergence emphasise different qualitative aspects of concurrently occurring gradual processes as complex systems evolve over time. In an educational setting, these concepts imply that it is important to look at the ways in which both introduced change and interactions between agents affect a classroom system as a whole.

Approaching Education from a Complex Systems Perspective

The commonly discussed properties of complex systems theory seem to offer potentially provocative new ways of structuring conceptualisations of the dynamic, co-forming nature of motivation in class groups. This and the following section therefore examine the existing literature regarding the application of complex systems theory to educational settings with a view to expressing how it can facilitate a deeper understanding of the interaction between self, environment and motivation in the language learning classroom.

Scholars who extol the applications and benefits of complex systems theory in educational research include Osberg *et al.* (2008), who argue convincingly that by considering education from the perspective of complex systems theory our understandings of 'knowledge' change. In much the same way, Larsen-Freeman (1997) applies complex systems theory to SLA, contending that individual language use and language change are one and the same when understood as processes of co-adaptation. From this perspective, knowledge is not a static, fixed body that is spatially conceptualised as external to a learner. Rather, complex systems theory encourages us to consider knowledge-and-reality as part of the same complex system that is co-adapting through time (Osberg *et al.*, 2008). As a result, while the question of *what content* is engaged with remains fundamental to learning processes, a complex systems approach to education would emphasise that content *is engaged with* and *responded to* (Biesta, 2006). As learning is understood to occur through processes of co-adaptation, complex systems theory implies that interactions between learners and content (and other members of the class group with their own 'content') are vital to individual development in an educational sense.

When learning is understood as a constant process of co-adaptation, some scholars of complexity argue that classrooms ought to be considered as *'spaces* for knowledge-producing networks' (Davis & Sumara, 2010: 859). Within such classrooms a dynamic, creative engagement with fluid content fosters learners in the classroom system – which includes both students and teachers – to 'respond, and hence bring forth new worlds' (Osberg *et al.*, 2008: 225). In such an approach, interactions in the classroom and connections between ideas are vital as the agents co-construct knowledge across their time in the classroom system. As Phelps (2002: 180) suggests, a complex systems understanding of education would posit that 'learning is occasioned'. The occasioned classroom space offers opportunities for agents to interact and co-adapt knowledge in the class group.

While an intriguing theoretical proposition, this vision of education and learning as a complex system may be of limited use unless it can be linked with the analysis of particular classroom systems, a point which highlights the difficulties of applying complex systems theory in education. Without such a foundation, firstly, there is a danger of suggesting that education *should change* to be like the picture painted above. Kuhn (2008: 186) describes this as a confusion of 'is' and 'ought', contending that 'from a complexity perspective, no matter how the classroom functions, it *is* demonstrating *its* manner of self-organisation' (emphasis added). Classrooms already *are* complex places. Although the discussion above provides hints as to ways in which complex systems theory may inform potentially more effective learning (although this will also depend on how we define 'effective'), we must not fall into the trap of believing that any classroom not aligning with this vision is therefore not complex. Secondly, it is impossible to ignore the critique of scholars like Hardman (2010), who suggest that the adoption of complex systems theory to understanding educational practice runs the risk of using metaphor for metaphor's sake. While conceding two possible benefits of the application of complex systems theory in education – to show that classrooms are sensitive, dynamic and difficult to describe, and to encourage research describing these sensitivities and showing how teachers deal with this complexity – Hardman (2010: 8) also cautions that metaphor in many cases 'replaces any real analysis of the specific system being described'. He concludes that in order for understandings from complex systems theory to be beneficial in education research, researchers must:

> ... first focus [...] on a classroom and carefully build [...] a description of *how interaction of individuals with each other and the environment can be described as a complex system*. This must be the next step in evaluating the usefulness of complexity theory to understanding classrooms. (Hardman, 2010: 8; emphasis added)

Hardman's (2010) arguments align with those of Richardson and Cilliers (2001) against the introduction to understandings of education of what they term 'soft complexity science'. As these writers contend, 'a new language with an old content will not work' (Richardson & Cilliers, 2001: 7). Merely borrowing metaphors from complex systems theory and inserting them into conceptualisations of education will not add anything substantial to these understandings. Hardman (2010) makes the essential point that if complex systems theory is to be used to understand education, it is necessary to base such understandings on both the philosophical underpinnings of complexity thinking and 'real analysis' of educational systems such as class groups. What then of such 'real analysis' based on complex systems theory used to understand language learners and classroom interactions?

Complex Systems Theory in Language Learning

Despite the fact that Larsen-Freeman made a ground-breaking connection between complex systems theory and SLA as far back as 1997, it has taken quite some time for researchers to apply these understandings to the study of language learning. However, recently there has been a spurt in theoretical and empirical work connecting complex systems theory and a variety of areas in applied linguistics, including work that considers language as a complex system (Ellis & Larsen-Freeman, 2009; Five Graces Group, 2009), first- and second-language development and acquisition from a complex dynamic systems perspective (Van Geert, 2008; Verspoor *et al.*, 2011), research into language learner agency (Mercer, 2011a), and the use of chaos theory to understand the nature of individual language learner identities (e.g. Sade, 2009, 2011).

Indeed, a growing body of work has begun to investigate language learning motivation from a complex dynamic systems perspective (see, for example, the volume edited by Dörnyei et al., 2015a). In general, this body of work highlights the importance of studying the dynamic features of change and non-linearity. In one such study, Finch (2010) investigated the experience of language learning with 74 undergraduate and graduate students in South Korea. He asked these students to write journals over one semester about their beliefs and opinions on language learning and teaching, and administered two surveys focusing on their past experiences of schooling and moments, actions or events during the semester that students perceived as having significance for their attitudes to learning and their future. The results led Finch (2010: 429) to argue for the existence of critical incidents or turning points in learning: students 'identif[ied] seemingly unimportant events which can easily be overlooked by teachers, but which can have disproportionate repercussions, depending on the noticing that occurs.' In another study, Paiva (2011) examined the language learning histories of 20 Japanese and Brazilian English learners. Like Finch, Paiva found there were distinct instances during which the students' motivational, identity- and autonomy-related trajectories altered abruptly. She grouped these events into two situational categories: students' first contact with English in junior- or senior-high school, and their diverse experiences outside school. Although these points of change were similar across the data analysed, the experiences and meanings that learners associated with these events showed great variety (Paiva, 2011: 70).

Nitta (2013) similarly found diversity in patterns of motivational change. His research with 190 students focused specifically on motivational trajectories over 26 lessons. He used two questionnaires: in order to gain an understanding of students' self-proclaimed general motivational orientation, a motivational factors survey was administered at the beginning of the research; and students were also asked to respond to another questionnaire repeatedly at the end of each lesson to obtain their perceptions of motivation on each particular day. Nitta then compared these two data sets to develop an understanding of general trends in motivational change. Although his results uncovered three macro-patterns of motivational change across the year at the group level, there was variation in the form and timing of change at the individual level: 'Some students' motivational systems changed smoothly and continuously, while other students experienced a period of more sudden and radical change' (Nitta, 2013: 287).

These studies clearly suggest that one key to understanding motivation is to find points of significant change over time. Such research is useful in that it fosters knowledge about the longitudinal dynamics of individual motivation. Yet it also reveals little from a phenomenological viewpoint of the way in which these individuals interact with and form the learning environment, or indeed their interactions with their fellow classmates. Taking a somewhat different approach, Yashima and Arano's (2015) study provides valuable qualitative insights into students' recollections of EFL motivation. These researchers used semi-structured interviews to ask 10 students about their motivation to study English over their four years at university in Japan, including their voluntary attendance at non-credit English courses and activities. The researchers then used the data to conceptualise the students' motivation at three different timescales: (i) fluctuations through moment-to-moment experiences (such as affective, contextual, social and cognitive perceptions); (ii) how these experiences contributed to personal meaning-making about English study over longer periods of time (typically semesters); and (iii) ways in which experiences consolidated into 'a value, or deeply internalised thought patterns or habits that direct[ed] the individual's learning behaviours for an extended period regardless of the daily ebbs and flows' (Yashima & Arano, 2015: 293, 302).

Although limited by its use of interviews in many cases long after the experiences concerned, Yashima and Arano's (2015) study reveals an intriguing framework for interpreting the non-linearity of students' motivational patterns over these timescales. It moreover hints at the vital role for situated connections between individual learners, other learners, and the emergent context in which they are interacting in the co-formation of classroom motivation. The necessity in classroom language learning research for consideration of both individuals and the situated environments in which they are participating is clearly articulated by Ushioda (2011a: 188), who draws attention to the 'mutually-constitutive relationship between learner and context':

> We cannot ignore the integral part played by the individual learner in shaping context and in shaping the input generated within that context. What L2 learners say or do, or choose not to say or do, how they behave, what they think, how they respond to their context mentally, affectively, verbally, behaviourally, will all contribute in complex ways to shaping and changing the developing context.

A study by Pigott (2012a) reveals the vital importance of context in a complex systems understanding of language learner motivation. Although rather limited in terms of the number of participants, from analysis of the qualitative interview data of four EFL learners at a Japanese university, Pigott (2012a: 27) contends that his study 'indicate[s] that motivation is contingent on interpersonal interaction and social and circumstantial context'. Through his study he came to criticise theoretical conceptualisations of motivation built around individual differences:

> Heterogeneities such as personality and ability may underlie motivation, but they do not seem to be at the forefront of the lived reality of motivation among these learners. Instead, motivation appears, at least to an extent, to be a function of context. (Pigott, 2012a: 42–43)

Such assertions find further support in the results of a study by Falout *et al.* (2013). Although not applying a complex systems approach, these researchers conducted a study with 466 Japanese university EFL students into the connections between motivation and the introduction of classroom activities to stimulate positive group dynamics. Falout *et al.* (2013: 257–258) found that participants in their study perceived interactions between their past, present and future ideas of English use as 'co-constructing constructs' and the students 'interpreted that motivational increases among these variables came from the influences of the communities in which they were practicing and learning English'. These results imply the shared formation of motivation across learners in learning groups in particular contexts.

Moving on

This chapter has focused on the potential of complex systems theory to inform understandings and research into classroom language learning motivation. Considering the framework of motivation I applied for the study reported in this book, it is important to bear in mind that Dörnyei (2009a) entitles this the L2 Motivational Self *System*. Indeed, he writes of learner action that 'although there is a plethora of factors, conditions, motives, etc. that can affect behaviour, these *work as a system* whose outcome is tangible for the individual at any moment in time' (Dörnyei, 2009b: 209–210; emphasis added).

The conceptualisation of educational processes and settings as complex systems offers a powerful set of insights with which to interpret motivation. However, few current studies of language learners and classrooms that apply complex systems theory explicitly seek to understand co-adaptation both at the level of *individual learners* and *across the whole* classroom system *from the perspectives of the members* of the system. Yet complex systems understandings would suggest the need in studying classroom language learning of taking just such a *dynamic, holistic* approach to conceptualising motivation. As Morin (2006: 6) argues, 'knowledge of the parts is not enough, the knowledge of the whole as a whole is not enough', but we must attempt 'to comprehend the relations between the whole and the parts'.

The following four chapters describe my approach to conceptualising motivation in the classroom based on these revised understandings.

7 Class Group as Open System

On the face of it, looking at motivation inside the foreign language classroom would seem to make relatively straightforward sense. Classrooms are the places to which learners come to study content deemed necessary for participation in the particular society of which they are members. Encircled by the four walls of the classroom, motivation to learn is the 'want' that students develop (or do not develop) through their experiences in these contexts. However, is the classroom in reality so finitely bounded an entity? Considering language learners in formal education, van Lier (2004: 194) clearly draws our attention to the necessity of also considering the classroom as an open system:

> The learners spend an hour or so in the classroom, but before that they have been elsewhere, and after that they will go to other places. There is no doubt that their activities elsewhere have an effect on what happens in the classroom, and the same naturally goes for the teacher. Classroom research ... has often treated the classroom as a bounded system, and studied the interactions and language in it without explicit connections to other contexts.

There are (at least) two crucial understandings forthcoming from van Lier's assertion. First, classroom motivation is open to aspects of the dynamic experiences of the learners that make up these spaces. Psychologically, students 'bring in' their experiences prior to the lesson, perhaps quite temporally removed or more proximal, as well as those they anticipate in their near or distal future. Secondly, by extension, we can also understand that learners in the classroom are involved with a multitude of different, open systems. If we take a student as our starting point and add some of the common socially and societally defined systems related to the classroom space in which this learner studies, we may arrive at an image like Figure 7.1 that at first seems relatively static and bounded.

Considering firstly education-related systems, the open nature of a class group is revealed if we recognise that at lower systemic levels students are made up of systems such as motivational or identity systems. These students

84 Part 2: 再見 Re-viewing

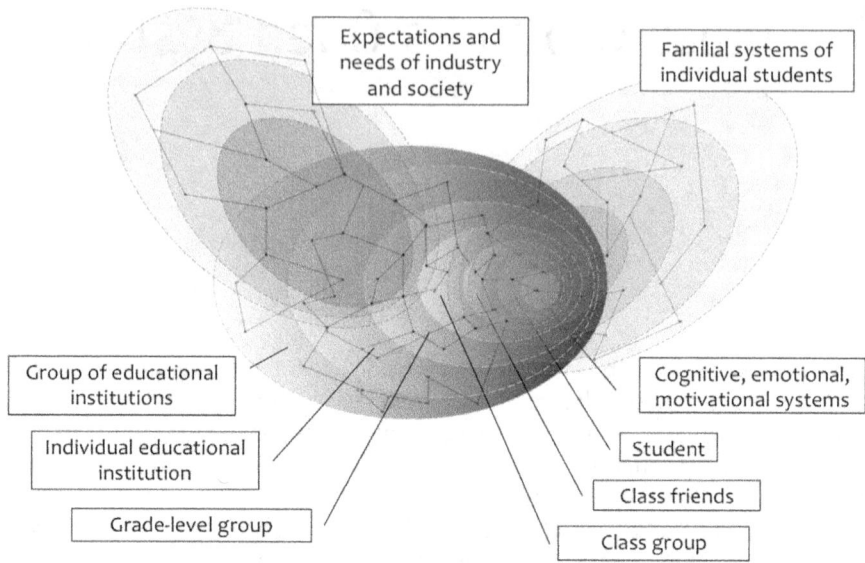

Figure 7.1 A *partial* abstraction of open systems related to a classroom learner
Source: Drawing on Bronfenbrenner (1979), Davis and Sumara (2006) and Haggis (2008).

are in turn situated in and form higher level systems such as class groupings, or the educational institution as a whole. The school or college may further be administratively bound to some kind of board of education or group of institutions. There are numerous other systems besides these overtly education-related systems which intersect at various levels. For example, students are not only part of a class group but are most likely involved with various dynamically evolving friendship groups (which might also span various classes and grade levels, or indeed friendships outside the particular educational context). They may be involved with after-school club activity or study groups, and are part of familial systems. In still other ways, learners are even interconnected with attempts by educational institutions to 'fit' functionally with expectations and the needs of industry and society. And these are without doubt only a small portion of the nested systems of which a learner is made up, is located in and jointly forms.

What a complex systems approach to conceptualising such open systems therefore encourages us to understand is that there is constant, multi-directional and multi-levelled interaction between these systems. Although our socialisation prompts us to define certain boundaries, in complex systems theory these borders are considered to be permeable and shifting, and might be more profitably conceived as interfaces (Radford, 2008). Due to the complex, open nature of these systems, energy is transferred via these 'interfaces' in non-linear ways.

In the classroom, Haggis (2008) claims that understanding education from a complex systems perspective means that students and teacher are affected by various of these 'higher' and 'lower' level systems. In my study, while I was essentially looking at participant reflections on interaction between self and environment through their experiences *inside* the classroom, I became aware that the analysis revealed this 'system' to be open to interactions with the surrounding environment. The class group that I chose to study was one temporally and spatially defined at the institutional level. It had a life cycle also determined by the Japanese academic year. However, analysis suggested the agents (students and teacher) that made up the class group to be also made up of and interconnected with innumerable other interacting systems. Drawing on the kind of complex systems conceptualisation of education outlined in the previous chapter, I came to understand that in this study change-action was introduced to the classroom *space* (Davis & Sumara, 2010). However, motivation was emergent from interactions within these *occasioned spaces* (Phelps, 2002) and systems external to the class group rather than as a direct result of the change-action. In response to various cautions against the blind introduction of complex systems metaphors to educational research (e.g. Hardman, 2010; Richardson & Cilliers, 2001), it is important to analyse research data for how multiple levels of interaction foster motivation – for example, interactions between members of the class group, between members and introduced change-action activities, and between members and external influences. The current chapter therefore commences discussion of analysis in my study by considering a number of ways in which a complex systems approach to the data analysis was able to reveal energy brought into the classroom system.

However, I wish to sound a note of caution with regard to the mutual exclusivity of the factors that emerge in the following discussion. From a complex systems perspective, self and environment would be considered co-forming and co-adaptive. In a similar vein, the categories that I discuss in this and the following three chapters ought not to be understood as independent from the others. In the majority of cases there is overlap, and indeed there is probably more overlap and blending than I am able to express in this discussion. The categories are not intended to be a default description, fixed and static. The relationships and interactions between the categories discussed are what I as teacher and researcher understood through my own interactions with the social environment of the classroom and my own experience and reading. This discussion is not intended to be a final statement about language classroom motivation, but is contextually (and temporally) based. I offer the analysis in the hope that it may facilitate further understandings and research trajectories relating to the interaction and dynamicity of self, motivation and environment in classroom foreign language learning, and indeed build on understandings of the L2 Motivational Self System.

Past Experiences and Initial Ideas of an Ideal Self

I proposed in Chapter 4 that one shared interest of action research and complex systems theory is the investigation of the initial state of a system. Although my study explored the development of motivation to learn of students in a class group over one academic year, past research into EFL motivation from Japan has shown that students' past experiences before joining any particular learning group will continue to play a role in the trajectory of their motivation (see, for example, Carpenter et al., 2009). Indeed, one form in which I understood the system as manifesting its open nature was the way participants drew on experiences from their past, in environments completely divorced spatially and temporally from the current system. These diverse past experiences influenced action and perception of motivation in the present. I will discuss these influences more in the following chapter. To commence the discussion in this chapter, I briefly look at some general themes that emerged from two change-action activities introduced in Cycle 1 of the action research. These activities provide insights into the kinds of past classroom English learning experiences and initial ideas of an ideal L2 self that students 'brought in' with them as they came to make up the class group (see Appendix D for instructions to students). Figure 7.2 summarises the themes from Cycle 1 of the action research.

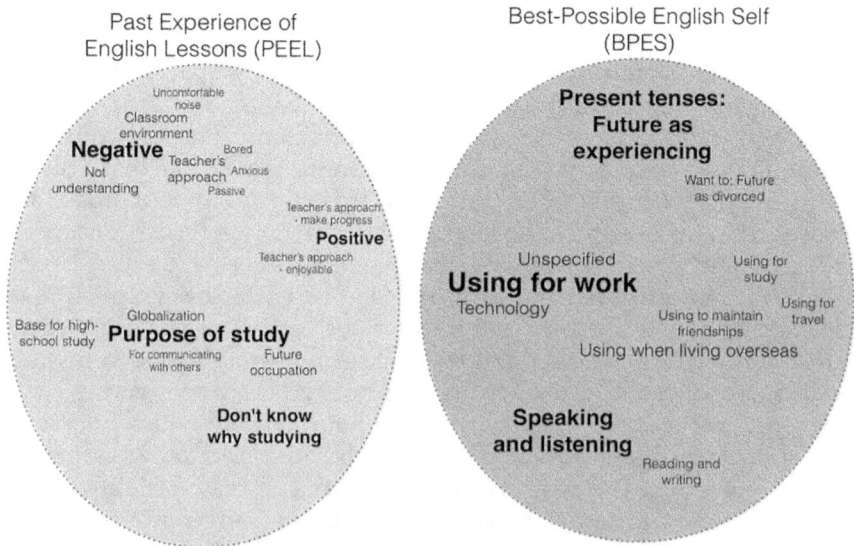

Figure 7.2 Summary of qualities of students' past experiences of English lessons and initial ideas of a best-possible English self

Past experience of English lessons

At the start of the academic year I asked students to reflect on their past experiences of English lessons from junior-high school. Analysis of the writing of students revealed that negative experiences of these lessons far outweighed positive experiences. On the one hand, the few positive experiences mentioned teachers' approaches to lessons: 'The teacher taught enjoyably, so it was fun', 'The teacher taught us enthusiastically, so we became smarter'. On the other hand, negative experience of lessons was split broadly into three areas, with the first also linking to the influence of the teacher. In congruence with past research from Japan finding demotivation stemming from teacher action (e.g. Kikuchi, 2013), many students reflected on teacher-centred, non-communicative experiences: 'The teacher just talked and talked, so it was very boring', 'The teacher wrote grammar on the blackboard and we just copied anything. I didn't learn'. Secondly, students wrote of their own or other students' lack of understanding in lessons: 'Lessons were too short – there were students who couldn't remember in the short time', 'Lessons progressed very quickly, so I lost track'. Thirdly, the classroom environments were also experienced in a negative way, being described at times as 'sleep-inducing because it was so quiet', while other students found the lessons 'weren't viable – students just did whatever they liked' or 'so noisy that I couldn't concentrate'.

Students also wrote of their understandings of the purpose of their English studies at junior-high school. While a small number made a connection to the promise of English in their future occupation, perhaps reflecting the rhetoric in Japanese society about the spread of globalisation and the apparent necessity of English, other students reasoned: 'So I can be useful in the global village', 'Because the world is becoming more globalised'. A final theme that emerged was a complete lack of understanding of the purpose of studying English at junior-high school: 'I don't know why', 'Because it was one of our lessons?', 'It needs to be studied?'

Initial ideas of a 'best-possible English self'

Around the same time, I encouraged students to project into the future and write specifically about their best possible English self. The analysis revealed some unexpected outcomes.

First, I identified different patterns of language that students used in writing (Wetherell *et al.*, 2001). Despite my previous experiences with students at the college, I was surprised that a majority of these middle-adolescent students wrote quite clearly as if they were visualising their future self in action by applying present tenses in sentence construction to express images of how they might be using English. As one student wrote, 'I'm still living in Japan. However, I'm using the internet that connects the people of the world to talk with people from other countries.' Another student, Akira, formulated a narrative:

> In the morning, I wake up. I flick the switch on my computer. Instantly, I understand all the information that comes in Japanese (it goes without saying), but also information from the countries on the other side of the Pacific and Atlantic oceans. The information on most sites is written in English. For example, Wikileaks is very famous, but it's written in English. But I can get information faster than anyone else. And then there're the emails. At 6 in the morning, I communicate with people in New York, on the other side of the Pacific – I can even have discussions with them. (Akira, BPES, 7/4/2011)

However, a handful of the students wrote using the Japanese 〜たい form (-tai – want to), which I interpret as representing qualitatively more of a separation of the present self from a removed future self: 'Even when I'm in Japan, when I'm asked the way by foreigners, I want to be able to guide them fluently in English. If I could speak English, I'd be able to feel at ease in any job.' Although this student extract contains images of a future self using English, the construction of the sentences suggests a division between the present self hoping these things for the future self.

While only a relative few students had expressed an understanding that their junior-high school English study had been in preparation for their future occupation, a second unexpected insight from the analysis was that a great number of students described a best possible English self using English for work. This writing fell into two categories. Some students made no clear reference to the kind of occupation they were envisioning. As Kazu wrote, 'I work as a manager for a large, foreign company, and don't really live anywhere – I travel all over the world' (BPES, 7/4/2011). Considering the focus of the college, many of the projections, however, explicitly mentioned occupations related to technology and engineering:

> I find my English useful when I develop robots in cooperation with people from overseas. I'm able to communicate with researchers from other countries. (Masa, BPES, 7/4/2011)

Although this activity revealed a great number of students who were very capable of envisioning fine detail to a future English-using self, another interesting finding regarded the content of these images. Congruent with past research literature (e.g. Rapley, 2010) finding young Japanese adolescents to hold a belief or hope that English *speaking* skills will be necessary for their future, students in my study also overwhelmingly envisioned forms of *verbal* communication that their best possible English self was conducting:

I'm working at the FBI. I work every day, and can take orders even in English. English is useful for things like everyday conversation, planning sessions at my job, or teaching my children. I can converse freely with people who live around me, or even the boss of my company. (Eiji, BPES, 7/4/2011)

Transportable Identities

Over the course of the year there were a variety of ways in which participants spontaneously wrote of identities other than primarily 'members of the class group' that played a role in facilitating motivation. I came to recognise that Zimmerman's (1998) concept of 'transportable identities' meshes well with a complex systems approach to analysis by providing a lens through which to examine such instances of participants 'bringing themselves' into the classroom. Zimmerman (1998: 91) introduces transportable identities as those that are 'assignable or claimable on the basis of physical or culturally based insignia which furnish the intersubjective basis for categorisation' – in other words, identities held through perceived attachment to certain groups or types of people. These identities are not simply 'given up' when people enter the classroom, but are transported with them wherever they go (although they may be more or less apparent in different contexts). Ushioda has recently expanded the concept to argue for motivation based on a more holistic understanding of language learners as not purely 'students':

> To the extent that we as teachers invoke and orient to students' transportable identities in the classroom and engage with them as 'people' rather than simply 'language learners'; to the extent that we encourage and create opportunities for them to 'speak as themselves' and engage and express their own preferred meanings, interests and identities through the medium of the target language; the more likely that students will feel involved and motivated to communicate and thus to engage themselves in the process of learning and using the language. (Ushioda, 2011b: 17)

Transportable identities as an adolescent: Peer relationships and personality

Adolescent development witnesses changes in the importance of peer group relations (Bukowski *et al.*, 2011). The participants' transportable identities as adolescent students in general, not solely members of a language class group, were apparent in their writing about the influence of friendships and social interactions in the classroom:

> The first lesson was a lot of fun. By going around the classroom, it helped my English, but it also helped me get to know other students that I don't really know so well yet. (Shun, LJ, 12/4/2011)

In the lesson, we changed seats and made new groups, then did self-introductions in English. Everyone in the new team I hadn't talked with before at all, but we interacted well together, so not only my English ability, but also my friendship circle improved – it was like killing two birds with one stone. (Mikihiro, LJ, 26/4/2011)

These extracts hint at the motivational importance students place on the development of friendships with peers, particularly at times of change in the structure of the classroom. Both students also allude to an emotional aspect. In the first extract, the lesson was enjoyable because it allowed Shun to get to know the other students. Mikihiro, however, expresses trepidation – 'everyone in the new team I hadn't talked with before at all', and then consequent relief – 'but we interacted well together, so not only my English ability, but also my friendship circle improved'. There was a subjective, emotional influence on motivation from students' transportable identities as developing members of certain peer groups.

One of the critical developments of adolescence is the attempt by young people to negotiate internally consistent ideas of different selves for different situations and roles (Harter, 2003). As the peer group gains increasing influence over actions, learners in the classroom may struggle with what appear at times to be incompatible expectations from those around them, such as their fellow classmates, teachers and parents. For instance, they must come to form a sense of self that can at one and the same time behave in a way deemed consistent with their own ideas of appropriate action for learning, their perceptions of the expectations of teachers, and yet also work to meet the approval of their peers. The ways in which adolescents negotiate these influences in the EFL classroom has been shown to vary markedly between individuals (Taylor, 2013). There was evidence in students' writing in my study of internal conflicts that arose as some students attempted to balance their roles as students trying to engage in learning opportunities with their identity as members of this or that adolescent peer group. The writing of one student, Jiro, gives an insight into his sense of appropriate classroom action, clashing a number of times with the behaviour of those around him, and a kind of obligation he seems to feel to re-channel the actions of other students: 'Near the end there were students that were playing about, but I couldn't tell them off' (LJ, 12/7/2011); 'There were some times when we got off-track when talking, so I want to take care that this doesn't happen again' (LJ, 15/12/2011).

Hinted at in the writing of Jiro, the individual personalities of students were also transported into the classroom and affected motivation. Another student identified himself as being a quiet person, an identity which evolved through experience in a lesson: 'Usually I don't talk so much, but during the lesson I could talk, so I was pleased.' These personality factors were apparent in student thinking and writing about English study, but also appeared to be part of their core self-concept:

I am just really bad at ad-lib. I'm not good at ad-lib even in Japanese, so even more so I'm not good at English ad-lib. So, at any rate, I want to become able to ad-lib in English. (Seiya, LJ, 22/9/2011)

I'm really apologetic to my teachers, but recently, my motivation to study hasn't gone up. This time's midterm [exams] I did without really caring … I'm a moody person, so depending on the day my attitude changes. Trying to fix that is my challenge at the moment. (Haruki, LJ, 24/11/2011)

Dörnyei (2005: 30) summarises past research into the role of personality in SLA, concluding that 'personality traits can be seen as potent modifying variables' that 'will have an impact on [students'] participation in a range of learning tasks'. These extracts certainly support such an assertion. The first student, Seiya, relates his disappointment at his own personality as being someone unable to improvise even as his native-Japanese self. However, he asserts his motivation to become a more flexible English user. It appears that he fosters a hope that his evolving second language identity may perhaps provide an opportunity to revise his personality, and to develop a more positive self-concept in general. Haruki does not discuss English directly, but recognises that his personality affects his motivation and attitude towards study. He perceives such a degree of influence from his personality as 'a moody person' on his approach to study that he defines the task of 'trying to fix that' as his primary 'challenge at the moment'. Students did not simply surrender such personalities at the doorstep, but transported these dynamic pictures of themselves into the classroom, affecting their actions in unpredictable, non-linear ways.

Transportable identities from students' personal lives: Outside experiences, hobbies and financial constraints

As the review of past research from Japan revealed in Chapter 2, for many students classroom EFL learning can be quite removed from their everyday lives. They struggle to see the relevance of learning a language that plays very little role in the community they see directly around them. This problem is exacerbated by classroom learning experiences that often allow only restricted opportunity for personal input and communication of students' own ideas through the language they study week in and week out for a great deal of their childhood and adolescence (Falout et al., 2008; Kikuchi, 2009). Participants in my study drew on diverse transportable identities from their personal lives, noting the way that activities in which they could make a connection with experiences from their own day-to-day lives were motivating:

Today we solved problems that we currently have. When we were doing that, I could write my own problem in English, so it really contributed to getting my skill to go up, I thought. (Ryo, LJ, 24/5/2011)

Students' motivation through making a connection between their English studies and their personal lives was also evident in their process of selecting one activity for English skill-building over the summer holiday period (see Chapter 5 and Appendix E). As the following extract written by Haruki illustrates, learners frequently based their initial decision of what activity to try on some aspect of their own life outside the classroom, and their motivation to continue was reinforced by their experience of making such a connection:

> Prior to Skill-building activity: I'm going to try to sing English songs at karaoke. I'm not good at English. So I thought I want to try from something close to me, so I chose singing. Everything will get in the way though (laugh). (Haruki, Skill-building activity, 20/7/2011)
>
> After Skill-building activity: I went with friends, so I could enjoy doing it. I felt English was close to me. I think I can continue this. (Haruki, Skill-building activity, 7/9/2011)

The analysis made it clear that students had lives and interests apart from being primarily 'language learners'. These interests frequently focused on conducting activities with friends and popular culture, such as music and *manga* comic books. There was a sense of the blended nature of students' identities whereby they mentioned a wish to be able to combine English study with their external interests. Such a combination would be more enjoyable and also more time-efficient. They wanted to focus on what was interesting for them as adolescents, and if English study could coincide with this, all the better. Sometimes such opportunities to make a connection with English study occurred through one-off experiences or events external to the language classroom:

> I had an experience that made me kind of realise that through doing things in lessons like having conversations of doing presentations in English, little by little I'm getting more practical English skill. In the summer holidays, when I went to Tokyo, I was asked for directions by a person from another country, and at that time, even though it was really wordy, I was able to say it so that the person understood me. I felt like this experience would be really important for me if I go out of Japan. I think there's no harm from studying English, so I want to study more from now on. (Yusuke, LJ Reflection 1, 5/10/2011)
>
> There was a time when, in the train that I ride every day, I didn't really understand the English that flowed my way [announcements] and when I looked it up in a dictionary I could think 'Oh, so *that's* what it meant!' I think that if only you try to use your head to listen to the English that you kind of listen to every day [in everyday life], it's so different. (Tetsuo, LJ Reflection 2, 9/2/2012)

Mercer (2011b) argues for a connection between experiences of language learning/use in formal and informal contexts and self-concept formation of foreign language learners. In her study, foreign language learners referred extensively to experiences of language use in informal contexts, that is, outside the classroom, as significant in their development of self-concept as language learners/users (Mercer, 2011b: 142). In the environment of the current study there may have been fewer opportunities for students to use English outside the classroom. However, elements from the transportable identities of students' personal lives – as someone who happened to be riding on a train, or having gone to Tokyo (not with the intention to use English) – allowed for opportunities to experience success with English in personally meaningful situations. These experiences again had an emotional dimension: Yusuke's satisfaction that 'I was able to say it so that the person understood me'; Tetsuo's sense of achievement from taking positive action to look up the meaning of a public announcement and realising 'so *that's* what it meant'. These positive experiences were transported into the classroom.

As is apparent from the motivational influence of situations or chances that only certain students encountered, there was great variety in the personal-life elements that students brought in to the classroom. Students also drew on connections with their personal hobbies:

> I often talk to people from other countries on online games, but although I can use the kind of simple English that I've learned up until now to say what I want a little, if there's a question from the other side I can't catch it well, and the conversation inevitably stops … (Kazu, LJ, 22/9/2011)

As Kazu's writing reflects, some students drew on their hobbies involving computer use to make a connection with English study. In similar fashion, Chik and Breidbach's (2011) comparative study of English language learners in Hong Kong and Germany uncovered the strong influence of media from outside the classroom, in this case popular culture, on learners' second language identity formation. In their study, students' engagement with popular cultural practices such as watching English TV programmes and video gaming motivated them to 'take their learning of English beyond the limitations of classroom practices' (Chik & Breidbach, 2011: 155). Learners' additional language identities and motivation developed through their choices to pursue these popular culture activities. While not mentioned frequently, occasional references by students in my study conversely hint at the way in which they made connections between pre-existing interests and their EFL study in the classroom. They hint at students' proactive attempts to build in additional personal relevance to their English studies, and understand their classroom learning as having a meaning for their lives outside the classroom. Kazu clearly recognises the limitations of what he has 'learned up until now', presumably in classroom study. His writing suggests that, for him, one strong motivation to continue to improve his English abilities is his vision of a personally defined ideal self that can interact effectively within the dynamic context of his hobby as an online gamer. If school study can align with this interest and more communicative focus, his motivation may become all the more potent.

The final way in which students drew on transportable identities from their personal lives relates to financial constraints on possibility. From the possible-selves literature, the motivational capacity of a possible self is effective when it feels plausible – realistic for that person in their own personal circumstances – and is in harmony with expectations from significant others or ideas of group membership (Dörnyei & Ushioda, 2011; Oyserman *et al.*, 2006). The following extracts are responses from a peer role-model session in which an older student came to a homeroom period and gave a presentation about his experiences going overseas:

> Today a student from [class name] talked to us about when he went to Canada. I thought that 400,000 yen is expensive. I thought that it seemed fun, but it's not good to make trouble for my parents, so I thought I'd stop. (Ryo, LJ, 1/2/2012)

> As [*yappari*] I think experience is important, I thought that I'd like to go overseas and learn various things. I thought that I want the school side to do their best with monetary support so that a lot of people are able to go. (Sayaka, LJ, 1/2/2012)

These comments hint at the influence of financial circumstances from the personal lives of these students on their images of the possibility of also going overseas. At 15–16 years of age these learners were still relatively young. The college had a policy of not allowing younger students to work part-time. Students were dependent on their families for financial resources. While Ryo notes the possible enjoyment that might be experienced in going to Canada, 'I thought that it seemed fun', he also draws on a recognition that '400,000 yen is expensive', particularly in light of his family circumstances: 'it's not good to make trouble for my parents, so I thought I'd stop.' Although it is unclear whether Sayaka envisages herself having enough money to go overseas, she wants 'the school side to do their best with monetary support so that a lot of people are able to go'. A plausible image of her peers (and possibly herself) being able to take part in the programme rests at least in part on the college providing financial assistance. The motivation of learners studying towards the possibility of going overseas and using English was clearly affected by transportable identities from their individual understandings of diverse family financial backgrounds.

Transportable identity of myself as teacher

The final aspect of the influence of transportable identities on the motivation of the open class group revealed in the analysis concerns my own identities and how they affected and were affected by interactions in the classroom system. As Hetherington (2013: 74) draws attention to, a 'complexity thinking perspective suggests that ... the complexity of the system in which the researcher is embedded may also emerge in unpredictable ways as a result of the researcher's interaction with the system'. The data revealed that there were times throughout the year when I explicitly drew my own identities as someone other than 'the language teacher' into the classroom.

Aguilar (2013: 13) has argued that teachers 'sometimes interrupt their "doing being teachers" within the second language classroom context, momentarily "doing being" someone else instead'. For instance, through activities in which I identified myself as a fellow language *learner*, students were able to reflect on language learning processes and their beliefs about language learning. In one activity I showed students a series of entries from a diary I had kept when studying Japanese (see Appendix E):

> I'd heard in a speech that [another English teacher] organised from an older student that if you are overseas for some time English will just seep in, but listening to the teacher's story today, I realised that you need to work hard if you want that to happen. Looking at the teacher's diary, I could see the result of continuing to work hard, and I thought that the teacher's effort was amazing. I don't have confidence that I can do the same, but I want to try at my own pace. (Reiji, LJ, 14/6/2011)

As might be evidenced in this extract, by transporting my identity as a language learner into the classroom and talking about my own experiences of learning Japanese in Japan, Reiji's beliefs that 'English will just seep in' if he goes to another country were challenged. Ryan and Mercer (2011) argue that foreign language learners often believe they can only progress to a certain, limited degree of competence through formal language study in a classroom and that, after some time, in order to develop their language skills further it is necessary to go overseas. They further assert that such mindsets have negative consequences, in that 'a strong belief in language learning as a natural process that is best achieved abroad situates the learner as a passive vessel absorbing language rather than as an active agent' (Ryan & Mercer, 2011: 170). By drawing in my identity as a language learner and showing in a visual way the effort to which I had gone, students were able to more concretely understand their agency in the language learning process. My own transported identity as a fellow language learner interacted with Reiji's motivation, such that he 'want[s] to try at [his] own pace'.

I specifically drew on my transportable identity as someone who had held various dreams at different times throughout my childhood and adolescence to introduce another activity in which students worked on developing a possible-self tree (see Appendix G):

> It took a while to get through my initial explanation, but I think using the photos of my past and talking about my dreams at those points in time, especially throwing in humour, seemed to really lighten things up and most students seemed to get straight into writing their ideas down. (RJ, 7/12/2011)

Richards (2006: 72) cautions that the explicit use of transportable identities by teachers involves an 'investment of self, with all the emotional, relational, and moral considerations that this invokes'. From the perspective of teachers and students, there are obviously limits to the extent classrooms are – or should be – places for sharing what might at times be highly personal aspects of their lives. However, in the course of the current study, it also appeared that drawing in my transportable identities allowed students to feel more at ease in thinking about their own future. Such overt employment encouraged students to reflect upon and compare their own ideas with new input:

> I was glad that I could think about the future in today's homeroom. Recently I've come to wonder about the meaning of being in kosen and was agonising about it. I'm in the X department, but I don't really have any interest in a future to do with X department. But like the teacher's dreams for the future changed many times, I thought that I want to search for the future in my own way. And, from now on I want to take my time and think about the future. (Aoi, LJ, 7/12/2011)

Absorbed Expectations

While the previous discussion has revolved around systems that may in some ways be conceptualised as 'internal' to participants, I turn now to influences at higher levels: At various times throughout the year I noticed in students' reflections hints of how they perceived expectations from society or the others around them regarding their future English abilities. Students' writing showed that for them English ability was understood as a necessary quality of membership of 'adult society' in Japan: 'I thought once again that when I become an adult, I'll have to use more English.' As is also evident in students' initial ideas about the purpose of their past English studies, there was a frequent thread that ran through their reflections about the processes of globalisation, leading to a sense of pressure from the 'world around them'.

Aoi's writing clearly evinces this idea of a pressure to study English towards participation in a future society in which globalisation has taken root: 'Through today's lesson, I thought once again how necessary English is for the globalising world, for my future when I go out into society' (LJ, 12/4/2011). As a further example of the ways in which student writing often revealed their perceptions of expectations, a peer role-model presentation introduced in Cycle 2 of the action research encouraged one student, Yuma, to write in great detail about the influence of the opinions of those around him on his ideas of future possibility:

> I think that I want to do some kind of work related to space. If I only could, I've even thought that I'd like to become an astronaut. But from all around, all I hear is, 'you're dreaming!' or 'get real!' And then, I've even been told, 'If you go overseas to where lots of international engineers come together, you'll have to speak not only English but many other languages too'. But listening to today's presentation about the overseas internship, and the fact that you don't have to have perfect English, my motivation has gone up. I might be following a dream too much, but I want to try! (Yuma, LJ, 11/5/2011)

These extracts from students suggest the influence of the socially constructed ought-to L2 self impacting on their own conceptions of future possibility as a kind of pressure. Yuma vividly reflects on the way in which the voices of those 'from all around' had chipped away at one of his conceptions of an ideal self. The new input that he receives from listening to the older student's presentation goes some way towards reinstating this image and reinvigorating his flagging motivation (although it must be said that his ideal self image of an astronaut would indeed require a lot of dedication and study to realise).

Recent research literature gives a conflicting picture of the influence on motivation and action of the ought-to L2 self in different contexts (e.g. Csizér & Lukács, 2010; Dörnyei & Chan, 2013; Kormos & Csizér, 2008; Lamb, 2012; Papi & Abdollahzadeh, 2012; Pigott, 2011). For example, the results of Csizér & Lukács' (2010: 6) study with adolescent Hungarian learners led these researchers to conclude that 'the lack of the emergence of an ought-to self dimension might ... be explained by the fact that the secondary-school participants are still relatively young to internalise the pressure the environment might put on them'. In contrast to such findings, research conducted in the Japanese context with similar secondary school learners found that 89% of respondents reported a stronger influence on their motivation from the ought-to L2 self than an ideal self using English in the future (Pigott, 2011: 544).

In the main, during the regular sessions involved in the current study, learners did not write clearly of how an ought-to L2 self might have affected motivation in the open class group. However, my interpretation of student responses from their learning journals prompted me to introduce an activity that directly encouraged them to write about and share their ideas of expectations connected to English from teachers, companies and family members (see Appendix G). While upon reflection I wish that I had also asked students to write of the expectations they perceived from peers, the responses to this activity allow some insight into the kinds of understandings of pressures and expectations regarding English they may have been bringing into the classroom with them.

First, the student writing of perceptions of expectations from teachers predominantly focused on levels of competence. A very few students believed their teachers anticipated high levels of competence for their English (all responses are from the Expectations activity, dated 11/1/2012): 'Want [me] to master [it]'; 'High English ability'. Conversely, the vast majority of students understood that their teachers envisaged only extremely basic English competence for them: 'The least necessary level of English (conversation, reading etc.)'; 'Able to use to the level least necessary in society'; 'Want me to acquire basic English ability'.

One potential problem with the soundness of this data is that, due to the vague nature of the term 先生 (*sensei* – teacher) in Japanese, it is unclear whether students wrote about their English teachers, their technology teachers, teachers in general, or even me as their homeroom teacher. This is an obvious limitation that would need to be addressed in future studies by being more specific as to *which* teacher expectations are being sought. It is also unclear why students arrived at these perceptions. Were there specific events or interactions with teachers that led them to such beliefs? Did their depersonalised experiences in past classrooms encourage them to sense that their teachers perhaps did not care about their learning? These are questions for future research into the development of the ought-to L2 self. Nevertheless, what is apparent from the data is that these students had clear ideas of what teachers expect of them regarding their English studies, and unfortunately these absorbed expectations were not on the whole positive. It is well documented how the expectations of teachers can influence student motivation and engagement in learning (Brophy, 1998; Dörnyei, 2001). As Dörnyei (2001: 34) puts it, 'if you [the teacher] show commitment towards the students' learning and progress, there is a very good chance that they will do the same thing'. Regrettably, the message that the majority of these learners brought into the class group was that teachers held quite low prospects for their English learning.

In contrast, learners' perceptions of expectations from companies regarding their English abilities not only featured pressure to attain a high degree of competence, but also included reference to specific tasks or purposes for which they might be expected to use English:

> English ability to the degree that can do business with foreign business partners. Can understand electronic communications correctly. (Eiji)

Level such that [I] can convey [my] will at meetings and presentations. (Tetsuo)

Not troubled with communication in English even in [my] area of specialisation. (Chie)

English ability to a degree that [I] can be active even overseas. (Seiya)

As the final extract from Seiya attests, students often believed that companies would expect them to use English when 'going overseas' or for 'communication with those overseas'. Ushioda (2013b: 5) has argued that in the present day the idea of 'foreign' language learning has in many ways become untenable due to the relative ease of both virtual and physical travel. However, the perceived expectations of companies these students brought with them into the classroom suggested that, for many, English is still something predominantly 'foreign'.

The expectations that students perceived from their families also revealed use of English outside Japan. However, in the case of family members, students had absorbed expectations of being able to assist in family holidays overseas through using English: 'Can interpret at travel destinations.' This was a surprising result, as most students in the study had never travelled overseas, suggesting that the chance of future overseas travel as a family would also be slight. What it is moreover possible to infer is that this focus on travel suggests that students had not developed understandings from their immediate family situations of the potential utility of English for their future occupations. Indeed, in parallel with the perceived expectations of teachers, student writing showed that many believed their families held very low expectations for their progress with English study:

Able to speak more than parents. (Yusuke)

Can do somewhat. (Reiji)

Not hoping anything especially. (Koji)

As Brophy (1998: 168) argues, 'each person has a unique motivational system, developed in response to experiences and to socialisation from significant others in his or her life'. For adolescent students, parents are one such significant influence. Research by Taylor (2013) into the self ideas of adolescent EFL learners in Romania found that neither their teacher nor their parents really expected English to play an important role in the students' future. Taylor also observed a gap between teacher/parent concerns and student conceptions about English. While the former primarily considered English an academic subject and held short-term expectations about grades and examinations, students 'could not emphasise enough how much they wished lessons would prepare them for real life' (Taylor, 2013: 119). The writing of the students in my study is perhaps even more shocking due to the apparent disinterest that some perceive from their households. While peers also play an increasingly important role, family members have probably been the most consistently close to learners over the years of their development. For students who bring into the classroom with them a belief that such family members are 'not hoping anything especially' for their English studies, motivation to learn must undoubtedly be affected.

Prosaic Contextual Influences

Considering classroom motivation from a complex systems perspective, I also became aware of seemingly prosaic contextual and temporal factors that nevertheless had an influence on the students' engagement in lessons. For example, during one period of the year that combined unseasonable heat with humidity, students were clearly affected by the environmental conditions: 'Today, to be honest, it was so hot, but I tried.' There were diverse reactions to these climatic conditions:

> Today we had a lesson when it was really hot. It was after sports lesson, so even more so my motivation disappeared. But at the start of the lesson the teacher said if you do something under harsh conditions, it will stick, and it will be useful anyway, and so my motivation went up, and I could concentrate on the lesson. It was really good. These conditions will probably continue, so I want to do my best. (Haruki, LJ, 28/6/2011)

The influence of physical conditions on class groups was also apparent in research conducted by Burns and Knox (2011). Through observations of classrooms, these researchers noted that the changing relationships between a number of factors from the physical environment, such as limited space, intense heat and poor lighting, produced classrooms unconducive to certain kinds of active learning tasks. Data collected from students in the current study refer only to heat and not to issues of space or lighting (the classroom we were using was perhaps the newest in the college, with ample space and sufficient lighting). However, the influence of a combination of factors is evident, as Haruki specifically mentions the physical environment and the factor of the timing of the lesson as affecting his motivation: 'so even more so my motivation disappeared.'

English sessions for these students were sandwiched between a first-period sports lesson and the lunch break. This timing meant that occasionally students recognised their motivation as fluctuating through hunger or their exertions in the previous period:

> Today, maybe because I was tired, I wasn't able to catch much when listening. Inside my head there were just all these question marks, and it was really terrible because I didn't understand at all. (Tetsuo, LJ, 10/5/2011)

The influence of the timetabling of the college as a whole was also apparent at different points in time across the school year. Interruptions to the regular weekly flow of lessons negatively affected student motivation in the class group. Students felt that their progress in certain English skills was impeded by a break. For instance, after the summer holiday break, Sayaka commented that 'After reading a long passage after a long break, I was surprised that I didn't understand at all' (LJ, 29/9/2011). Frequently students mentioned that their comprehension of my English or that of textbook DVD listening tasks was being affected by such breaks:

> Trying to do listening after a long break, I couldn't catch anything, so I panicked a bit. Rather than usual lessons, where I take them quite calmly, I felt like I panicked more in this lesson. I want to take the next lesson more calmly. (Seiya, LJ, 10/11/2011 – after college festival break)

As might be evidenced from these extracts, the influence of a break in study often had an emotional element. Coming back from their daily lives in a Japanese society in which very little English is used to the English lesson environment, students struggled to relocate a self being able to comprehend this language. As Seiya's extract testifies, while 'usual lessons' – presumably those other content lessons taught in Japanese – were met with more positively valenced affective responses even as students readjusted after a break, the English lessons at times created more of a burden. Student mindfulness of the effects of breaks was further apparent when they wrote of 'not wanting to forget' the feeling of motivated action they had experienced in a lesson:

> Next week and the week after there's the college festival and a holiday that means no lessons, so I want to try not to forget. I want to take the next lesson like this, cooperating together in our team. (Reiji, 20/10/2011)

The importance placed on exams in the college and the effects of their timing on motivation was also evident from student writing. In my initial review of the Japanese EFL motivation literature (Chapter 2) I determined that the frequently mentioned pressure from high-stakes entrance exams was not likely to affect the participants' EFL motivation just after they had entered the college. However, regular school-wide tests held four times a year did influence students' engagement in the English lessons. As the following extract suggests, even though there was no mid-term exam for the English lessons that were the focus of this study, Fumihiko's motivation was clearly affected by his consciousness of the impending college exam period:

> Today I took the English lesson with lowered motivation, so I didn't have energy to think of products. But I still think I at least tried. This is the last lesson before midterm exams, so I wanted to try my best, but I was more worried about exams. (Fumihiko, LJ, 24/5/2011 – before midterm)

As Fumihiko's extract reveals, students often voiced tension between a perceived necessity to study for exams and their engagement in lessons. There was a clash as the influence of something 'outside' the direct lesson environment, the college timetabling of exams, was brought in.

Similarly, prosaic dynamic influences on motivation have been found in the language learning classroom by Waninge *et al.* (2014). In their study with young learners (aged 11–12) a number of participants reported a sudden upward turn in their motivation towards the end of one particular observed lesson. However, when the researchers checked the source of this motivation with respondents it had very little to do with the lesson content at all, and was rather due to 'Only one more hour and this school-day is over!' (Waninge *et al.*, 2014: 717). Although perhaps seemingly trivial and often neglected in theoretical representations of motivation, similar contextual and temporal influences had a substantial *in situ* impact on students' perceptions of motivation in the current study.

Reflecting on Openness

In many ways my conceptualisation of the class group as an open system meshes with considerations in a case study approach to research. As Hetherington notes in linking complex systems theory with case study:

> Choosing boundaries to set around a case entails focusing in on particular aspects and thus excluding other aspects and therefore reducing the complexity of the case. ... It also means that however the case is bounded, the multiple interactions and connections with systems beyond that defined as the case make it impossible to set limits on the research due to the infinite range of interactions that impinge on the case itself. (Hetherington, 2013: 79)

Although I drew on the L2 Motivational Self System to conceptualise motivation in this study, aspects of the analysis discussed in this chapter brought to my attention the open nature of motivation across the whole class group. Rather than purely ideas related to the language learning self affecting motivation, the analysis suggests a more integrated, situated and complex picture of motivational influences on members of the foreign language classroom.

Extending the theoretical Figure 7.1 from the introduction section to this chapter, Figure 7.3 shows a revised representation of the interacting systems 'brought in' to the class group and affecting motivation which became apparent through the analysis of participants' writing. At 'lower' nested systemic levels, the personalities of individual students influenced their motivation and actions within the classroom. Students were also in turn affected by interactions with 'higher level' systems such as influences from family, hobbies and

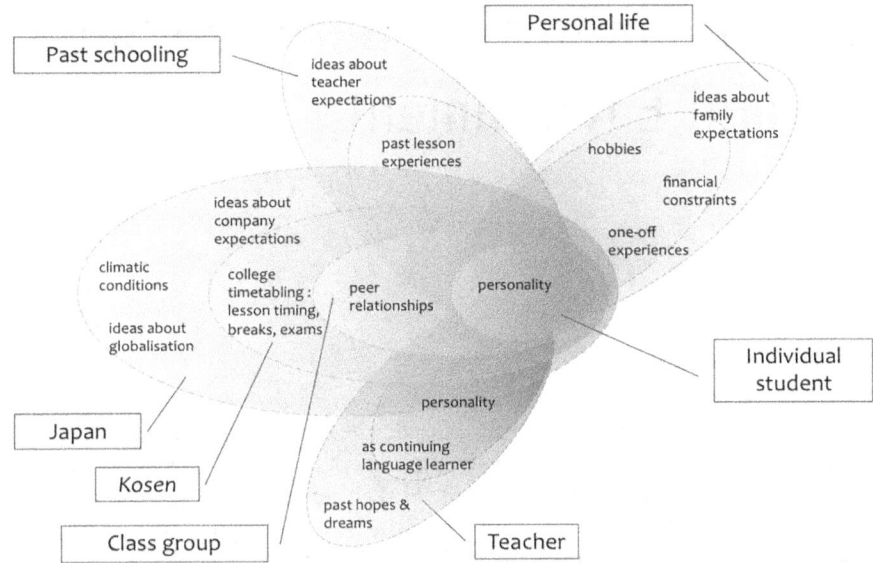

Figure 7.3 An abstraction of the multiple 'external' systems revealed through analysis to be interacting with students' motivation in the classroom
Source: Drawing on Bronfenbrenner (1979), Davis and Sumara (2006) and Haggis (2008).

one-off experiences, as well as their relationships with peers and the teacher in the class group, the effects of the timetabling in the college, and their understanding of expectations from significant others and the society around them.

What the analysis suggests is that the boundaries not only of the above systems, but also of the L2 Motivational Self System, are permeable. As such, what may be drawn on as a significant influence on motivation for one member of a class group may have little effect on another, or not exist in the same form as an influence. Difference is significant (Byrne & Callaghan, 2014), and 'variability in data is not noise to be discarded but is part of the behaviour of the system' (Larsen-Freeman & Cameron, 2008a: 73). The analysis illustrates that students' ideas of ideal self, ought-to self as absorbed expectations, and their learning experiences within the classroom are influenced constantly by situated interactions with innumerable systems 'external' to the three proposed elements of the L2 Motivational Self System. While the analysis reveals certain trends for groupings of influences from outside the direct class group on the motivation of members within the classroom, the 'openness' suggests that energy is transferred in non-linear ways through these interactions.

I continue my analysis in Chapter 8 by looking at a different dimension of interactions, employing the complex systems metaphor of a *state space* to explore the dynamic co-adaptation of self and environment fostering motivation of students in this class group.

8 Co-adaptation Between Self and Environment

Among a variety of influences from outside the direct learning environment, the previous chapter revealed the strong presence of ways in which learners 'bring themselves' into the classroom. How then do students' ideas of self evolve and interact within the context of the foreign language classroom and influence their motivation? Dörnyei's (2009a) conceptualisation of the L2 Motivational Self System is comprised of the *ideal L2 self* and *ought-to L2 self* – self aspects – and the *L2 learning experience* – influences from the environment. Complex systems theory encouraged me to notice in the data the integrally interactive nature of these elements of the L2 Motivational Self System: the here-and-now environment adapts the self of class members, just as the self of these same class members adapts the environment. There is *co-adaptation*, whereby the self and environment interact over time with mutual causality – change in one system fosters change in other, connected systems, which also feeds back to co-influence the original system (Larsen-Freeman & Cameron, 2008a: 233). In this chapter I draw on the complex systems theory concept of a 'state space' to examine how these self and environmental aspects co-adapted as a system in the context of this study.

A state space is a metaphor visualising all the possible states in which a system could be at any point in time (Larsen-Freeman & Cameron, 2008a: 46). Within this space, there are usually certain states or areas which might be relatively more stable 'attractor states' or unstable 'repeller states' (Thelen & Smith, 1994). In my study, I applied a definition of motivation as referring to 'a cumulative arousal, or want, that we are aware of' (Dörnyei, 2009b: 209). Motivation is by definition valenced, or 'directional'. By revisiting the data, I became aware that there were dimensions of participant writing which reflected such 'want' connected to some areas of the state space. Participant writing returned to these areas of the state space frequently over the particular span of time involved in this study. I consider these dimensions as more stable attractor states in the motivational state space. On the other hand, there appeared to be dimensions that suggested 'unwantedness'. Considering motivation as a 'want', I conceptualise these areas as repeller states that were more unstable. Finally, complex systems theory proposes that there may be 'control parameters' that play a significant role in affecting and channelling the trajectories of movement around state space (Byrne, 1998: 171). In outlining the possible scope of such control parameters in education, Larsen-Freeman and Cameron (2008a: 54) discuss the actions and intentions of the teacher as some possible control parameters for the trajectory of learning of the class group. In a similar fashion, in the current study these control parameters acted as processes – mechanisms bridging between the environment and self that directed motivation.

Figure 8.1 provides a diagrammatic visualisation of the discussion in this chapter. I represent the three different parts of the L2 Motivational Self System with merged circles as a kind of motivational state space. Within this state space I have visualised motivational attractor states revealed through the analysis as basins and a motivational repeller state as an uprising or mound. I position the octagonal control parameters as bridging between the environment and self. Furthermore, Figure 8.1 also includes the influences from outside the direct classroom system discussed in the previous chapter, shown with bidirectional arrows.

This model reflects my interpretation of the dynamics of motivational co-adaptation in this classroom system. This said, a model runs the risk of oversimplifying and giving a picture of static, isolated elements. As I have argued throughout, importance should be placed more on combinations, relationships and interactions. Moreover, it must be remembered that the extracts in the sections that follow are a partial and selective representation of the ongoing motivational co-adaptation. To draw on the words of Cilliers (1998: iii), 'instead of trying to analyse complex phenomena in terms of single or essential principles', my understanding acknowledges 'it is not possible to tell a single and exclusive story about something that is really complex'.

In what follows I introduce three sets of 'nested' motivational attractor and repeller states showing co-adaptive interaction between parts of the L2 Motivational Self System. The discussion will focus on the way in which analysis revealed the co-adaptive nature of interactions between the L2 learning experience – the environment – and the ought-to and ideal selves – the self. The final section of the chapter briefly examines how the analysis showed these nested states to be influential over different periods of the year of study.

Nested Motivational States Related to English Use

The English lessons in this study used a task-based approach. One of the key principles of task-based language teaching is experiential learning in which learners learn by doing, using the additional language (Nunan, 2004). Particularly in the first half of the year, perhaps as students were adjusting

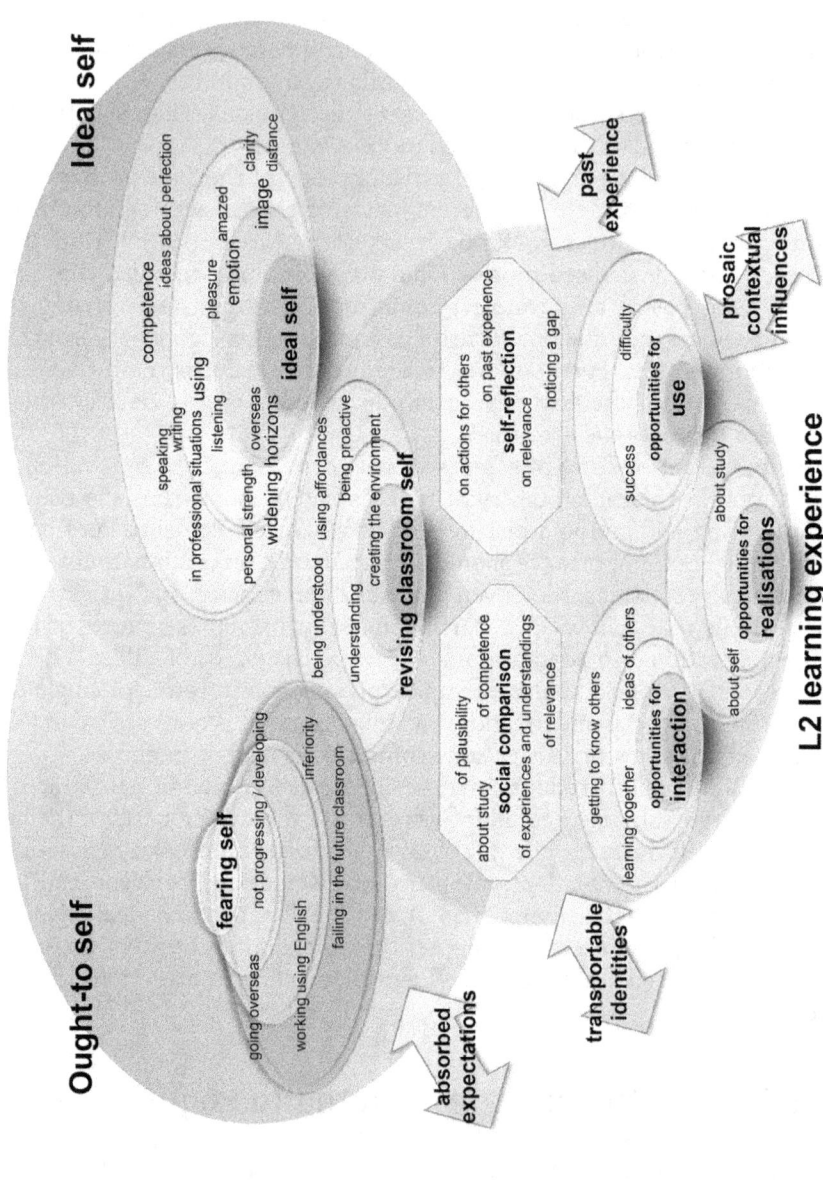

Figure 8.1 State space of the L2 Motivational Self System in this class group

to the new lesson style, these *opportunities for language use* appeared as a strong motivational attractor state:

> Through discussing with classmates in English, as we are all non-native English speakers, I became more confident in using English, and could discover new things. I want to use English, watch, and speak, and get more confidence with English. (Aoi, LJ, 19/4/2011)

Students gained more confidence through using English, which in turn fostered a desire for further learning. Opportunities for the use of English allowed students to experience success in a variety of ways. As might be recalled from the previous chapter, many students initially held negative perceptions of their experiences in past English classrooms due in part to not being able to understand the input from the teacher. As one student wrote, chances for meaningful receptive use of English in comprehending fostered motivation 'when I could catch the teacher's English, and could understand it'. However, the experiences of success – in comprehending and otherwise – that the opportunities for use allowed did not only revolve around myself as teacher, but were also frequently connected with attempts at undertaking tasks. These attempts were often linked to emotional states:

> At first I had no idea what to write when I tried to imagine about the picture, but I tried to use words I already know, and I was really happy when they were correct. In fact, I was moved! (Yuma, LJ, 26/4/2011)

> When we said the reasons, I tried positively to use English. I was worried whether my English would get across, but when it did, I was relieved. I thought that I want to try using even more English next time. (Yuma, LJ, 10/5/2011)

These two extracts from the same student reveal a similar, iterative pattern to his emotions in response to being presented with opportunities to use English. In the first extract, Yuma writes of his initial worries when faced with attempting to use English towards completing a task. However, when his attempt meets with success he writes of being 'really happy'. He then further stresses this emotional state: 'In fact, I was moved!' Written a few weeks later, the second extract reminds us of the social face of being an adolescent foreign language learner working to complete a task in the classroom: Yuma again notes emotion linked to the opportunity for language use in that despite trying 'positively to use English' he was 'worried whether my English would get across'. The unease of going out on a limb and attempting to communicate in the foreign language classroom is no doubt all the more intense as learners take their first tentative steps in a new class group. Despite being around one month after the start of the Japanese academic year, Yuma's writing shows his nervousness at this point. Emotion also, however, plays a key role as he becomes motivated to 'want to try using even more English next time' through his experience of being 'relieved' when he was able to experience success in conveying his message communicatively.

From the analysis, it appears that *self-reflection* acted as a vital control parameter, guiding the trajectories of students' motivation through this area of state space. In complex systems theory the present development of the system is critically dependent on past development (de Bot *et al.*, 2007). As mentioned in the previous chapter, students often 'brought in' their past experiences to make comparisons of past and current use of English in the classroom. Students reflected on their experiences of a self who had previously not had opportunities to use English, comparing these past experiences with their more favourable current use of English. As one student, Jiro, remarked, 'I've not ever really tried to write my own thoughts in English, so it was good to be able to think' (LJ, 26/4/2011). Another student, Hide, was even more overt in his comparison: 'As I thought, it's better to actually use English than just always studying grammar' (LJ, 12/4/2011).

Self-reflection also played a critical role as students developed understandings of their own abilities, making comparisons of past and current competence in reaction to their experiences in the current classroom environment:

> Today I did a presentation. There was a time before when I did a presentation, but compared to that time, this time I could definitely do it better, so I felt like I've improved. But I still only know very simple words, so I want to learn more words so that I can use those words to do a better presentation. (Kanata, LJ, 8/6/2011)

The review of the Japanese EFL motivation literature in Chapter 2 revealed the importance of students' own perceptions of competence on their motivation (e.g. Carpenter *et al.*, 2009; Falout & Maruyama, 2004; Hiromori, 2003; Tanaka, 2009; Tanaka & Hiromori, 2007). This extract provides a look into the cognitive processes that students go through as their ideas of competence evolve. Kanata reflects on perceptions of progress in competence across lessons. He perceives that he 'could definitely do it [a presentation] better' than previously. However, his self-reflection channels the direction of his motivation by noting difficulties as to where he is currently, where he wishes to be, and how he might make further progress.

The use of language in the classroom encouraged learners to write of an *ideal self* purposefully applying English in future professional situations:

> I thought that the English we *used* when we made business cards, and then introduced ourselves and our position was really useful. So when I get out into the working world, and can *use* this when meeting with

people from another company, I hope it will be understood. (Tetsuo, LJ, 19/4/2011; emphasis added)

I think I'll have to do many presentations in my work in the future, so I want to get better at doing them. This time the message didn't get conveyed so well, but I could at least grasp the flow of a presentation, so I want to increase my presentation ability one step at a time, so that I can make *use* of it in my future. (Kazu, LJ, 8/6/2011)

Research by Ronfeldt and Grossman (2008) has shown that through opportunities for successful experimentation, educational programmes can afford scaffolding to learners in their development of images of future roles. These extracts reveal students making a connection between their present use of English in the classroom and possible future English use. In the first extract, Tetsuo writes as if future English use is almost a given fact: 'So when I get out into the working world, and can *use* this when meeting with people from another company, I hope it will be understood.' Kazu also recognises English as a kind of requirement for a future self who will 'have to do many presentations in my work in the future'. He then draws on the challenges and difficulties experienced by the present self to aim towards a future self using English: 'so I want to increase my presentation ability one step at a time, so that I can make *use* of it in my future.' The following student discusses how his image of a future self using English changed over the year through success in the English lessons:

One year before I couldn't really have an image, but using English in the company for things like a presentation, I became able to have an image. [These] lessons are so good, because I can be good at English a little for [them]. (Jun, LJ Reflection 2, 9/2/2012)

One of the giants of classroom motivation theory and practice, Brophy (1998: 60) is often quoted for the following insight: 'The simplest way to ensure that students expect success is to make sure that they achieve it consistently.' While there is always the possibility of failure in the communicative foreign language classroom, Jun's writing reveals how he makes a connection between the *use* of English in lessons and development of an image that at the start of the year he 'couldn't really have'. He then ascribes great importance to his experiences in the English lessons in fostering an image of a capable English-using self, because 'I can be good at English a little for [them]'.

However, not all opportunities for language use connected with a positive self-image. Images of a self that students were fearing acted as a kind of *repeller state*. This state represented an area in the motivational state space that was more unstable and reflected 'unwantedness', the opposite of the 'want' of motivation. I introduce the progressive-tensed *fearing self* rather than the more traditional 'feared self' in order to draw attention to the dynamic experiencing of this self that was apparent in participant writing. Expressions of a fearing self emerged in connection with students' current experience of English use and were often emotionally connected to a lack of progress (emphasis added):

> Trying to do the phone conversation, it was harder than I thought. I thought it would be pretty difficult to actually do smoothly. *If I don't do my best from now on* ... (Taka, LJ, 6/10/2011)
>
> Compared to everyday conversation, business English has many difficult words, so I thought it was difficult. And I also *felt a sense of crisis* that I can't just stay this way of not even being able to do everyday conversation. (Chie, LJ, 29/9/2011)

As Chie vividly writes, these extracts reveal 'a sense of crisis' felt because of the current experience of difficulty in the classroom. The fearing self is something very potent and clear for these students, with Taka's last sentence hinting at an almost menacing nature of the fearing self: 'If I don't do my best from now on ...' However, I also understand that these students feel the feared self as possible, but something that can be avoided through a revision of action: 'I can't just stay this way.'

As the previous two extracts show, present learning experiences encouraged students at times to write of ideas of a fearing self in quite a general temporal sense. Students furthermore wrote of a temporally proximal fearing self using English in the classroom. For example, one student made a comparison of his comprehension of my spoken English between past and current experience: 'Today was the second lesson, but I thought I could catch less of the teacher's English than last time.' He continued in the next sentence by making a revision of a future self in the following lesson: 'I want to catch more words in the next lesson than this time.' Although not overt in his writing, an implication I understand in the space between these two sentences is that he fears a continued downward spiral in the following lesson in which he also may not be able to understand.

However, rather than the kind of debilitating state representative of foreign language anxiety, students frequently wrote of a kind of proximal future self acting in the future classroom. I developed the term *revising classroom self* to represent this evolving conceptualisation. One form of revising classroom self that connected to the opportunities for language use was an image of being proactive in future classroom English use. These self-ideas were constant works in progress, developing and adapting through the experience of lessons. For instance, one student reflected on the difficulty of attempting to achieve a self-determined goal – 'Near the end I tried to use only English, but I couldn't do it and used some Japanese' – to which he then revised his idea of a self in future classroom activities: 'Even simple English is ok, but I want to try to use only English.' Other students wrote of similar revisions:

> I could discuss seriously and positively, so I was pleased. I'm studying after lessons, and looking up words before lessons, so I want to continue studying like this. Next time I want to try speaking again, so my English ability goes up. (Jun, LJ, 17/5/2011)

Jun attributes his current success in a discussion using English to his study outside the classroom. This experience of success not only provides positive reinforcement that the activity outside class time is worthwhile, but also fosters a revising classroom self-image as someone who will 'try speaking again, so my English ability goes up'.

Reminiscent of the use of possible selves as kinds of 'stepping-stones' into the future discussed in the literature (Dörnyei, 2009a; Oyserman & James, 2011; Pizzolato, 2006), there were also cases when students linked their current experience in using English to their future selves at different time frames. As is evident in the following extract, on occasions these descriptions of a self-across-time connected their present use of English with a future revision of self in the classroom, while at times students also linked these ideas to the more distal future. As such, these revising selves were connected not only with the English classroom and class group, but also with other English lessons and the developing futures of students:

> I really felt that I'm becoming able to catch English. I'm beginning to understand the meaning too. If I pile things up [experience] I'll become able to do it, so I thought that I want to try harder in [this] English lesson. I want a little more chance to touch English. When I thought of sentences, I couldn't think of compound phrases. So I want to remember lots of compound phrases from now on. And also there were many parts of grammar that I didn't know, so I want to try hard in grammar study too. (Tomoe, LJ, 20/10/2011)

The influence of connections between opportunities for language use and emerging self-ideas was far more evident over the timeframe of the first half of the year of this study. A second set of motivational states nesting opportunities for interaction with self-ideas was recognisable through the writing of participants across the entire year.

Nested Motivational States Related to Interaction

Ushioda (2011b: 21–22) argues that 'it is through social participation in opportunities, negotiations and activities that people's motivations and identities develop and emerge as dynamically co-constructed processes'. Students wrote from the very start of lessons about the motivating aspects of a variety of *interactions*. Some of these opportunities allowed them to get to know the identities of their peers. As one student, Makoto, remarked about a mingling activity near the start of the academic year in which students introduced themselves, 'When we exchanged business cards, I enjoyed being able to get to know interesting facts about other classmates' (LJ, 19/4/2011).

The opportunities for interactions also provided motivation via students being able to think together. Through cooperation with other class members, students were able to experience successes that they might not have been able to achieve independently. As the following extract suggests, these experiences led to motivation towards further interaction in later lessons:

It was really difficult to think of 5 questions in English. I'm not so good at English, so thinking of 5 questions and writing them was really difficult. But after using a dictionary to make the questions together as a group, there was a real sense of achievement. So I thought that I want to discuss lots in our group again in the next lesson. (Aoi, LJ, 10/11/2011)

The motivational capacity of the opportunities for interaction furthermore arose from chances to exchange ideas and learn with peers. Understood with complex systems theory, the class group involved much redundancy: members shared cultural backgrounds, similar first language and roughly equal social status. Redundancy assists 'systemic coherence' through the capacity 'to enable interactions among agents' (Davis & Sumara, 2010: 858). Interaction during tasks was fostered by redundancy as it helped students to share understandings. However, intrinsic motivation from the diversity of members of the system also emerged as a result of the range of different ideas and approaches that students were able to bring to tasks. Ryu was quite clear about the benefits of this diversity when he reflected on an activity in which student groups had to examine information about an imaginary product and make an enhanced proposal:

Today we thought all together about improvements for various ideas. Everyone had their own ideas, and I could realise things that I couldn't realise by myself. (Ryu, LJ, 13/10/2011)

These opportunities for interaction were also frequently linked with affect through the connections students could feel in their groups. Interactions fostered positive emotional states and attachment with fellow class members, while the dissolution of such attachment often led to negative emotions, as reflected in the following extract:

With the cooperation of the team members I was able to make English sentences and get the data together. I was *really pleased* that we did the work so quickly and efficiently that there was almost time left over. This is the last lesson with these members so I'm a bit *sad/lonely* [*samishii*]. (Yuma, LJ, 1/12/2011; emphasis added)

Although in many senses the opportunities for interaction were intrinsically motivating, *social comparisons* that students made also acted as a control parameter to guide their motivation related to interactions. Students compared with others to revise their ideas of the plausibility of a self using English in the near and distal future. For example, during activities in which students received information about the use of English by older students at the college they socially compared with others whom they perceived as being similar to themselves (Oyserman *et al.*, 2006), influencing perceptions of future possibility. In response to the role-model presentation about an engineering internship overseas, Shun compared his ideas with those of the speaker:

I don't really know much about my future, and even more so I've not even been able to imagine the possibility of working overseas. But listening to today's presentation, I felt strongly that this possibility is a lot closer to me than I had thought. (Shun, LJ, 11/5/2011)

Such social comparison of plausibility also channelled motivation in opportunities for interaction in the English lessons:

When we were speaking English in our groups, rather than just using one word, there was a student who could use whole sentences, so I was really impressed. When I can't say something, I always just use Japanese, so I thought that I want to learn from the other student's example and speak like them. And there was another student who didn't think about English in complicated ways, but just tried to have fun with it. I thought that English is just a language like Japanese, and if only I change my way of thinking, I might be able to speak like this student. (Sayaka, LJ, 10/5/2011)

That social comparison would play a role in the motivation of the 15–16-year-old students in this study is not overly surprising, considering that this period of adolescent development is marked by an increasing awareness of pressure from society to construct different selves for varying roles and relationships and attempt to build a coherent picture of the self (Harter, 2003). Indeed, Harter (2003: 623) argues that this phase of development sees adolescents 'often morbidly preoccupied with how they appear in the eyes of others'. Sayaka socially compares her own current capabilities – '[w]hen I can't say something, I always just use Japanese' and the actions of other students: 'rather than just using one word, there was a student who could use whole sentences'; 'there was another student who didn't think about English in complicated ways'. She adjusts her ideas of plausibility as a result of these social comparisons: 'I thought that ... if only I change my way of thinking, I might be able to speak like this student.' The opportunity for interaction provided the chance for motivation, but it was her social comparison of plausibility that directed the trajectory of this motivation.

Dörnyei and Ushioda (2011) emphasise that one of the conditions for motivation through the L2 Motivational Self System is that a future state is not perceived as certain to occur without effort. Through such social comparisons, students were also able to reflect on their approaches to study. Some students made social comparisons with others relating to their own level of effort in studying: 'At first today we thought about the goal we'd set at the start of second semester. Everyone had been doing something, even a small thing, to move towards their goals.' This student then reflected on his own efforts – 'But I haven't been doing anything, so I got uneasy' – before altering his ideas of effort: 'So I think I'll change it to a smaller goal that I can achieve soon.'

Through social comparisons during opportunities for interaction, students altered their ideas about what was possible for an *ideal self*. For example, after the first role-model presentation one student wrote of his change in ideas: 'For my own future, not just working in Japan, but also working overseas would be cool, I thought.' He then connected this revising of image with his perception of the current Japanese working environment – 'At the moment, lots of Japanese companies are heading overseas' – before linking the future possible-self with a necessity for action in the present: 'so I'd like to try working overseas as an engineer. So I was made to feel strongly the importance of studying English.' Another student's image of the competence of an ideal self altered:

> What I was most surprised about was that even though he didn't understand everything that the local people said, they could still communicate. At the moment I'm pretty bad at English, but as kosen has such a system for helping students to do work experience overseas, I think I'd like to try it. (Teru, LJ, 11/5/2011)

Teru's writing suggests that he previously held a belief that competence in English required 'perfection', being able to comprehend all input. However, through the interaction with the presenter's ideas he receives negative feedback about this understanding. He alters his own image of an ideal, competent English-using self to be someone who may not 'understand everything that the local people [say]' but 'could still communicate'.

In a similar fashion to the opportunities for language use, opportunities for interaction also at times elicited negative social comparisons connected to a *fearing self*. Indeed, Kim (2009: 277) defines the ought-to L2 self as 'originat[ing] from an L2 learner's apprehension of failure' which 'reflects the external demands from other members of the community'. One way in which students wrote of a fearing self was through the ideas they expressed of perceived inferiority with others. They became more aware of this perceived lack through interactions. However, rather than being envious of others, many students appeared to feel a kind of pressure to be able to act in similar ways or have similar experiences:

> When friends said they did an [overseas] home-stay, or lived in England, I thought I want to get close to English so that I don't lose out to those kinds of experiences. (Sayaka, LJ Reflection 1, 5/10/2011)

Sayaka reveals a fearing self quite distal and removed from the classroom. The extract expresses a strong sense of perceived expectation. Sayaka compares herself with peers who have experience overseas, and notes that she doesn't want to 'lose out to those kinds of experiences'. This comment suggests that, for her, a failing self would be someone who doesn't have such experiences with English in the future.

Pressures from perceived expectations in the community of the class group led some students to write of a fearing self failing in the classroom. At times this pressure seemed to come from ideas of failing during interaction in the future classroom, while at other times students expressed an internal sense of not wanting to inconvenience others through deficits in action in the classroom:

> I troubled the other team members with my presentation, so I felt regretful. I thought that it's difficult to say what I thought in Japanese with English expressions. I felt strongly that my study of English grammar is still not sufficient. (Chie, LJ, 8/6/2011)

There were also more positive ways in which opportunities for interaction fostered ideas of the proximal, *revising classroom self*. A set of extracts written independently by two students in the same group from the same date vividly suggests how the current experience of interactions in the classroom affected ideas of a revising classroom self co-creating the lesson environment:

> Today, like the teacher suggested, I tried even more than normal to use English positively. But the other members in the group didn't really try to use English, so I also couldn't use it. But when I tried to use English, from then on, mostly the other members also tried to use English. I thought, rather than waiting for someone else to start trying, it's important to start by myself. From next time, I want to try speaking by myself, and create an atmosphere in which English is spoken. (Nao, LJ, 28/6/2011)

I couldn't use very much English when we had to talk about good and bad points of different products. But I could use English to discuss together to decide which product was the best. At this time, I saw another team member really trying to use English in this discussion, and so I felt like I wanted to speak in English too. I think that if someone doesn't start by using English like this student, then we'll naturally just use Japanese, so I want to try using English right from the start in next lesson. (Sayaka, LJ, 28/6/2011)

Davis and Sumara (2006: 105) contend that there is 'an underlying "win-win logic" of complex unities. ... A win-win logic suggests that one agent's situation will likely improve if the situations of his/her/its nearest neighbours improve. A "we" is usually better than an "I" for all involved'. In the previous extracts, both students write of their parallel experiences at the beginning of an activity. Although Nao wanted to use English, she receives negative feedback about the appropriateness of her intention: 'the other members in the group didn't really try to use English, so I also couldn't use it.' This lack of use is confirmed in Sayaka's extract. However, there is a turning point when Nao attempts to use English anyway: 'But when I tried to use English, from then on, mostly the other members also tried to use English.' In her new attempt, she receives positive feedback from the environment suggesting her revised behaviour to be appropriate. This turning point is clearly understood by Sayaka as well: 'At this time, I saw another team member really trying to use English in this discussion, and so I felt like I wanted to speak in English too.' These experiences encourage both students to write of a revising classroom self more proactive in making the environment for learning. As Nao reflects, 'I thought, rather than waiting for someone else to start trying, it's important to start by myself. From next time, I want to try speaking by myself, and create an atmosphere in which English is spoken.' Sayaka's revising classroom self is in parallel: 'I think that if someone doesn't start by using English like this student, then we'll naturally just use Japanese, so I want to try using English right from the start in next lesson.'

Although also evident in homeroom periods in which possible-self activities were introduced, motivation emergent from the nesting of opportunities for language use, opportunities for interaction and self-ideas was more prominent in the English lessons. A final set of motivational states nesting opportunities for realisations with self-ideas was noticeable to a greater degree in direct connection with the introduced change-action.

Nested Motivational States Related to Realisations

Opportunities for realisations were perceived as motivating by students. While some of these realisations concerned English study in particular, students also made connections with aspects of their personalities or ways of thinking. These realisations frequently encouraged students to write of powerful motivation towards future action:

> There's not usually occasion to think about what kind of personality I have, or what's bad, so I couldn't think of things very quickly. I'm pretty simple, so just by thinking carefully and writing about what I should fix about English or myself, I'll get the feeling of 'I'll try my best from today!' So I'm appreciative of the teacher that does homerooms or lessons that raise my motivation. As [*sekkaku*] I've got this feeling of wanting to do my best, I want to do what I can. (Sayaka, LJ, 7/12/2011)

> Today was a really strange homeroom. I'm really shy and get nervous easily, so what the teacher taught will be really useful, I thought. ... It was a really meaningful homeroom. I felt like I could understand the importance of imagination. I want to always imagine, and keep chasing after the future me. I had the feeling that if it's me, I can do anything. (Yuya, LJ, 12/10/2011 – Guided-imagery activity)

As these extracts suggest, although I introduced change-action into the classroom system, the ways in which students interpreted this 'noise' and made realisations through these opportunities were various. Reflecting a vital property of complex systems, control was decentralised (Davis & Sumara, 2006). Although Sayaka mentions her appreciation of myself as teacher for introducing different activities, she resoundingly places herself as the focal point of her agency: 'As I've got this feeling of wanting to do my best, I want to do what I can.' Her voicing of choice reveals interactions between motivation and affect through her experiences in the classroom. In response to a guided-imagery activity, Yuya's extract suggests an extremely strong experience of motivation from his ideal-self image: 'I had the feeling that if it's me, I can do anything.' His writing also uncovers his dynamic interpretation and reinterpretation of his affect towards the session, as it was initially 'strange' yet became 'really meaningful' through reflecting on his personality and the role of imagination.

In an iterative process, the learning journals fostered motivating realisations for students by allowing them a space to both retrospect and prospect. The use of reflective journals encouraged individual students to construct an increasingly holistic understanding of the interactions between their past experiences and their current, emerging state that appears to have added to their sense of agency:

> By writing the learning journal every lesson, I could reflect upon the lesson, and think of a little goal for the next lesson. I feel like every time when I made these little goals, my motivation went up a little more. And

by reflecting upon the lesson, I could be refreshed for the next lesson. (Jiro, LJ Reflection 1, 5/10/2011)

Both *self-reflection* and *social comparison* acted as control parameters to channel the motivation of students related to realisations. First, students reflected on relevance through a connection between the self in the present and a future self in general. This connection was particularly noticeable in writing concerning the Possible-Self Tree activity (Appendix G):

> Through comparing things like bad points about myself now and my hopes for the future I realised that I can't keep going the way that I am. By expressing that in a picture I could realise the position that I'm in now, and I got a real shock. (Hiro, LJ, 14/12/2011)

Student motivation to learn is connected with the need to feel there is a purpose to what one is doing, a factor commonly found in studies of classroom motivation and demotivation (Agawa *et al.*, 2011; Jang, 2008; Reeve *et al.*, 2002). In congruence with such findings, students frequently wrote of exploration of the meaning of their English studies and why they were studying. For instance, one student reflected: 'From now on I want to understand the purpose of what I'm studying when taking the lesson.' This self-reflection guided their motivation as students made realisations through the environmental opportunities. Building on qualities expressed by many students at the start of the research of ideas of the purpose of study and a best-possible English self, the meaning of study was usually ascribed to professional situations in the future, with these realisations linking to a desire for action. In the following extract, Ken's writing clearly illuminates the way in which conscious appraisal of these opportunities encouraged motivation:

> ... *when I think about it*, I feel like the English for saying my opinion will be useful when I work at a company in the future. *If I concentrate* on something like that when I'm studying I think it will lead to greater skills. (Ken, LJ, 13/10/2011; emphasis added)

The writing of students concerning the two role-model presentations introduced as change-actions also reveals the way in which social comparisons directed students' motivation. Near-peer role modelling has been discussed as beneficial in language learning through its capacity to show learners similar others succeeding, fostering the notion that comparable success is possible for oneself also (Murphey & Arao, 2001; Yashima, 2009). Student writing moreover suggested a social comparison of the relevance of English study – 'if it's relevant for this older student, it's relevant for me too'. At 15–16 years of age, the requirements of obtaining full-time employment were temporally removed from these students. The role-model presentations played a key function in encouraging students to realise this was a process that, like the presenters, they too would need to engage in. Through making social comparisons with the presenters, the presentations provided the opportunity for students to realise the relevance of their English study, that it connected to their possible future in the form of the near-peers:

> I thought that in only a few years' time I'll have to get a job. Watching today's presentation, I thought that wherever I work, in Thailand, in America, or even in Japan, I'll need English. So rather than just superficially doing English in lessons, I realised that it's for my future, so I thought I want to study English more than before, and make it useful for my future. (Mikihiro, LJ, 11/5/2011)

In response to opportunities for realisations, students' motivation was also influenced via making social comparisons of their experiences and understandings with peers. Two entries relating to the session in which students compared their own experiences in junior-high school English lessons with those of other students are illustrative:

> I understood that there were a lot of students at other junior-high schools that felt English lessons were boring. It was a very interesting activity, because there's usually no chance to ever hear about what the English lessons of students at other schools are like. (Chie, LJ, 12/4/2011)

> It was interesting that there were very few students that had written similar ideas to mine. (Yuya, LJ, 12/4/2011)

A little background is required to understand how diversity and redundancy in the class group encouraged these students to make realisations through social comparison that were quite different. Chie encountered other students who thought their previous English lessons were 'boring'. Cross-referencing with what she wrote about her own past experiences, she also perceived junior-high school English lessons as of little interest. Her encounters with other students who brought similar experiences to her own led to positive feedback in social comparison – her understandings were reinforced. On the other hand, Yuya writes overtly of negative feedback: 'It was interesting that there were very few students that had written similar ideas to mine.' Through cross-reference with what he had written about his experiences, he wrote negatively about past English lessons. However, during the activity there was sufficient diversity in the experiences of other students that Yuya happened to encounter students with different – perhaps positive? – recollections. This diversity and redundancy of ideas spread across the class group fostered motivation and interest through making social comparisons. It also reflects the non-linear nature of the complex motivational system of the class group – although the same change-action was introduced to the class as a whole, the outcomes for individual students varied as they interacted with others in the class system.

Through these opportunities for realisations, students wrote of their *ideal self* becoming closer. They linked words that expressed the perceived distance of their future English-using self with action from the present. As Yuya commented at the end of the year, 'The 'English-using myself' is something that's near yet far, but I want to try hard and become [it]' (LJ Reflection 2, 9/2/2012). The opportunities for realisations pushed the quality of the ideal-self image to change:

> One year before I was thinking that I'd really never have to use something like English. Because I was thinking that if I entered a company within Japan I'd get away without using English. But at present in companies within Japan as well there are people from other countries working, so I'm imagining using it to communicate or using it for dealings with other countries. (Haruki, LJ Reflection 2, 9/2/2012)

A future self needs not only to exist in a particular domain, but also have a sufficient degree of detail if it is to be motivating (Dörnyei, 2009a). The clarity of detail of a future English-using self was particularly noticeable in comments that students wrote about the guided-imagery activity (Appendix F). Tetsuo visualised a self competently using English, spurring him to want to move closer to his image: 'Me of a few years later was really able to talk with friends in English a lot. I want to become like that' (LJ, 12/10/2011). While student writing revealed these images as not always complete or well-formed, the reflection processes during opportunities for realisations fostered a renewed cognisance of future self-ideas:

> This time, perhaps because I was relaxed, even though I was able to see the image of me of some years later, images like my clothes were scattered around like pieces of a puzzle, and I thought that I need to think about what's in front of me by myself, and choose it by myself. (Eiji, LJ, 12/10/2011)

Student writing further revealed a realisation of a range of perceived benefits of the ideal self, often through the development of a kind of personal strength:

> I thought that there are so many convenient products now. And they all get better and better all the time, so I wondered at the persistence of companies that make them. And I thought, so that I can become

someone who works at a company like that, I'll do my best to study English. (Teru, LJ, 17/5/2011)

Teru realises a connection between an activity discussing different technological products and the kind of company he wants to work at in the future. His next statement also recalls the ought-to self, his expectation that to 'become someone who works at a company like that' English is a requirement. However, Kubanyiova (2009: 323) has argued that what was initially an externally motivated possible self (an ought-to self) might develop over time into a more internalised ideal self. Teru's use of phrases such as 'so that *I can become* someone who …' (suggesting possibility rather than pressure) and *'I'll* do my best' (rather than *I have to* do my best) suggests the process of such internalisation.

Possible selves gain motivational momentum when there is a connection with a person's emotional system (MacIntyre *et al.*, 2009: 47). When students made realisations about a future self using English, these images frequently involved expressions of emotion. For example, in reflecting on the first role-model presentation, the writing of one student reveals an emotional element in her realisation that an ideal self who 'could speak English smoothly' like the presenter would be 'amazing'. Writing of the same opportunity, another student reflected that he 'was amazed to see him [the presenter] speaking English fluently with the teacher before the presentation', before clearly linking this emotional perception with a future ideal self: 'so I thought I want to become someone like this.' The peer role-model presenter's competence was incorporated into this student's image of future self with concrete, positively valenced affect.

While far less evident than in the other nested motivational states, representations of a temporally distal *fearing self* also emerged as a repeller state connected with the opportunities for realisations. Students sometimes expressed apprehension when imagining a future self overseas because of a perceived lack of English ability. In introducing change-action and information that suggested the possibility of a future using English, the opportunities for realisations in many ways challenged students to move out of a perhaps comfortable state in which they imagined no such need for themselves. Yet although they were at times worried about going overseas because of predicted difficulties with English, learners also seemed to perceive that remaining only in Japan would also be a failure. As one student wrote: 'I got scared because I definitely wouldn't be understood. But … it's no good to just stay stuck inside. I think I want to try going overseas sometime.' In some ways, what this theme suggests is the kind of push-pull effect that Dörnyei and Ushioda (2011) contend might be forthcoming in self-based motivation: An ideal-self image provides a pulling force while a fearing self fosters a push.

Students also occasionally referred to a fearing self connected to working using English. The reflections of one student about a video I screened showing

Japanese company employees studying English are illustrative: 'In today's lesson I watched a video and understood that even though English is necessary for working people, they weren't actually able to use it.' Rather than concentrating on how people were shown attempting to improve their English in this video (which was the major theme), he focuses on their lack of ability. The opportunity fostered a realisation of a fearing self who is similarly unable to respond to a perceived expectation that 'English is necessary for working people'.

Moving temporally closer, participants wrote of a *revising classroom self* using the various opportunities or affordances in the environment. There was realisation that effort expended over time would benefit the future self. As the following extract suggests, students noted these realisations as encouraging them to act in the present:

> Today we improved our product. I understood that even after the product is complete, it needs to be improved. I felt like study is kind of the same. Even if there's only one answer, what's important is the feeling of wanting to search deeper afterwards, I thought. I want to not forget this feeling, and make use of it from now on. (Fumihiko, LJ, 13/10/2011)

Students used the opportunities to reflect with the learning journal to make realisations about their actions in the day's English lesson and ideas of near-future action. For instance, one student wrote, 'Today I couldn't make a chance to speak English from myself. Even if a little, I think I should have spoken English.' She then directly refers to this realisation as fostering a revising classroom self for the following lesson: 'Making use of this reflection, I want to make sure I use it [English] next time.' Other students similarly wrote of realisations fostering ideas of a revising self using the opportunities in the environment both outside and inside the classroom for my English lessons:

> Today I made a report. Now, I tried to use as much as possible expressions I'm learning in the other English [lessons]. I thought that if I use them in this kind of chance, then they'll seep into me. In a normal lesson it's mostly just listening to the teacher's speech, but [these English lessons are] look, listen, write, and everything, I take a lesson by using, so I think I want to keep trying to use [English] from now on too. My expressions might be mistaken, but I think there's a meaning to using, so I want to not worry about failures and just challenge. (Kazu, LJ, 1/12/2011)

Chances were there in the environment to be used, and when there was experience of them being used appropriately, realisations guided further intention towards revising action within the classroom.

The refocusing of the action research to include more activities allowing students to think explicitly about their images of self (Cycles 4 and 5) fostered a change in consciousness of self and the connection between this recognition and action. I bring this section to a close with the words of Taku, who clearly expresses the iterative nature of these processes:

> At first my image was hazy. I hadn't thought about that kind of myself [*jibun*] before. By becoming conscious of that kind of thing, I was able to turn my eyes to the future. Even now the image is still hazy, and I don't really know about the future. But now, there is a me who is doing his best to make an image. I can really feel that even just through that, it's different from the me before. (Taku, LJ Reflection 2, 9/2/2012)

Reflecting on Co-adaptation in State Space

A complex systems approach to analysis facilitated very rich understandings of aspects of the L2 Motivational Self System co-adapting in a kind of motivational state space. I argue that this notion of a state space affords a more realistic vision of the interaction between self and environment in classroom language learning. It encourages recognition of the dynamism and co-forming nature of these processes rather than focusing on primarily self or environment as distinct elements.

By examining these processes of co-adaptation longitudinally over the timescale of the year of study, it was possible to discern certain trends in the stability and prominence of the nested states. Figures 8.2–8.4 depict the

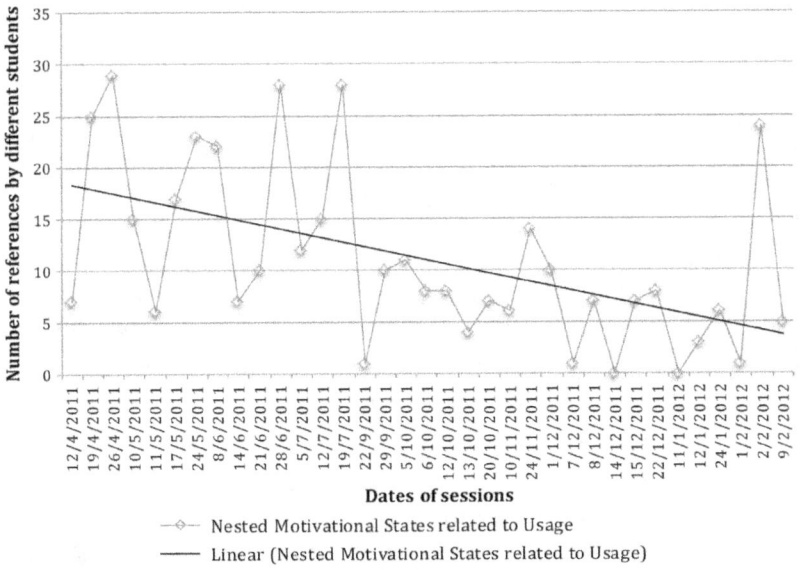

Figure 8.2 Graph showing the evolution of nested motivational states involving co-adaptation between opportunities for language use and self-ideas

124　Part 2: 再見 Re-viewing

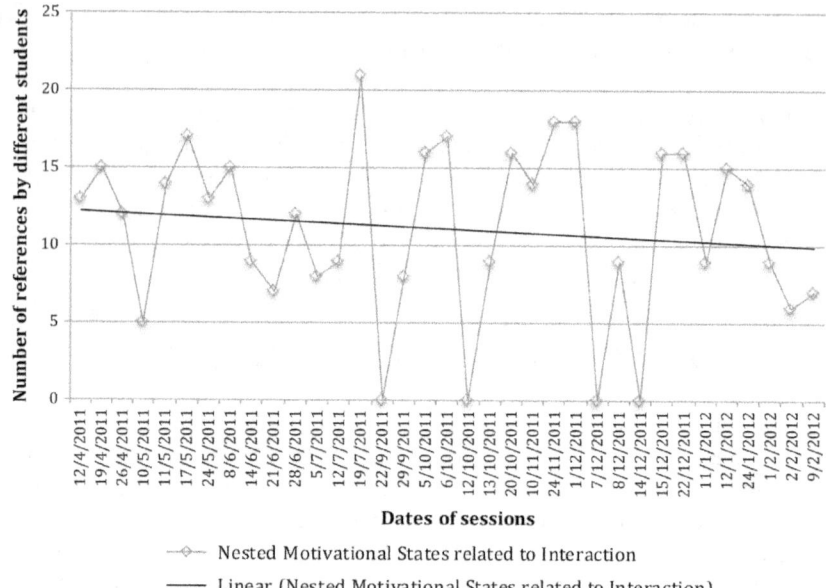

Figure 8.3 Graph showing the evolution of nested motivational states involving co-adaptation between opportunities for interaction and self-ideas

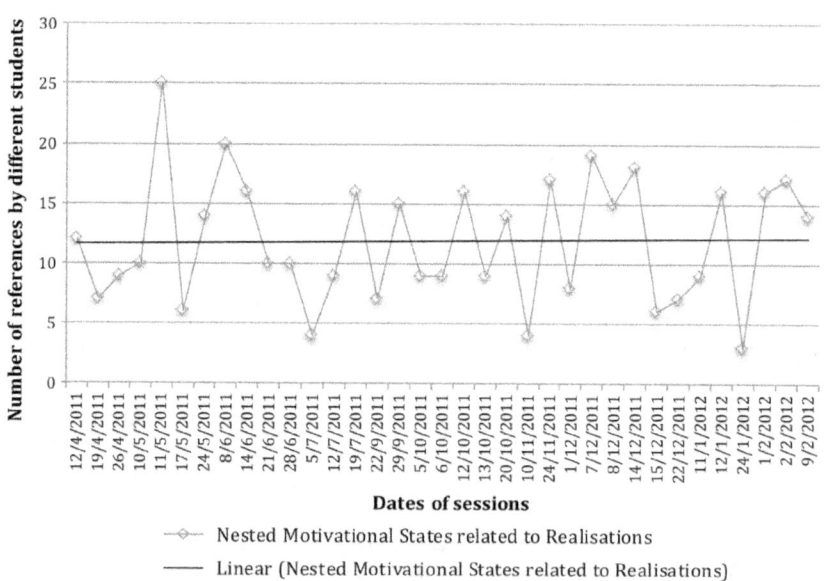

Figure 8.4 Graph showing the evolution of nested motivational states involving co-adaptation between opportunities for realisations and self-ideas

evolution of these three nested motivational states by plotting the number of references by different students to a particular state against the dates of the relevant sessions during the year.

The graphs give a clear sense of the way in which different classroom environments involving different activities were perceived as having some effect on motivation or alternately having very little effect. What is further interesting from a pedagogical point of view is the way in which, as far as can be discerned from student writing, opportunities for interaction and realisations remained relatively motivating throughout the year, whereas student motivation in response to the opportunities for language use appears to have decreased. Although only speculative, perhaps the change from a more traditional, teacher-centred lesson style in junior-high school to the task-based lessons witnessed a surge in motivation through the intrinsically motivating novelty of using English. The gradual decrease in motivation in this area of state space also, however, suggests the need for teachers to provide activities that somehow might sustain this freshness of using English.

Nevertheless, this conceptualisation of co-adaptation between self and environment suggests the extremely agentic role that each participant (students and teacher) has in forming possibilities for the language learning classroom (motivational) system and also constraints on action. Self emerges as a fluid process of choice making and understanding – in a motivational and affective sense – in dynamic interaction with the situation at hand as members themselves co-form the classroom context. It also evolves out of iterative understandings of past experiences and future potentials. Juarrero (2002: 252–253) eloquently summarises such a notion of an agentive self:

> Yesterday's choices affect today's options, but choices made today will also bias those options available tomorrow. The environment coevolves with us. ... In a process of continuous landscape reconfiguration, each step enhances or diminishes the downstream options available to the organism. That is, each choice alters both the availability and probability of future steps. We are not passive products of either the environment or external forces. In a very real sense we contribute to the circumstances that will constrain us later on.

In the following two chapters I revisit the data to look at ways in which such individual agency also co-formed motivational change in the class group as a whole.

9 Motivational Phase-shifts and Self-organisation Across the Class Group

Worldwide, a large proportion of foreign language learning takes place in classrooms with students moving through the turbulent period of adolescence. Taylor (2013) has argued that truly communicative classrooms offer unique opportunities for such young people to express themselves at a key point in the development of their identities. Yet, as discussion in earlier chapters has hinted, the communicative classroom also places more responsibility onto the shoulders of learners. It may offer a quite different and at times perplexing freedom in comparison with previous study experiences. While teachers can attempt to support students in their efforts to adjust, how do learners themselves make adaptations that foster a communicative classroom facilitative of learning?

In this chapter I turn to the ways in which a complex systems approach to analysis encouraged an understanding of certain timescales across which the agents and environment of the classroom space co-adapted to form the motivational landscape of the class group as a whole. In particular, the chapter explores the co-formation of motivation in the class group connected to the move to a communicative lesson style.

Phase-shifts Related to Transitions

At certain points in time, systems can become very sensitive and exhibit far-from-equilibrium conditions (Guastello & Liebovitch, 2009). At such points a phase-shift may occur as a kind of transformation in which the system as a whole changes to a very different form or direction of action (Byrne, 1998). However, it is not merely one final event or experience to which we can attribute the causation of any sudden change, but the combination of interactions between the developing present and all that has gone before.

The transition to new lessons as phase-shift

At the start of the year, student writing clearly revealed how motivation was influenced by a difference in environments. From the experience of their separate junior-high school English lessons, there was a transition for students to the new classroom space of English lessons at their new college. These lessons applied a communicative, task-based approach to language learning. As such, one of the primary changes was to a classroom in which a great deal more English was used than in students' previous classroom experiences. This abrupt difference in lesson style led students to worry about their ability to understand:

> It was the first lesson. It was fun. In contrast to lessons at junior-high school, the teacher spoke in English, so there were parts that I didn't understand, but I want to gradually get used to English. At junior-high school, the teacher just read whatever text was in the textbook, so this lesson was a breath of fresh air. I want to do my best to be able to listen to English. (Tomoe, LJ, 12/4/2011 – first English lesson)

Many learners expressed unease at the transition to the first English lesson due to worries about understanding in an environment that probably involved a great deal more English use than they had experienced before in their junior-high school lessons. However, they also articulated the formation of what I termed in the previous chapter *revising classroom selves*, that is, proximal ideas of a self in the future classroom. Based on their experiences of the initial lesson environment, students referred to a revising classroom-self being able to understand English. Moreover, as Tomoe reflects, for a great number of students experiences in the presently unfolding classroom space offered 'a breath of fresh air' compared to past experience. From data collected in action research Cycle 1 in which students wrote about their experiences of English lessons before entering the college (Appendix D), the majority of learners (38 of the 41 students) wrote of negative experiences. They attributed these negative experiences to three main factors: the teacher, a lack of comprehension, and the classroom environment. These elements came together to create lessons at junior-high school that for many students were 'sleep-inducing' and 'boring'. In response to the transition to the new English lessons, students invariably wrote of their experience as pleasurable, leading them to make predictions of future enjoyment of *this* space:

> Even though today was the first lesson, it was actually fun. I wasn't able to like my junior-high school English lessons, but I think I'll be able to like these kosen lessons. Because I'm actually feeling that I'm enjoying English. I guess that the content will get harder and harder, but I

want not to forget this feeling of 'it's fun'. You can use English in various situations like for interacting with people, so I want to study seriously so I can become able to use English. (Satoshi, LJ, 12/4/2011 – first English lesson)

Recalling discussion in the previous chapter, many students referred to language use as being motivating in the opening lessons of the academic year. Satoshi also remarks on a sense of enjoyment, and moreover makes a connection between 'study[ing] seriously' and becoming able to 'use English in various situations' in the future. Not only at the very beginning of the year but over the first few weeks of lessons, participants reflected on their adaptation to the 'new' system and its way of doing things, including their testing of its boundaries:

I understood well the style of [these] lessons. From before, I wasn't so good at doing conversation in English, so I was worried whether I'd be able to do it, but it went well, so I was very happy. And there were many new words that came up, so I thought that I want to study them seriously. The teacher got angry, but I think everyone will get more and more into these lessons. It's only the second lesson, but already I feel like I've been made to think deeply a lot. (Seiya, LJ, 19/4/2011 – second English lesson)

Adaptation to the new lesson environment is evident in this extract in the form of positive and negative feedback. Seiya draws on his past perception of his ability, writing that 'from before, I wasn't so good at doing conversation in English' to predict the outcome of action in the current system: 'so I was worried as to whether I'd be able to do it'. However, his attempts at action in the current system met with success, positively reinforcing that *this* kind of action would be appropriate in *this* system. The outcome was also contrary to the expectation of failure in that 'it went well', providing negative feedback to such a prediction of the future, and a resultant feeling of pleasure: 'I was very happy.' Finally, Seiya's mention of an incident in which 'the teacher got angry' is also noted in my research journal, and suggests these shared experiences near the start of the year to have been critical for the motivational trajectory of the class group:

Who knows how things will turn out now? My class were just on another planet today. In the end I had to stop them, and have a 'stern word' or two. So now, of course, I feel terrible ... Who knows what dynamics came together to create that, what, mess? Looking around as they were making their business cards, only about half of them seemed to actually be getting into the spirit of things. ... Then there was a mingling activity, using these business cards to meet 'co-workers'. Once again, it seemed as if precious few students were really getting into things, imagining that they were working at this company. (RJ, 19/4/2011 – second English lesson)

This extract provides a sense of the way in which my own motivation was severely influenced by my experiences in the classroom on this day. I begin the entry by focusing not on the activity of students, but on the outcome of having 'to stop them, and have a "stern word" or two' because of the 'mess' that the lesson became. The outcome has a crushing effect on my ideas of future lessons with the class group, leading me to worry about 'how things will turn out now'. The source of my concern appears to be the perception that a communicative mingling activity was met by 'precious few students [...] really getting into things'. In complex systems terms, I received negative feedback that something about this activity on this day with this class did not foster the kind of learning environment I had been anticipating. However, rather than conceiving of these interactions taking place in the distinct timescale of the activity in the classroom, Lemke's (2000) use of the concept of heterochrony is facilitative towards understanding my frustration: my preference for communicative activities that encourage students to share their ideas in interaction has built up over a longer timescale through my language teaching career and postgraduate studies. This built-up belief in such activities as effective for language learning clashed with the *in-situ* perceptions of students' engagement on this day. In fact, student reflection on this same lesson suggests that I need not have been so harsh on myself as a teacher for 'scolding' the students:

Today we were scolded because we were being too noisy by the teacher. It reminded me that already two weeks have passed since the entrance ceremony, and I'd gotten a bit lazy. I'll try not to let this happen again. I want to change the class back to a good atmosphere again. (Haruki, LJ, 19/4/2011 – second English lesson)

Haruki's writing bears witness to the class members testing the boundaries of appropriate behaviour by 'being too noisy'. However, far from my fears of a devastating effect on future lessons with the class group, my response seems to have had a critical dampening function on this form of student behaviour. It also allowed Haruki the space to affirm his resolution to work together in the co-formation of a more positive classroom environment: 'I want to change the class back to a good atmosphere again.' Haruki's determination (and that suggested by many other student reflections about this lesson) gives vital insight into the processes of co-adaptation occurring constantly in learning groups: the classroom I would walk into the following week would be a different space.

My entry about the next lesson provides evidence of this change. It also reveals the ways in which I was motivated over the week between these two lessons to come to terms with student levels of ability and how I could scaffold their learning more effectively in the task-based lessons:

> Well, that was great. I don't know whether it was the students that changed, or me (probably both), but this week's lesson was so incredibly better than last week's. ... The activities (for example, an info-gap to find out and imagine about a product; and getting put into new teams – new seating – and introducing themselves to other team members) seemed to go well, and many more students were trying to use English this week. ... I'm also getting a feel for the types of activities that might go well, and the need to repeat phrases over and over, and review things they've learnt, so that it sticks. I'll get to work on revising some upcoming lessons, where I've realised some things I had planned probably wouldn't go well. (RJ, 26/4/2011 – third English lesson)

Hiver's (2015) study of teacher immunity showed that teachers' adaptations to experiences in their daily practice and how they accept these adaptations as part of their identity can influence how teachers cope with stress. Drawing on my experiences with the class group up to this point, this extract reveals motivation to adapt my teaching approach to 'repeat phrases over and over, and review things they've learnt, so that it sticks'. The extract gives the sense that my confidence as a teacher, founded in part on my belief in communicative, interactive methods, has been restored through my perception that 'the activities ... seemed to go well, and many more students were trying to use English this week'. The extract suggests the form in which my identity as a competent teacher has likely built up through repetition of numerous similar experiences across a still longer timescale. However, rather than attributing the outcome that the lesson was 'so incredibly better than last week's' to only my own adjustments, an implicit recognition of co-adaptation is also revealed in my puzzlement as to 'whether it was the students that changed, or me (probably both)'.

The class group learned from this experience of negative feedback about appropriate forms of behaviour and the system settled into a region of its state-space that was relatively stable. Nevertheless, change is vital to complex systems (Larsen-Freeman & Cameron, 2008a). Indeed, Morrison (2006: 2) argues that complex systems that are stable will 'die or move towards entropy – systems *need* disequilibrium in order to survive' (emphasis in original). There was still constant change in the interactions between members and their testing of boundaries. The class group reached another critical point later in the year. The writing of many students implied their awareness of events in a lesson early in the second semester that marked it out as another particular phase-shift in the trajectory of the system. For instance, one student wrote '... we were scolded by the teacher. It's the second time.' While he reflected back on the previous instance of behavioural intervention by myself as teacher, he also connected the current phase-shift with a reaffirmation of his intended action: 'I'll take the lesson seriously from next time. Because I want to study English.' Other students similarly recognised this lesson as pivotal for the motivation of the class group:

> Today [we] were cautioned by the teacher that there was too much talking off topic. Actually, I think that this lesson is a good chance to actually be able to use English, but I also think that with every lesson there's more talk off topic. That's me just being lazy, but also me not having enough motivation for English, I thought. I want to, by myself, realise again that these many chances to use English are very important, and concentrate on raising my motivation for the next lesson. (Koji, LJ, 6/10/2011 – Semester 2, third English lesson)

Koji's extract is informative from a complex systems perspective as it draws attention to the gradual change to the current tipping point: '... I also think that with every lesson there's more talk off topic.' It appears that my intervention as the teacher prompted a timely reminder of the affordances of the lesson environment towards being able to use English, and Koji writes of retraining his motivational trajectory: 'I want to, by myself, realise again that these many chances to use English are very important, and concentrate on raising my motivation for the next lesson.'

The transition to new groups as phase-shift

Further, concurrent motivational phase-shifts occurred on a different timescale when students changed to new groups in the English lessons. As part of the curriculum that we were using, students were rearranged into groups of four members at four points across the year. Although students did not study exclusively in these groups, the curriculum required that they conduct discussions and collaborative projects important to their 'work' at the imaginary international company together with these members. The writing of the learners at these points of change again reveals their co-adaptation as they worked with the other members to co-create a new group environment in which they could communicate effectively to work together:

> In this lesson we worked together in a new group, teaching each other as we went. I tried to start conversation, so that things went smoothly. We could all say our opinions well, so it's a really good group and I think we will make good lessons. I want to keep it like this. (Nao, LJ, 29/9/2011)

The transition to a new group was an emotional experience as students drew on their transportable identities and renegotiated membership and group form. I wrote of one such transition in my research journal:

> Students seemed really *unsettled* today. Perhaps it was that they got into new seating arrangements from the start of the lesson? Anyway, there was a lot of excess chat that took a number of tries by me each time I wanted to get students' attention for them to actually be quiet. This said, some groups seemed to be really *happy* with their new arrangements – Ken, Fumihiko, Taichi and Ryu – the soccer boys – worked really well together, even using English – a far cry from the silence that Ken and Ryu showed in their previous groups. (RJ, 8/12/2011; emphasis added)

The emotional aspect of transitions to new groups was also evident in students' writing. Communicative classrooms are inherently social places, yet these adolescent students at times encountered the kind of self-doubt and unease in embarking on new social relationships that is a hallmark of this period of youth development (Harter, 2003). As one student remarked in transitioning to a new group for the second time, 'I was *nervous* talking to someone I'd never talked to before, but I feel like I could convey my ideas'. While they interacted to negotiate the new group form, students expressed apprehension about their experience of the new group and worries as to whether the group could function effectively:

> I got into a new group, but I feel like we are all over the place. There's no way we'll be able to do a presentation together if we continue like this, so I think we need to come together more as a group. (Seiya, LJ, 29/9/2011)

The transition for Seiya is clear: 'I got into a new group.' This shift required co-adaptation between four new members. However, the co-adaptation did not proceed smoothly, as he writes they were 'all over the place' in their interactions. He draws on his own past experience and understanding of the function of groups in this environment to state that 'There's no way we'll be able to do a presentation together if we continue like this', before hoping for smoother co-adaptation of the group in the future. Such comparisons with previous experience of groups sometimes reinforced expectations, while at other times comparisons revealed additional possibilities for action in the new group. The transition to a different working arrangement offered the chance for a 'new start' and change each time:

> When I tried discussing in the new group, I thought that compared to the last group everyone in this group can say their opinions. At the time of the self-introductions [they] translated into English quickly, so I thought

it was *amazing*. Today I couldn't take part so much in the discussion, so I want to become able to say my opinion next time. (Sayaka, LJ, 8/12/2011)

It was good because study in a new team started, and different opinions to the group from before came out, so I could take the lesson with a fresh feeling. (Eiji, LJ, 29/9/2011)

Lewis (2005: 175–176) understands phase-shifts in complex systems as a kind of 'trigger event' during which 'the orderly behaviour of the system is interrupted by a perturbation, resulting in a rapid loss of orderliness and an increase in sensitivity to the environment'. Such trigger events – as in this case transition to a more communicative lesson environment that afforded both fears about understanding and hopes for the future, as well as movement to make up new working groups in the classroom – may mark the beginnings of a new process of self-organisation of the system as a whole.

Self-organisation: Fostering Communication

While the concept of a phase-shift describes abrupt transformation of the system as a whole as it reaches a 'tipping point' (Gladwell, 2000), a complex systems perspective encourages understandings that there is also constant change over longer timescales in systems. One form of such gradual change is known as *self-organisation*. This process involves systems altering their internal structure and forms of behaviour adaptively and spontaneously to deal with and influence their environment. A complex systems approach to analysis brought to my attention a key quality of such self-organisation, that of *functionality* (de Wolf & Holvoet, 2005). In the current study, English lessons required communication for the development of new, imaginary technological products in the setting of the international company at which students were 'working'. Without any direct instruction on my part, there were a number of ways in which students motivated themselves towards making the classroom spaces – the environment – more communication friendly. The class group spontaneously arranged itself into patterns of behaviour more effective in responding to and forming the environment.

A self being understood

As noted in the previous chapter, students' revising classroom self ideas depended heavily on their interpretations of experiences during lessons. Particularly near the start of the year, learners wrote of their initial fears about not being able to understand due to an increased use of English in the classroom environment. Through activity and interaction, they frequently reflected on their actions and hopes for a revised vision of a classroom self being understood in communicative situations:

> I think it's important to say clearly your opinion in a loud voice. And it's also important to look at the other person's face, and listen carefully to their opinion. This time, I think I did the listening part ok, but by looking at the other person's face, I could tell that my voice was a little quiet. Next lesson I want to be conscious of whether my message is actually being conveyed to the other person. (Nao, LJ, 10/5/2011)

Nao shows deep retrospection on her actions from a communicative standpoint. She firstly breaks the task into two elements that she perceives as important: 'say clearly your opinion in a loud voice' and 'look at the other person's face, and listen carefully to their opinion'. Through reflection, she gives herself a passing grade for the listening side of the activity, but perceives negative feedback about language production: 'by looking at the other person's face, I could tell that my voice was a little quiet.' She finally writes of a hope for a revising self in the classroom in the next lesson as someone 'conscious of whether my message is actually being conveyed to the other person'.

Students at times devoted an entire entry in their learning journal to a revising classroom self acting so that others would understand them:

> There's no point if [people] don't understand what I'm saying, so I want to read so that it's easy to catch. And, when I'm reading if I think it's difficult to understand changing, and making it so that the time matches well, I want to adapt myself to the requirements of the moment. (Sayaka, LJ, 24/1/2012)

Writing about the following lesson, the above extract evinces prediction of co-adaptation. Sayaka describes her classroom self in the next lesson as being able to 'adapt myself to the requirements of the moment' in reaction to her prediction of a situation in which communication may be hindered: 'when I'm reading if I think it's difficult to understand changing, and making it so that the time matches well.'

A self acting for others

Vallacher and Nowak (2009: 388) have argued that 'individuals in social interaction modify their respective thoughts, feelings, or action tendencies to promote coordination over time in these features of experience'. As is also evident in Sayaka's extract above, students at times wrote about their actions as overtly focusing on fostering the understanding of the other person in communicative situations in certain activities:

I wasn't able to say what I wanted with good English sentences, but through using gestures, and non-grammatical phrases like 'it's safe' 'it's not originality' [English in original] to explain, it seemed like my ideas were conveyed, and the other student answered with similarly hesitant English. Not grammar, but communicating with others using English. I learnt that this is the real '[English lesson]'. (Akira, LJ, 8/6/2011)

I think the interview went well. I consciously did things like looking in the direction of the other person, or showing them the sheet when necessary. Both of us aren't good at English, and there are times when it's really hard to understand, but amid that, when what I wanted to say got across or I could understand I was so happy, I got the feeling of wanting to try harder. Of course I want to work hard on things like pronunciation, but I really want to take care of this feeling of 'trying to convey'. (Nao, LJ, 24/11/2011)

Although there was no explicit understanding enforced that students ought to work to enable the comprehension of their classmates, student writing quite often revealed a very clear picture of some of the spontaneous ways through which they acted for others. Sometimes experiences in a lesson encouraged students to write of a revising classroom self more supportive of others in the future classroom. As one learner remarked, a commonly noted form of support was through choosing vocabulary predicted to be comprehensible to others: 'We have to present properly for 4 minutes. ... So that everyone can listen and the meaning gets across, I want to try as much as possible to use simple words.' At other times, student extracts revealed reflection on supportive actions they had taken in the lesson they had just experienced. Reflecting about a final project in which students had to make a video advertisement to present to the class, Kazu wrote about a range of concrete actions his group took to support comprehension: 'It's important that things get across properly to the person watching, so we put in kind of elaborations to the video ... looking at the camera, and to make the action easy to understand, we tried using extra props' (LJ, 2/2/2012). As Kazu's extract implies, students also wrote of occasions where there was a clear recognition shared by group members of attempting to foster a more communication-friendly space:

As we were doing the presentation, we thought about how we could make the English easier to understand for listeners, so we made our English better. Even when we listened to other presentations, there were lots of things I could learn from other students. My own communication ability went up a level, I think. (Ryu, LJ, 19/7/2011)

Ryu writes of his group's attempts at fostering communication 'for others' in the real-time flow of actually doing a presentation: 'we could make the English easier to understand for listeners, so we made our English better.' He then discusses the way in which he could learn from other students through listening to their presentations. His choice of the word 'communication' in the final sentence, rather than 'English', is indicative of the way in which interactions and social comparisons with others fostered motivation towards supporting communication in the classroom system. Perhaps as students themselves struggled to comprehend their peers and my English, it appears that many became progressively more proactive in their attempts to also allow the understanding of others in the class group. Such realisations were unscripted – the system had decentralised control with regards to fostering a more communication-friendly space.

A recognition of co-adaptation of the classroom environment

As the following extract illustrates, the co-forming nature of the classroom context was explicitly addressed in the writing of some students:

> Today was mostly group-work, and we could work together well in our group. I used a little Japanese, but even so, I'm definitely using a lot more English than before. I want to keep working like this, making an atmosphere in which we can use English together to work towards our presentation. (Taku, LJ, 21/6/2011)

Students reflected on their actions as influencing the formation of a more communication-friendly classroom environment, as well as the way in which the actions of others affected their own behaviour. Taku articulates the experience of being able to 'work together well in our group' as connected to 'making an atmosphere in which we can use English together'. He wants to 'keep working like this'. His writing hints that if there were not this group-created atmosphere he would not be 'using a lot more English than before'. The writing of another student at the end of the first semester illustrates how opportunities for communication in English were supported by others, and this student's hope to continue in the co-creation of such an environment:

> When I was studying English, there were words the meaning of which I didn't know, or couldn't read, but by teaching each other [with other students] I could understand, and so I enjoyed studying English. And by understanding, I got more confidence because I could do it, and so this teaching together really gave me more motivation. So [these] English lessons and homeroom periods, along with helping me to feel the fun of studying English, have also taught me the importance of cooperating together with other students. Through teaching each other and discussing together, I've been able to enjoy studying English. So from now on as

well, in the same way as up until now, I want to make motivation to study English together with classmates. (Hiro, LJ Reflection 1, 5/10/2011)

Dörnyei and Murphey (2003: 74) refer to research by Levine and Moreland (1998) that found 'groups working in dangerous, impoverished or confining environments ... develop particular forms of interaction suited to the conditions they face (e.g. in order to take coordinated action and reduce conflicts among members)'. The English classroom environment was not as harsh as that in the study referred to by Dörnyei and Murphey (2003). However, movement from experienced difficulty to the co-formed development of motivation through interacting with other students is clear in Hiro's writing: At first Hiro experienced challenges to his capacity to communicate functionally in the classroom because 'there were words the meaning of which I didn't know, or couldn't read'. Nevertheless, through 'teaching each other' he becomes able to understand, and notes this as key to his being 'able to enjoy studying English'. He finally reflects on the co-created nature of motivation from this experience: 'I want to make motivation to study English together with classmates.' The writing of a number of students across the year reflected such cognisance of the shared nature of the evolving classroom context. Another point of particular interest from Hiro's writing is that he includes not only his experiences in the English lessons but also homeroom periods as assisting him to 'feel the fun of studying English' and the importance of 'cooperating together with other students'. Such a comment evinces once again, as discussed in Chapter 7, the open and blended nature of classroom spaces. These English lessons were not happening in a vacuum.

Reflecting on Functional Pattern-building: The Self-organising Whole and Parts

In summary, the analysis suggests firstly that transitions can be seen as a kind of particularly sensitive period in which, in the environment of education, radical phase-shifts in the motivational trajectory of not only individuals but also a *class system* may be possible. As evident in Chapter 7, writing by students of their perceptions of past experience of classroom English learning was predominantly negative. As students encountered the new lesson style or moved to make up a different group these transitions opened up further possibilities and challenges, in which they could reframe new, possible classroom selves based on their understandings of the developing environments.

Occurring alongside these transitional phase-shifts, the analysis moreover revealed that the class system gradually self-organised over the year as students motivated themselves and others to become a more

138 Part 2: 再見 Re-viewing

communication-friendly group as a coherent whole. Students noted the co-adaptive nature of a classroom context more facilitative of communication and the actions that they were taking, saw others taking or projected a future classroom-self taking. The growth in student reflection on fostering communication is clearly shown in Figure 9.1, which plots the number of references by different students against the dates of English lessons across the year of the study. Despite a dip in September (possibly due to the English lesson involving predominantly the viewing of a video), the number of references made by different students to fostering communication in the classroom shows a steady rise over time.

While Figure 9.1 graphically evinces a dynamic, gradual increase in the number of student references to fostering communication, it ultimately shows a linear representation of development. It does not give a facilitative sense of the agent-level 'spread' of this system-level self-organisation. Proponents of complex systems theory would urge that a representation of the parts of a system is not sufficient (such as the individual participants), nor a representation of the whole as a whole (such as the graph in Figure 9.1) (Morin, 2006). Complex systems understandings draw attention to the need for representation of the relations between the whole and the parts – in this

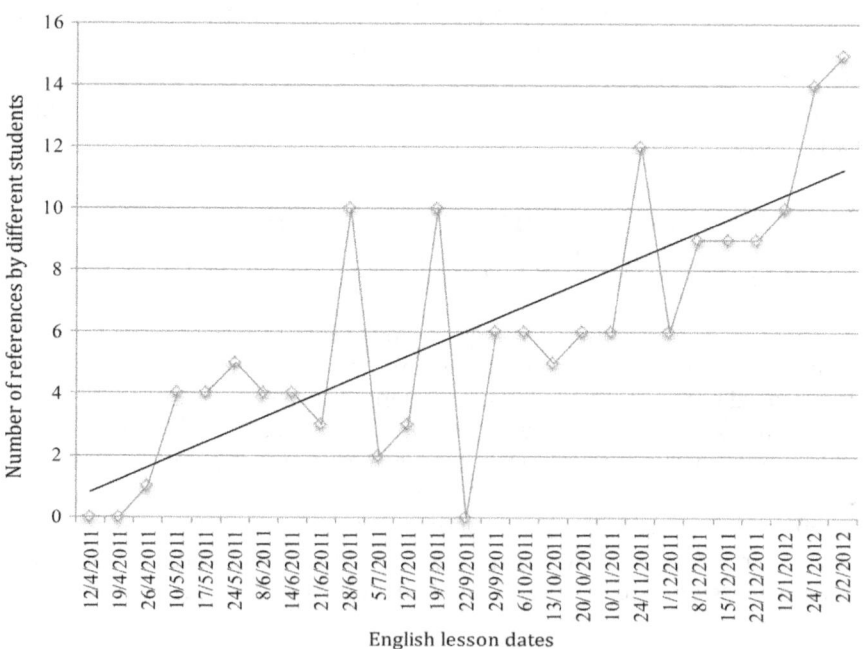

Figure 9.1 Graph showing increase in number of student references to fostering communication in the English classroom

Motivational Phase-shifts and Self-organisation Across the Class Group 139

case, both the discussed forms of behaviour of individual students, and the group-level self-organisation.

A further tool from the complex systems literature useful for visualising the developing *form* of self-organisation *across* the class group is 'multiple threading' (Davis & Sumara, 2006). Multiple threading can be used to represent diverse voices that emerge from texts or data to make up a single group

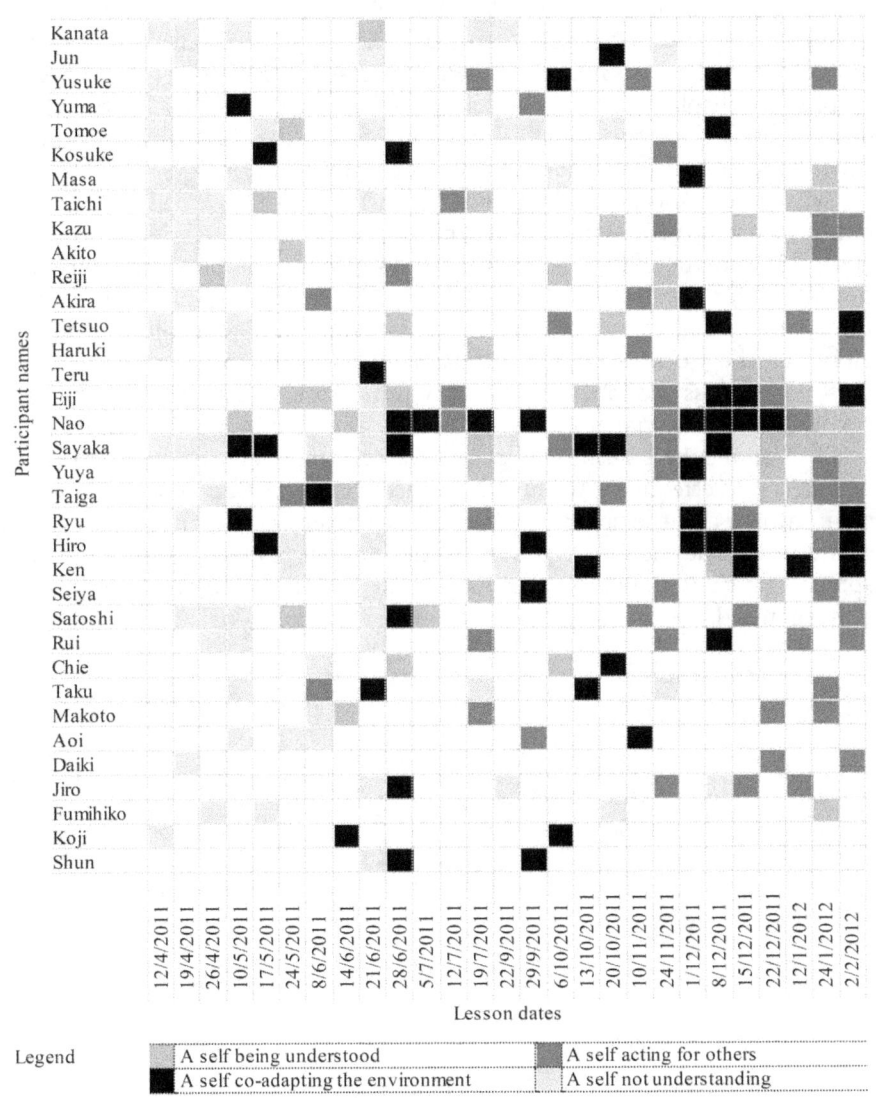

Figure 9.2 Multiple threading (Davis & Sumara, 2006) representation of the self-organisation of motivation in the class group towards fostering communication

narrative. While some of these voices may provide only occasional interjections, others may be more sustained, and the various strands may overlap at times (Davis & Sumara, 2006: 162). Figure 9.2 represents the form of the motivational self-organisation in this class group. Included are references to the three areas of a self being understood, acting for others and co-adapting the environment. I have also included references to a self not understanding, particularly noticeable in the phase-shift related to transition to the new lesson environment. As is evident, not all of the students contributed to this growing narrative (only 35 of 40 student voices are visible), and some contributions are more or less pronounced or sustained. However, this diagram graphically displays the differing strands from students that I interpret as evocative of the motivational self-organisation of the class group towards a functional form that might better foster communication.

My understanding of the self-organisation that developed in this class group returns to the decentralised nature of control in a complex system (Davis & Sumara, 2006). The tasks that students were presented with and discovered for themselves in the classroom spaces allowed them the opportunity to reflect on strategies that might facilitate smoother communication. However, the processes of self-reflection and social comparison by the members of the class group were, naturally, unscripted. The classroom system encouraged functional adaptation towards a more communication-friendly space. The members within the class group wrote of revising their actions to operate more effectively within this space through co-adaptation with the environment and the other members of the classroom. As students' histories of interaction developed, so too realisations about fostering communication spread. There was not one driving agent for this change – the system self-organised.

10 Novel Motivational Emergence in the Class Group

While much of the rationale for task-based language teaching and learning focuses on the effective features of individual tasks (see, for example, Willis & Willis, 2007), Benevides (2010: 22) argues that weaving task-based learning experiences together into a 'themed, task-based' curriculum allows for the 'development of meaningful contexts and content wherein relatively authentic communicative language acts can take place'. Over the year of study, in the regular English lessons of which I was a teacher, learners had 'worked' at an imaginary company that developed new technological products using the textbook *Widgets* (Benevides & Valvona, 2008). They had been involved in various groupings, using English to create their own original technological product ideas, had selected some of these to 'go into production', and had improved the designs and features of these products (see Appendix A for a brief outline of the English course). As a final assignment, the groups created and video-recorded short advertisements to 'sell' the products. Across the last six weekly English lessons of the academic year, student groups worked on this final project, preparing, recording and finally showing a four-minute video that combined information plus persuasive situations – an 'infomercial' – advertising one of the new, imaginary products that they and other students had developed over the year (see Appendix G for more details of the project).

Although every class group exhibits collective behaviour in different forms, the writing by participants about this project and the final lesson in which they shared their infomercials revealed very clearly a kind of novelty at the whole-class group level that de Wolf and Holvoet (2005) argue is representative of *emergence* in a complex system. De Wolf and Holvoet (2005: 3) write that complex systems exhibit emergence when '... there are coherent emergents at the macro-level that dynamically arise from the interactions between the parts at the micro-level. Such emergents are novel w.r.t. [with respect to] the individual parts of the system.' In conceptualising a class group as a complex system, the emergent behaviour at the macro-level (the whole-class level) is not readily reducible to the agents that make up the system at the micro-level (the students and teacher). That is, emergence is a bottom-up process that fosters novel macro-level, collective behaviour.

While I was not aware of it at the time, the procedure that I followed in identifying this motivational end-state and looking backwards at the context of its emergence shares some similarities with the method of 'retrodictive qualitative modelling' proposed by Dörnyei (2014). As Dörnyei argues:

> Even very complex systems tend to arrive at certain salient outcomes, and although we cannot predict in advance what these outcomes might be, when we see them we recognise them. ... By tracing back the reasons why the system has ended up with a particular outcome option we produce a retrospective qualitative model of its evolution. (Dörnyei, 2014: 85)

However, two caveats ought to be discussed. First, present applications of retrodictive qualitative modelling (e.g. Dörnyei, 2014; Chan *et al.*, 2015) have initially identified certain learner 'archetypes' as a motivational outcome (through focus groups with teachers to define learners by particular adjectives). The researchers then obtained data from learners whose motivation fitted the qualities of these archetypes, and traced back the reasons for the motivational end-states of these learners at the point of the research. In this approach, conceptual categories come first, and then the histories of real humans who match these categories are examined to produce a fuller understanding of why certain individual motivational end-states came about. In contrast to such a process, in my study recognition of the class-group motivational outcome was arrived at in a more spontaneous fashion. My perception as a teacher as well as the writing of students about the final, infomercial presentation lesson drew my attention to this motivational end-state naturally occurring in the context of this language learning project. Secondly, despite a common understanding in complex systems theory that a present end-state of a system is reliant on the complete history of what has come before, it is not feasible to try to investigate all of the interconnecting systems across various timescales (van Geert, 2008: 185). We need to confine the history of the system to a specific length of time in order to make it reasonable to investigate its dynamics. While it may seem an arbitrary decision as to at which point we 'cut' the history of a system, on occasion timescales may make themselves apparent from the context of study. For the sake of analysis, I confine my interpretation to the natural timespan – six weeks – of the particular project in question. In what follows, I use a process similar to retrodictive qualitative modelling to: (i) trace the contours of the emergence evident in the final infomercial session; (ii) identify the main forms of interaction in the system over the six weeks of the project; and (iii) use complex systems theory to understand some of the conditions of emergence revealed in the analysis.

An Emergent Motivational Outcome

My own words recorded in my research journal straight after the final lesson give an insight into my excitement about the novel emergence at the whole-class level:

> That was great. With a capital G. I said to the students at the end of the lesson that I laughed so much my bones hurt. It was just a fantastic atmosphere, and I really felt like all the students were so INTERESTED in what every other student had made. There were various technical hitches, like controlling the volume, and not being able to get the video up on the big screen, but it all came together. And the students were laughing together too. No AT involved. I don't really know what else to add. (RJ, 2/2/2012; emphasis in original)

My observation must surely be one shared by numerous teachers: at some time, for some reasons, with some class, things just work, enabling 'a fantastic atmosphere', and despite challenges 'it all came together'. My writing reveals one of the dimensions of this emergence as being a *sense of enjoyment*: 'I laughed so much', with the students also 'laughing together'. The following student extract reveals similar enthusiasm:

> Today we watched all the recorded videos by everyone. It was so, so much fun. Everyone had a proper story, and expressed themselves with facial expressions and movements as well, so they all did it really well. I haven't had chances to do something like this, so I'm really happy that I could experience it. I thought, it'd be good if English study was conducted like this – everyone having fun while they are studying. (Koji, LJ, 2/2/2012)

In parallel with writing in my research journal, Koji's extract reveals a kind of emotional synchrony that was evident in the writing of many of the students about this final lesson. There was a shared sense of enjoyment as one aspect of the emergence, as Koji's writing intimates: 'It was so, so much fun'; 'I thought, it'd be good if English study was conducted like this – *everyone having fun* while they are studying' (emphasis added). Koji's writing moreover shows an additional dimension to the emergence – that of the *sense of quality* of the infomercials: 'Everyone had a proper story, and expressed themselves with facial expressions and movements as well, so they all did it really well.' The writing of another student exemplifies this connection between the emotional experiencing of watching the infomercials and the perception of quality: 'All the videos were done to a really high level, so I was amazed.'

The following student's excerpt is of particular interest as it evinces the idea of 'transportation', the experience of 'being transported into a text' whereby participants' 'imaginative resources have them feeling removed from their surroundings and completely engaged in the world created by the author' (Green & Donahue, 2009: 241):

> All of the products of the teams, I could watch being interested and having fun. As I was watching, there were some products I began to want to buy, so those parts I thought again were amazing. (Tomoe, LJ, 2/2/2012)

The products were all imaginary ideas that students had initially proposed earlier in the year as a solution to their individual everyday problems. Students then worked with various products over the year. Despite on a conscious level *knowing* that the products in the infomercials were all imaginary, Tomoe describes her feeling of wanting to buy them. Implicit in her reflection is her perception of the quality of the infomercials, in that she felt a sense of transportation such that when she 'was watching, there were some products I began to want to buy'. Indeed, Green and Donahue (2009) argue that one of the primary influences on the extent of transportation into a story is the quality of that story. Moreover, Tomoe's mention of emotion is linked to this quality: 'so those parts I thought again were amazing.'

An extract from another student, Mikihiro, more directly addresses both of these dimensions of enjoyment and quality:

> Today I did [watched] the product presentations of other teams. On top of the *quality* of all the groups being *really high*, they were *funny* and I *couldn't watch without laughing*. Today was something special befitting the very last presentation for the year's [English course]. (Mikihiro, LJ, 2/2/2012; emphasis added)

In fact, Mikihiro's extract is revealing from a complex systems perspective as it illustrates three commonly discussed characteristics of emergence: radical novelty, coherence of the whole, and dynamism (de Wolf & Holvoet, 2005: 4). First, as previously evinced in my own writing in the research journal and student writing, Mikihiro's extract shows the novel detail of the emergence – the shared senses of enjoyment and quality. Secondly, the whole-class nature of the emergence across a coherent 'whole' is revealed when Mikihiro defines the lesson 'today' as 'something special' which was 'befitting the very last presentation for the year', remarking on the final session as contributing to a kind of closure. His use of the phrase 'something special' again attests to the radical novelty of this whole-class phenomenon. Moreover, there is another important idea in his last statement. The final session did not occur divorced from everything else. The 'special', novel atmosphere that developed in the final lesson was 'befitting' because of all of the experiences during the year. Emergence is dynamic as gradual change in a system over time sometimes results in a novel end-state (which will also be the beginning of renewed change). While I have used the natural timeframe of the final project as the boundary of the current analysis, Mikihiro's writing reminds us that in fact emergence commences and continues over longer timescales as well.

Identifying Interactions in the Context of Emergence

As a member of the class group that had experienced this final lesson, I was intrigued to investigate what the data suggested may have played a role in motivation fostering novel emergence. The writing of de Wolf and Holvoet (2005: 4) offers a valuable hint. These researchers argue that the collective behaviour of emergence is 'implicitly contained in the *behaviour* of the parts if they are studied *in the context in which they are found*' (emphasis added). Although under complexity understandings emergent behaviour at the macro level cannot be simply traced back in a linear fashion to agents making up the system at the micro level, the behaviour of these agents in context can provide clues as to what fosters the macro-level behaviour. In the complex classroom system, this claim hints at the utility of looking at the interactions (forms of behaviour) that participants noted in the build-up (the context) to the final lesson.

It is impossible to trace or understand all the influences that led up to this final space (and indeed, if we could, it would not be emergent). However, the reflections of students and observations from my research journal over the six weeks of the project offer insights into some of the interactions taking place in the system. I number the extracts below to more readily facilitate an interpretation of the importance of these interactions to the emergence.

Interactions between students and task requirements

Students interacted with the requirements of the set task and for many the assignment was perceived as being *challenging*:

> Extract 1. We continued to decide the content of the advertisement. *It was difficult* to think of an advertisement that would get others' interest, but I want to do my best next time too. (Rui, LJ, 12/1/2012; emphasis added)

Urdan and Turner (2007: 308) synthesise a range of research into classroom teaching practices and the development of competence motivation of students, arriving at a recommendation to 'assign moderately or appropriately challenging tasks'. There is nevertheless a delicate balance along a continuum of the difficulty of the task assigned. As most of us know from experience, tasks that are too difficult often lead instead to resignation and a sense of defeat. In the classroom, if students perceive the requirement as unobtainable, they may alternatively resist the challenge and become disengaged (Urdan & Turner, 2007). This phenomenon is also reflected in the possible self literature: motivation is in part forthcoming from our ideas of what is plausibly possible for us to achieve based on understandings of our own particular current circumstances and abilities (Norman & Aron, 2003; Ruvolo & Markus, 1992). If we envisage a future self as highly unlikely given our present position, motivation to move towards this possible self will be lessened. As the following extract suggests, in the case of the infomercial task, for a majority of students there was, however, a *sense of achievement* as different parts of the project came together and moved them towards this future self completing the task:

> Extract 2. We finished the script!! Someday when we have time I want to film it all together. We'll produce it well!! (Yusuke, LJ, 24/1/2012)

Although a short entry, Yusuke's reflection offers key insights into his engagement with the task requirements in the general sense of *achieving work targets*. His use of double exclamation marks after his initial statement clearly gives voice to his positive affect at having reached this stage of the project, perhaps as a mix of excitement and relief came together. His next statement hints at the open nature of his motivation, as he seems both worried yet also hopeful of being able to find time to conduct the filming for the project amid the other commitments in his daily life. Finally, though, his extract suggests one impact of being able to feel a sense of achievement at this stage of the project. He again employs double exclamation marks to affirm his motivation to work towards the goal. Many students reflected on both of these aspects of challenge and a sense of achievement in their learning journal entries concerning the final lesson:

> Extract 3. Thinking of the English text by ourselves, understanding it, remembering it in Japanese and then in English, having various accidents, and adjusting the camera was all really hard, but this is the first time I was able to speak English for such a length, so it was really good. (Tetsuo, LJ, 2/2/2012)

> Extract 4. At first it was difficult to speak English continually correctly and so that it would be easy to catch, and on top of that as it was in front of a camera I got all strangely nervous, so at first it didn't go well. But up until now I hadn't done this kind of thing, so it felt pretty fresh, and so I gradually became able to enjoy it, and as I got used to it, it progressed more smoothly. I was able to use this much English, so it became a good experience. (Ken, LJ, 2/2/2012)

In these two extracts Tetsuo and Ken mention challenging elements, how different aspects of the assignment were 'all really hard' and that 'it was difficult to speak English continually correctly and so that it would be easy to catch'. Although some of their writing again refers to work targets, reminiscent of the first motivational attractor state discussed in Chapter 8 it also reveals another critical aspect of the sense of achievement being connected to *succeeding in the use of English*. As Tetsuo notes: 'this is the first time I was able to speak English for such a length', with Ken defining the experience by this success: 'I was able to use this much English, so it became a good experience.'

Furthermore, among the members there were different functions that each group member could perform in response to the task requirements. Students drew on their personal experience, past learning and abilities to *find their own role*, as the following extracts from two different students reflecting back upon their activity in the same group evince:

> *Extract 5.* For the filming, firstly it was difficult to find somewhere to record it. ... Seiya did the editing, and I didn't do anything, but it looked really hard, so I'm really grateful. (Masa, LJ, 2/2/2012)

> *Extract 6.* It was really hard to make the video. ... In the infomercial I don't appear much, and I don't say very much, so at first I felt really apologetic to my team members, but I was happy that I could be useful in editing the video. (Seiya, LJ, 2/2/2012)

Seiya writes that 'at first I felt really apologetic to my team members' because he did not perceive himself as making enough of a contribution in the actual filming. However, he does finally feel 'happy that I could be useful in editing the video'. His activities suggest how, through the different function that he could perform – the editing – the group was able to achieve its purpose. His vital role towards achieving the task requirements is acknowledged by Masa when he writes: 'Seiya did the editing, and I didn't do anything, but it looked really hard, so I'm really grateful.' Masa recognises his own limitations, and as a result is thankful for Seiya's contribution. From a complex systems perspective, the task requirements involved 'enabling constraints' (Davis & Sumara, 2010: 859) such that students focused on certain functions that each was more capable of performing towards completing the task.

Supportive interaction between participants

While in some cases group members moved into such roles relatively naturally, there was also negotiation during *interactions between members* in the form of *support* and *cooperation* in working towards the final showing of their group infomercials:

> *Extract 7.* Today we thought about a commercial for our own team's product, and wrote it in English sentences. At the start, because we had to write everything in English I had anxiety, but through thinking together with the people in the group, my anxiety disappeared. And it gradually got more fun, so my motivation towards studying English went up too. (Makoto, LJ, 22/12/2011)

> *Extract 8.* We couldn't finish the story. But with everyone in our group we did things like using dictionaries so we could make about 1/3. We threw around various ideas to do with recording it on a cell-phone and discussed so that we can make an interesting [video]. Lots of great ideas come from everyone, so I'm looking forward to completing the story. (Tomoe, LJ, 12/1/2012)

In the first extract Makoto articulates how initially he was worried, faced with the group task of 'writ[ing] everything in English'. As the lesson continued, though, he realised that this was not a role that he had to take on all by himself. Through cooperating with his group members he could make progress, enjoy the activity and gain motivation. The second student, Tomoe, seems to place an admission that her group couldn't make as much progress as she might have hoped for right at the start of her entry: 'We couldn't finish the story.' However, after writing about the cooperation in the group, she ends the entry with: 'Lots of great ideas *come* from everyone, so I'm looking forward to completing the story' (emphasis added). Her use of the verb form 'come' rather than the past tense 'came' suggests that her anticipation of the continuation of such cooperation fosters her motivation towards finishing the task in the following lesson. As intimated in these extracts, the cooperation of members worked to address their individual concerns and worries about the challenging nature of the task:

> *Extract 9.* At first when we made the film I was really nervous, but as we were doing it, it was fun, and my nervousness dissolved. Also, it was really difficult to move while speaking English so I failed any number of times, but there was assistance from everyone in the team, and we could safely finish making the film. Through cooperating together with friends and supporting each other to make the video, I feel like my relationships with friends got deeper. (Hiro, LJ, 2/2/2012)

In fact, these extracts are highly suggestive of one of the three basic psychological needs from Ryan and Deci's (2002) self-determination theory of motivation, that of the need for relatedness. This need involves both a feeling of connectedness with others as well as caring for and being cared for by those others in a group (Ryan & Deci, 2002: 7). As Murphey *et al.* (2012: 223) assert in considering group dynamics in formal language learning situations, 'feelings of acceptance in the classroom ... are more likely to lead to feelings of security and well-being in students, who also exhibit autonomous and self-regulated behaviours' and 'have greater interest and engagement in academic activities'. As Hiro's reflections illustrate, interactions between students supported them to extend themselves when they faced obstacles and to feel secure in their actions.

Informative interactions between participants

Lastly, *interactions between participants* in *seeing the endeavours of others* preparing for the final showing of the infomercial *shared information about similar experience*. Despite the project being intended (and graded) as a group project, Kosuke's reflection below suggests the way in which groups received assistance from members outside their group:

Extract 10. I recorded not in the classroom but in the hallway. Because I couldn't remember all of the lines, it was really difficult to say them smoothly. But it was fun because, for example, people from other teams gave us help with applause sounds for the recording. (Kosuke, LJ, 24/1/2012)

Other students reflected in their writing about the final lesson on the observation of peers during preparation engaged in similar processes as well:

Extract 11. I saw both my own team, and here and there other teams, seriously engaged in preparing for today. And all that's left is how that comes together in video. But whatever the result, I'm really happy that I could try my best, could cooperate for today's 4 minutes. (Eiji, LJ, 2/2/2012)

Extract 12: Thinking about the whole process of recording the video, it was really fun. ... I did things like staying behind [after school] to be even somewhat useful to my group. (Akito, LJ, 2/2/2012)

The extract from Eiji adds further detail to the way in which these interactions with other student groups was perceived: 'I saw both my own team, and here and there other teams, *seriously engaged* in preparing.' Through seeing other students preparing, Eiji receives first-hand information about the efforts to which they went, spurring curiosity to view the infomercials to see 'how that comes together in video'. Although in the second extract Akito does not directly discuss 'seeing others', an entry recorded in my research journal adds context to his mention of 'staying behind'. During the course of this final project, on one occasion I happened to go to the homeroom classroom at around seven o'clock at night:

> *Extract 13.* When I opened the door, I saw some students recording infomercials for my lessons. There were many other students around as well, and they all looked to be having a great time – fouling up bits led to a lot of laughter (from me too, in the short time I was able to take in this scene). ... (RJ, 31/1/2012)

These extracts hint at a key component of the coherence of the class group – a shared group history. The homeroom classroom was a common place for students to gather and unwind after lessons were over for the day. By making use of this space, experiences were shared across the class group. Such interactions between the members of the class group, myself included, in seeing the actions of others preparing the infomercials – even staying behind at the college for a number of hours after lessons had finished for the day – may have further fostered the shared senses of enjoyment and quality evident in the emergent atmosphere of the final lesson.

A clearly anomalous case

The majority of reflections by participants concerning the infomercial project were overwhelmingly positive. However, I would not do justice to the complex makeup of the classroom system if I did not include a further extract that also suggests the diversity of experience leading up to the final session, this time from a student who did not enjoy the process:

> I really honestly thought that I really couldn't be bothered filming. But actually trying to do it, it was a little fun, so that was good. I hope it's done well. But I thought I don't want to do this anymore. (Kanata, LJ, 2/2/2012)

For many students it appears that a variety of experiences in the preparation leading up to the final session may have fostered the eventual novel emergence of the classroom atmosphere on that day. However, Kanata's writing just before the infomercials were screened reveals his detachment from the whole process when he notes 'I hope it's done well', suggesting that he had not actually watched the finished product of his own group. His experience of the preparation, in that he 'really couldn't be bothered filming' ends with his realisation that 'I don't want to do this anymore'. The existence of a diversity of such cases is not only a given in complex systems theory, but is also in line with the experiences of most teachers. Such a case hints at the utility of the different applications of complex systems theory to understanding *individual* language learner motivational trajectories across time as discussed in Chapter 6 (e.g. Paiva, 2011). A similar approach could examine the individual 'trace' of students such as Kanata who express negative motivational tendencies. Doing so may well elicit further nuanced understandings about why some students display apparent apathy and detachment even when a majority of classmates recognise a positive sense of motivational emergence (Sampson, 2016).

Reflecting on Conditions of Emergence During this Project

Dörnyei (2014: 89) contends that by looking backwards from a motivational outcome with retrodictive qualitative modelling the aspects uncovered might be 'so essential that they can reasonably be expected to be echoed in other situations as well'. Pigott (2012b: 356) takes task with such a proposition, however, arguing that this form of abstraction draws complex systems approaches too close to the simplification of traditional positivist research. I tend towards a middle ground: I agree with Dörnyei (2014) that it is both possible and useful to attempt to discern similarities in processes that lead up to a certain motivational outcome. What Pigott's (2012b) perspective reminds us of, however, is the need to remain cognisant that the qualities and paths of these processes may differ quite radically by context. It is vital to bear in mind that insights are contextually based. My analysis is restricted to the motivational emergence in this one class group during the course of this language learning project. In what follows I draw on a number of interrelated properties of complex systems to understand shared elements revealed through the interactions in this context.

Co-adaptation

One important process revealed in the analysis of interactions is that of co-adaptation, whereby the system elements (agents, context) adapted in response to each other. In a class group, a member is at the same time both an agent and part of the context, in that they are interacting with other agents. As such, any form of behaviour alters the environment at the same time as it alters the agent (Larsen-Freeman & Cameron, 2008a). Both the agent and the environment 'learn', and the system changes dynamically.

From a complex systems perspective, the analysis uncovers such mutually influencing co-adaptation. For example, the context adapted the agents by imposing certain constraining requirements of the project task. Student writing reveals reflection on the challenging nature of these requirements (Extracts 1, 3, 4, 5, 7), but also their processes of adapting through supporting one another (Extracts 7, 8) and finding their own roles (Extracts 5, 6). In a bi-directional process, agents also co-adapted with each other in their groups and with members of other groups. These interactions in turn adapted a growing sense of self-efficacy to move towards a positive task outcome in groups (Extracts 7, 8, 9), and a resultant sense of achievement (Extracts 2, 3, 4). While complex systems theory warns against the ability to make future predictions from past events (Larsen-Freeman & Cameron, 2008a), it would appear that a significant key to fostering the emergence of the motivational outcome across the whole-class group was the sharing of information. Murphey *et al.* (2012: 225) discuss one aspect of group dynamics in the language classroom as involving the idea of 'emotional contagion', whereby cognitions and emotions are linked between group members. By sharing their enthusiasm (as well as witnessing the lengths to which others were going) (Extracts 9, 10, 12, 13), students and groups again co-adapted the context by encouraging each other and pushing the boundaries of what was possible as an outcome of the set task (Extracts 10, 11). This constant co-adaptation between the context/agents seems to be one of the defining processes in the build-up to the emergent motivational end-state.

Directed motivational current

Dörnyei *et al.* (2015b) and Muir and Dörnyei (2013) have proposed the idea of 'directed motivational currents' to refer to heightened periods of motivation for additional language learners. These periods involve an extended engagement in connected tasks or activities, experienced as rewarding because they link to a clearly defined and highly valued, emotionally satisfying outcome (Dörnyei *et al.*, 2015b). In the context of my study, both the analysis of the final lesson and those lessons leading up to this motivational end-state clearly show such personal significance and positive emotionality. Moreover, directed motivational currents are said to 'emerge from the alignment of a number of personal, temporal and contextual factors/parameters' (Dörnyei *et al.*, 2015b: 103). My analysis uncovers parallels with these discussed elements.

First, students' understanding of the infomercial project as a set of clearly defined, linked tasks (Extracts 3, 4, 7) hints at their recognition of a specific triggering stimulus that initiated the process, as with that involved in a directed motivational current. Secondly, in Extract 11 Eiji writes just before watching the infomercials of his strong desire to see 'how that comes together in video' and his anticipation of 'today's 4 minutes' (the length of each infomercial video). These comments reveal the nature of his motivation being directed towards goal achievement and a vision of this outcome. However, while Dörnyei and associates (2015b) argue that a visionary component is a fundamental feature of directed motivational currents, this element does not on the whole receive such overt mention in the data. This said, extracts concerning the final lesson and some in the build-up to this lesson reveal the kind of intense involvement in a project that Dörnyei *et al.* (2015b) contend is associated with such a vision (Extracts 11, 12, 13). Additionally, Extracts 3, 4 and 8 evince the way in which the process of preparing the infomercial itself fostered the shared development of an image of the outcome. Finally, Dörnyei and his colleagues (2015b) propose that sub-goals acting as progress checks along the path to a project outcome and a related sense of fulfilment are defining factors in a directed motivational current. Many of the extracts from students in my study clearly reveal how groups defined their own sub-goals, and positive emotion as students felt a sense of achievement at being able to 'tick off' these tasks on the way to the final infomercial showing (Extracts 2, 3, 4, 7, 9).

Diversity and redundancy, neighbour interactions, and distributed control

Davis and Sumara (2005: 316) argue for four conditions related to emergence in educational social collectives: *diversity, redundancy, neighbour interactions* and *distributed control*. While I did not explicitly set out to create conditions that might encourage the motivational emergence, I contend that the analysis reveals each of these aspects in the build-up to the outcome of showing the infomercials.

First, groups of four students worked together towards the task outcome. In many senses each group contained much redundancy, in essence 'having multiple copies of the same part' (Page, 2011: 228) in the form of the agents making up the group. Group members shared many similar qualities (such as shared cultural backgrounds, similar first language, and roughly equal second-language ability and social status) and a shared purpose in the activity of making the infomercial. This redundancy allowed the sharing of information (Extracts 10, 11) and experience (Extracts 9, 11) across agents in the system. Secondly, and related, the roles that the students played within their groups and through cooperating together reveal diversity in finding adequate solutions to the challenges of the task at hand (Extracts 5, 6, 7, 8). However, this cooperation would not have been possible if there were not also redundancy allowing the members to maintain interactions. Thirdly, the ways in which students wrote about observation of their peers hint at exchange of ideas, as neighbours interacted, groups helped other groups, and they were able to share a similar purpose (Extracts 10, 12). Indeed, part of my own positive 'emotional contagion' (Murphey *et al.*, 2012) towards the infomercial project as an agent in the system was revealed in the analysis as developing from neighbour interactions with the other agents when I saw students staying after regular school hours to work on the task (Extract 13). Finally, the challenges, difficulties (Extracts 1, 3, 4, 5, 7) and ultimate sense of achievement (Extracts 2, 3, 4) relate to the distributed control of the task. Although I, as the teacher, set the outcome (an infomercial) and certain details (a video, in English, 4 minutes in length), the processes that students undertook in this shared project were various, and were further influenced by their observations of and interactions with others. The analysis suggests that these complex conditions, and undoubtedly more besides from outside the scope of the current investigation, interacted to foster the novel motivational emergence of the project and the last lesson.

Part 3
相互
Reciprocity

11 The Landscape of Classroom Motivation

Rather than a static, fixed end point, I envisage that one outcome of this research is the development of new emergent possibilities. These new possibilities interconnect with and owe a great deal to previous research enterprises. I recognise that my interpretations and understandings are part of human knowing that is ever pushing into the 'adjacent possible' through ceaseless novelty (Kauffman, 2008). As Kauffman (2008: 127) argues, however, 'salients are almost certainly created in specific "directions" in the space of possibilities, which in turn govern where the system can flow next into its new adjacent possible'. Although the previous chapters have also included discussion of the analysis with reference to existing literature, this and the following chapter aim to draw together my experience of the research process with a discussion of the theoretical, pedagogical and methodological implications of the study as a whole. While presenting a brief overview of results, in this chapter I introduce some of the 'salients' emergent from my study that contribute new possibilities for motivation theory. Through this discussion, I hope to encourage movement towards a richer, holistic exploration of the complexities of classroom motivation.

Two of the fundamental aims of my research were related to developing a more complex understanding of my students' motivation for English learning by exploring the influence of their ideas of an English-using self. In what follows I examine the ways in which my findings suggest classroom language learning motivation to be integrally founded on interactions between self-ideas, perceptions of experience by individual language learners and the co-constructed class environment.

Individualised, Dynamic English-using Self Ideas

One of the primary findings from the present study is that, far from being disinterested 'blank slates', the self-representations of these adolescents were filled with highly elaborate, individualised detail that emerged over the course of the study.

In order to gain a clearer understanding of the students making up my class group at the start of the research I developed two instruments to enquire about their past experience of English lessons and future ideas of a best-possible English self. Students related overwhelmingly negative perceptions of previous English learning connected to the teacher's approach, a lack of understanding and classroom environments that were not conducive to learning through being too noisy or too quiet. The vast majority of students connected a purpose for their previous English lessons to the rhetoric in Japanese society about English being useful due to the spread of globalisation. Only a very few students thought these lessons to be useful for future work. Other students explicitly stated that they did not understand the purpose of their previous English study.

Regarding a best-possible English self, a particularly surprising result was that from the very start of the study students' writing revealed clear images through the use of present tenses by the majority. In contrast to learners' understandings of the purpose of *past* English study, these *future* ideas in the main revolved around using English for an occupation. There was a strong tendency towards imagining speaking and listening to English, with students writing of concrete activities they imagined undertaking using English. The clarity of these initial images of a future English-using self provided a sharp counterpoint to my experiences with previous, older students at the college. At the time, I was quite astonished by this outcome.

Understood in the context of research into life transitions, students' past experiences in junior-high school English lessons shine some light on this result. Transitions are intricately linked with self-concept (such as ideas of an ideal L2 self). From the field of identity psychology, Oyserman and James (2011: 125) summarise a range of research on the links between life changes and possible selves/identities:

> Transitions are often accompanied by changes in the accessibility of, commitment to, and beliefs about the likelihood of attaining a particular possible identity. These changes may occur slowly as new challenges unfold developmentally, or they can occur relatively quickly as new challenges present themselves due to unforeseen circumstances.

Transitions to new educational settings have also been found to offer the opportunity for language learners to reassess their self-concept in this domain of their life (Mercer, 2011b), as well as providing challenges as they readjust to the possibility of new ways of study (Malcolm, 2013). As Plimmer and Schmidt (2007: 65) write, during life transitions 'focusing on a positive possible self can liberate people from less appealing current states'. In the present study, despite students noting predominantly negative experiences of past English learning with only vague or no concrete idea of the purpose of these studies, the transition to the new college provided a chance to redefine themselves in a new context. Part of this revision included imagination of a future English-using self linked to the vocational focus of science and technology at the college. The transition to the new educational context and the activity of writing about their best-possible English self encouraged students to express hopes that, finally, their English study might connect to an aspect of their future self.

Building on these first attempts to gain insights into students' ideas about English study, over the year of research I also collected data through change-action activities and from learners' regular English lessons with me to investigate their ideas of an English-using self emergent from experience in the classroom. My analysis found these adolescents to hold vivid ideas about an ideal L2 self, a fearing self, and a more proximal revising classroom self. Students' representations of each of these selves shared certain common general thematic qualities, summarised in Table 11.1.

One vital understanding from my study was that although common themes emerged, students' perceptions of language learning experiences, self and motivation were highly personal, individualised and contextualised. Regarding the ideal self, participants made connections to their lives outside the classroom. They wrote about one-off experiences such as a chance encounter that added detail to their English-using self-ideas, or made links to their individual interests, such as not being able to communicate when playing online games (Chapter 7). The analysis in Chapter 8 revealed strong emotion connected to students' ideal self-images as 'amazing' or 'great', and also a visual element, such as the components of an ideal self 'scattered around like pieces of a puzzle'. Students also picked up on different aspects of their experiences over the year to revise their ideas of the plausibility of an ideal L2 self: for some this revision was influenced by individual perceptions in interactions during classroom activities; others through idealising a peer role-model speaker; yet others based their revisions on understandings of

Table 11.1 Common general qualities of L2-related self ideas of students

Ideal self	Competence, positive emotion (amazement, pleasure), a sense of clarity and 'closeness', using English and a sense of widening future horizons
Fearing self	Anxiety about going overseas, fear of inferiority, fear of failure in the future classroom, fear of not progressing in language proficiency (in both the short and long term), and worries about working using English
Revising classroom self	Being understood and understanding, being proactive, using affordances and chances, and creating the learning environment

their familial financial circumstances. In congruence with these results, through using interviews with Japanese learners, Kojima-Takahashi (2013) found participants mentioning a variety of unique types of ideal L2 self not commonly included in closed-ended questionnaire research. The qualitative nature of the data in the current study illustrates that students' ideal self-images are individualised based on their perceptions and understandings at a particular temporal moment in their specific life situation.

As one aspect of the content of the ideal L2 self, students wrote of using a variety of different English skills in their futures. Amid such detail, despite a range of tasks in the English classroom involving interaction with written texts, the limited mention of a future English-*reading* self stands out. One can only speculate as to why learners' experiences in lessons did not encourage such recognition. One possible explanation may again be sourced from students' descriptions of their past English lessons at junior-high school. The predominantly negative experience of these lessons was in many cases linked to a teacher-centred lesson style. Some students specifically mentioned the 訳読 (*yakudoku* – grammar translation) pedagogical method. Learners may have associated this intensive reading and one-to-one translation with their negative experiences at junior-high school. The grammar-translation method was also used in other English lessons students had at the college. While they encountered more communicative requirements to interact with written texts in the English classroom in my study, the negative impact of these other experiences may have been so powerful that even with new input they did not, or could not, develop future images of a self reading English. A further reason for such a discrepancy may lie in Japanese adolescents' beliefs about EFL learning. As I remarked in Chapter 7, research literature (e.g. Rapley, 2010) shows that Japanese junior-high school students hope that English *speaking* skills will be necessary for their future beyond education. In a similar vein, research by Ryan (2009b: 416) exposes the sense that for many young Japanese people being able to speak English engenders a certain social status. In some social groups it is considered 'cool'. As such, adolescents appear to be more drawn to the positive image of an ideal self speaking English in the future.

It might be tempting to ask, 'So what if the students did not refer to reading? Is it not enough that they at least expressed images of an ideal L2 self using other skills?' This is one point at which contextualised expectations (i.e. the ought-to self) become important. Notable from past research is that both kosen teachers and university academics believe the skill of reading to be fundamental for engineering and technology students (*Koseneigo kenkyuuiinkai*, 2008). Lack of student mention of reading English as part of an ought-to self (let alone an ideal self) in the current study reveals a large gap in understanding between learners and those charged with preparing them for life after formal study. If the skill of reading is genuinely vital for Japanese technology students' futures, this gap in understanding suggests the crucial necessity of introducing some kind of rationale to allow students to more clearly understand this need and develop an ideal L2 reading self. It is also possible that extended engagement with reading materials in a more communicative or meaning-focused form, such as extensive reading, might foster students' images of an ideal English-reading self (Ohata & Fukao, 2014).

The analysis furthermore revealed students writing about deeply personal, emotional experiences of a sometimes menacingly real fearing self. Dörnyei (2009a) includes a self we do not wish to become as part of the ought-to L2 self. Chapter 8 found students mentioning a fearing self that at times connected with their perceptions of the broader expectations of others (i.e. the ought-to self). At other times the fearing self connected with a narrower focus on failing in the future classroom. Such a fearing self seemed not to be related to expectations, but was rather an internalised ideal: *'ideally,* I do not want to be this failing self in the future.' The 'want' of this motivation stemmed from an internal desire to be (more) competent in the future classroom. This dualism suggests the fearing self to be conceptually different from the ought-to self, although in some cases learners may experience the fearing self as a form of pressure or expectation.

The difficulty of operationalising and distinguishing between the ideal self and the ought-to self has also been highlighted in the literature (e.g. Apple *et al.,* 2013; Boyatzis & Akrivou, 2006; Costa Ribas, 2012; Dörnyei & Ushioda, 2011). As I emphasised in Chapter 8, Kubanyiova (2009: 323) has suggested more of a continuum from an externally motivated ought-to self to an internally motivated ideal self. In a similar fashion, with regard to the fearing self in particular, the analysis from my study implies that this self may stem by differing degrees from more internalised or externalised sources.

In the main, my analysis did not uncover specific student mention of an ought-to self during the course of regular learning journal writing. Unfortunately, underlying beliefs about perceived expectations from an ought-to self only really became apparent through my explicitly asking students to write about and compare these ideas in the Expectations activity (Chapter 7).

The ought-to L2 self, then, is somewhat of a quandary. As I discussed in Chapter 7, recent research literature gives a conflicting picture of its influence on motivation and action in different contexts (e.g. Csizér & Lukács, 2010; Dörnyei & Chan, 2013; Lamb, 2012; Papi & Abdollahzadeh, 2012; Pigott, 2011; Taguchi *et al.,* 2009). Pigott's (2011) research in the Japanese context found that adolescent learners perceived a far greater influence on their motivation from the ought-to self than from an ideal L2 self. Furthermore, of particular relevance to my study, research by Apple *et al.* (2013: 65) with Japanese science and engineering major students revealed motivation stemming less from ideas of an ideal or feared self, and more from ideas of expectations. Their study with 654 students ranging from the final year of senior-high school to doctoral level found that two aspects to an ought-to self played a vital role in students' EFL learning motivation: awareness of a societal expectation to do their best in their role as students; and pressure to contribute to Japanese society in their future as the next generation of Japanese engineers and technologists (Apple et al., 2013: 66). Similar findings were forthcoming in a study by Huang et al. (2015) with Taiwanese undergraduate students. These researchers found that social role obligations and an ought-to self connected to perceived expectations about career advancement strongly correlated with students' intended learning behaviours in English lessons. Once again, however, while these studies provide strong statistical support for the influence of the ought-to self on Asian students' EFL motivation, further work is necessary to uncover the qualitative detail and dynamics of change in ought-to self ideas.

Perhaps one lesson that may be learnt based on recent research is that the motivational influence of the ought-to L2 self (and indeed all of the parts of the L2 Motivational Self System) is contextually based. Lamb (2012) conducted a valuable study with English learners in three distinct contexts in Indonesia (a metropolitan city, a provincial town and a rural district). Among his results, Lamb (2012) found that, while pupils in the metropolitan and provincial schools shared certain aspects of motivation, there was a distinct difference in that the provincial students placed a higher value on instrumental motives for learning English. He concluded that the families of students in provincial areas 'took pains to impress on their children' the value of 'English to gain entry to more prestigious higher education or careers' (Lamb, 2012: 1009). That is, the ought-to L2 self was more developed for learners in this particular geographical, educational and familial context. In a similar vein, research by Dörnyei and Chan led these authors to argue that the existing body of research suggests that:

> While externally sourced self-images (i.e. the images that are usually categorized under the rubric of the ought-to self) do play a role in shaping the learners' motivational mindset, in many language contexts they lack the energizing force to make a difference in actual motivated learner behaviours by themselves. (Dörnyei & Chan, 2013: 454)

Particularly in light of the research by Pigott (2011), Apple et al. (2013) and Huang et al. (2015), my findings imply that situated explicit exploration of the dynamic processes by which the ought-to self develops for learners in some contexts and connections between the ought-to self and other dimensions of (possible) self hold great potential as an area for future research.

Regarding the L2 Motivational Self System as a whole, Taylor (2013: 32) criticises its conceptualisation for not including a present, actual self. My evolving understanding based on this study, however, is that a present notion of self might best be included as part of the 'learning experience' element of the system. Analysis from my study found self-representations to be (iteratively) dynamic and contextually based on present experience. My research shows students to be constantly revising their ideas of an English-using self based on their individual interpretations of past and present experiences. The lesson environments provided students with chances to experiment with 'provisional selves' (Ibarra, 1999) by testing them out in the classroom and making their own judgements about the effectiveness of their actions. Processes of self-reflection and social comparison during these experiences guided the students' motivation. As Ronfeldt and Grossman (2008: 43) argue, education can provide 'a place to begin the iterative cycle of adaptation by providing opportunities to observe, experiment with, and evaluate provisional selves as an explicit part of crafting a new … identity'. Learners also formed what I termed *'revising classroom selves'*. These images were proximal ideas of a self using English in the future classroom, for example, in a way that fostered communication more effectively. Future revising classroom-self ideas also depended heavily on students' interpretations of their experiences during the lesson. The possible-selves of participants were works in progress, constantly being readjusted and renegotiated through experiences and interactions within the classroom and from outside it.

An unfortunate trend in researching possible selves has been a conceptualisation of these images as fixed. As Henry laments:

> Because of the use of experimental and questionnaire-oriented methodologies, research in both mainstream psychology and in [SLA] has tended to 'freeze' current and ideal selves, presenting them as photographic stills rather than moving pictures. … Language speaking/using self-guides are better regarded as *dynamic* structures, the phenomenological qualities of which can be highly variable. (Henry, 2015: 93; emphasis in original)

The findings from my study imply that the detail of self-representations builds up through individual experiences and suggests the need for a longitudinal focus on real, unique people in dynamic contexts when studying the L2 Motivational Self System. It is not enough to ask students to reply to a questionnaire once or twice. As my recognition of continual co-adaptation between the environment and self suggests (Chapter 8), by the time any questionnaire has been collected and analysed, the self images of respondents will have evolved into different forms with different qualities based on their continuing experiences.

Echoing previous research, a final insight from a practical perspective appears to be the need to foster a connection between the instantiation of distal possible-self images and more proximal goals. As discussed in Chapter 2, based on survey results, Otani (2001) was damning of the vagueness of what he termed the 'big English motivation' of his students founded in obscure ideas of globalisation. In contrast, the students in my study wrote in great detail about the actions of a best-possible English self at the commencement of the study. However, even though the data revealed them to be writing of ideal-self images, the students themselves seemed to become less cognisant of these images as the study progressed. I introduced a variety of change-action to encourage learners' awareness of the existence of their own ideal self. With all that is going on in the life of adolescents (particularly transitioning to a new educational context), let alone their study in other subject areas, these opportunities to notice their images, to feel English as a useful aspect of their future, seemed to be of crucial importance. The change-action and experiences of using English successfully in the classroom gradually fostered a recognition of a connection and 'closeness' to the ideal L2 self.

Nevertheless, as Otani's (2001) study also found, it concurrently seemed to be a constant struggle for learners to take concrete steps above and beyond their regular efforts in English lessons to move towards their ideal self. Put simply, as far as the data reveal, my attempts at encouraging student goal setting did not have much impact on their motivation and action. My study did find that the possible-self tree activity (Hock *et al.*, 2006) encouraged students to realise that action in the present forms future possibilities (see Chapter 8). Time constraints in the context of the current study prevented the use of additional stages from this intervention. In order to examine how teachers can assist students to consolidate and more concretely connect the ideal L2 self with sub-goals on the road to these images, a useful direction for future language learning motivation research would be to investigate an integrated programme continuing with the action-planning stages from Hock *et al.*'s (2006) intervention.

Complex Systems Theory and the Importance of Interactions in Classroom Motivation

Conceptual comparison with the properties of complex systems allowed me to produce a much more satisfying interpretation of the 'messiness' of the contextualised, dynamic motivation of the human members making up the class group. In Chapters 7–10 I developed a representation of motivation that pushes towards the kind of 'real analysis' of a classroom, answering Hardman's (2010: 8) challenge to explore 'how interaction of individuals with each other and the environment can be described as a complex system'. I summarise this representation in Figure 11.1 by connecting these understandings with groupings of the properties of complex systems (see Chapter 6).

Complex systems theory was instrumental to the present study because it draws attention to the range of actions and interactions that influence motivation and ideas of self at various levels and across diverse timescales (e.g. de Bot, 2015). An analysis of the students' writing led me to propose one shared understanding that the classroom system was 'open' (Chapter 7).

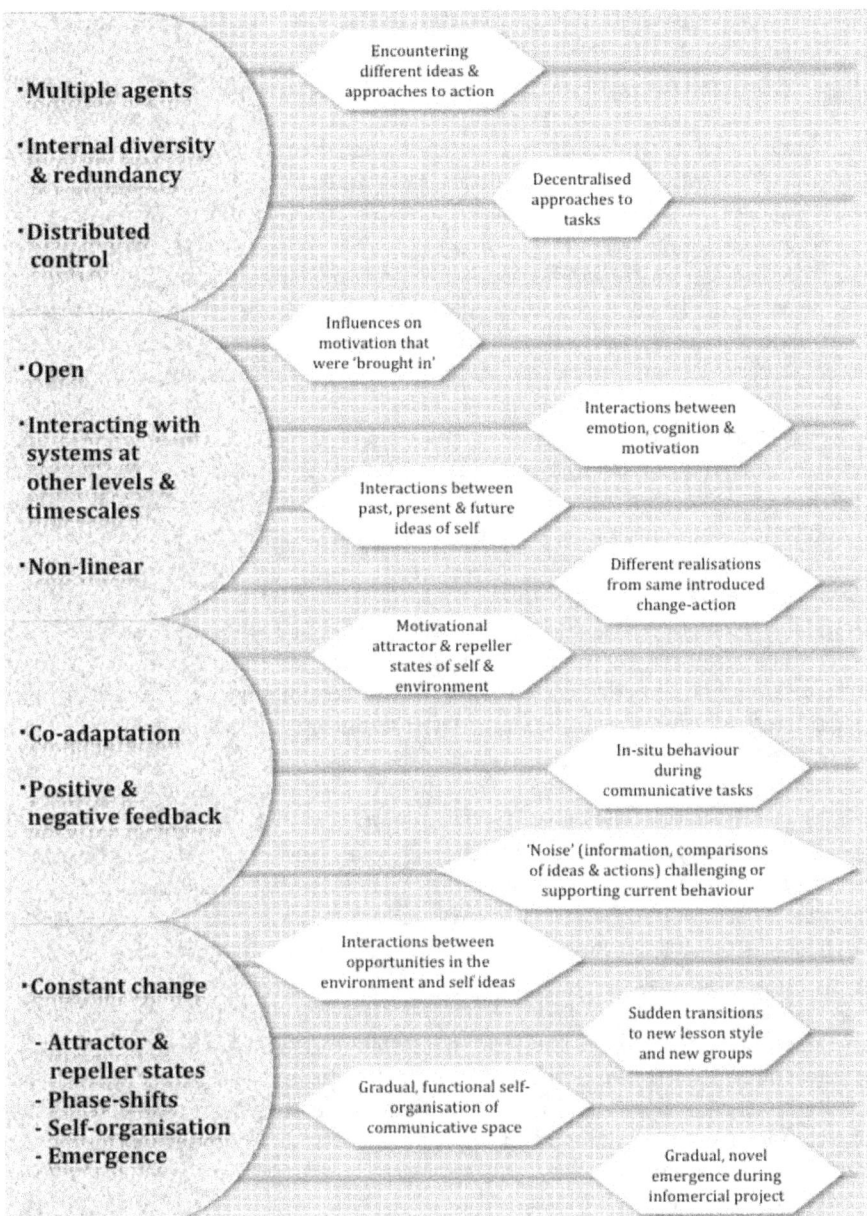

Figure 11.1 A summary of understandings emergent from the current research and their connections to the properties of complex systems

Students' self-ideas and their motivation in the classroom were influenced by interactions with a variety of elements that were 'brought in' from outside the class group. I drew on the notion of transportable identities (Zimmerman, 1998) to conceptualise the way in which participant writing revealed the influence on motivation of their identities as adolescents and as students in general, their individual personalities, personal circumstances, and some of the transportable identities of myself as the teacher. Further to these interactions with elements outside the direct class group, the analysis also revealed the influence on motivation of prosaic things like timetabling, and hinted at the potential influence of individually perceived expectations from significant others. These experiences and conceptualisations occurred and interacted across different timescales and influenced engagement in the classroom as well as ideas of future action.

A second shared understanding that emerged from the analysis was that within the classroom interactions between the learning environment (learner-external) and learner self-ideas (learner-internal) fostered motivation (Chapter 8). Students recognised certain types of opportunities as motivating: opportunities for language use; opportunities for interaction (between class members and between understandings); and opportunities for realisations. Processes of social comparison with other students and self-reflection on their experiences and understandings guided their motivation. Motivation for these participants developed through interactions between experience of self during such opportunities and their evolving images of an ideal self, a fearing self and a revising classroom self.

In Chapter 8 I developed a representation of this motivation which drew on the complex systems concepts of co-adaptation and a motivational state space. The analysis showed that there was nested, motivating interaction between the opportunities presented in the classroom spaces and the development of student self ideas. These opportunities are in many ways similar to the concept of 'affordances' in sociocultural theory. Swain *et al.* (2011: 149) write that an affordance is 'a property of the environment which offers the possibility of action to an individual', but also that 'which ones are taken up and used will depend on the person's goals and what is seen as useful to attain them'. During lessons and homeroom periods, adaptation occurred through negative feedback loops, as beliefs, understandings and perceptions of behaviour were challenged in an environment ripe with opportunity. In parallel, some forms of behaviour were explored and found appropriate, fostering positive feedback loops and reinforced understandings of the usefulness of these affordances. The learning experience provided scaffolding for the development of more detailed L2 selves, and interactions between the learning experience and these L2 selves fostered motivation.

Furthermore, the analysis draws attention to interactions between not only the learning environment and self, but also between cognition, affect and motivation. MacIntyre *et al.* (2009: 47) make a strong argument that L2 possible selves without an emotional element lack motivational power for the individual, remaining as merely a cognitive construct. Indeed, the close-knit interactions between affect and motivation can be observed in the way that affect is argued to 'orient cognitive and social activities' through 'creat[ing] dispositions, orienting not only action but also thinking and the way of being in the world' (Cahour, 2013: 67). In Chapter 7, participant writing about different elements of their identities that were transported into the classroom setting frequently revealed links between affect and motivation. Throughout Chapter 8, affect, cognition and motivation were shown to be intertwined: students reflected on their experience of lesson and homeroom activities as affectively 'moving', 'pleasing' or 'worrying'. This experience tied in with the development of motivating possible-self ideas (cognition) that were in themselves also at times fear inducing or at others 'amazing'.

Interactions between affect, cognition and motivation encourage more holistic understandings of language learner motivation, summoning possibilities for those involved with language education to assist students by engaging all three elements. As Op 't Eynde and Turner (2006: 374) assert:

> Teachers, parents, and society place importance on students' cognitive acquisitions over students' emotional feelings about the learning processes. By further developing a researched understanding of the various interrelated and integrated ways in which cognitive-emotion-conative [motivational] processes function within academic learning ... we [will] be able to demonstrate to teachers and parents that the emotions students experience during academic lessons, students' motivational energy for engaging in the learning process(es), and students' acquisition and use of academic knowledge and skills are undeniably, inextricably linked.

A final shared understanding regarding the learning spaces in this study is that interactions, such as those between the opportunities presented in the classroom spaces and the self ideas of individual students, or between cognition, affect and motivation at the same time alter the (motivation of the) class group as a whole. Students' individual actions and reflections lead to revised forms of behaviour. But they do not act alone – they co-adapt in reaction to and with the other members that form the class group. That is to say, through such seemingly individual processes, at a different level, participants also co-form the classroom context. A complex systems approach allowed me to understand from the data that in a classroom setting, actions and interactions co-form possibilities for future action and motivation in the class group.

Chapters 9 and 10 in particular focused on the development of motivation in the class group as a whole from three perspectives. First, the analysis found transitions to the new lesson environment and new groups to be phase-shifts in the motivational trajectory of the whole-class group of which the participants were cognitively aware. These transitions were further connected with emotions such as anxiety, relief and a sense of shared belonging. Secondly, the revising classroom selves of participants revealed them as intending and acting to make better use of their learning environment. Students reflected on their own actions and those of others they encountered during activities. The classroom conditions enabled the possibility of the spread of self-reinforcing motivation (Arthur, 1989). I conceptualised this spread as motivational self-organisation of the class group to foster communication. Thirdly, in the analysis of data concerning the final infomercial project, the cognitive appraisal of quality, and the emotional experiences of achievement and enjoyment interacted positively with the participants' motivation as a class group. I examined the interactions noted by the participants across the span of the six-week project to conceptualise this whole-class motivation as an instance of emergence.

As a theoretical motivation framework I initially drew on Dörnyei's (2009a) L2 Motivational Self System. While I apply this framework throughout, as the study progressed my understandings have also gravitated towards Ushioda's thinking regarding a 'person-in-context relational view of motivation'. Ushioda's (2009: 217) approach involves the idea that the motivation of real people (not defined purely as 'learners' or 'teachers') emerges through processes of 'personal meaning making in social context'. In terms of classroom motivation, she asserts that 'it is through social participation in opportunities, negotiations and activities that people's motivations and identities develop and emerge as dynamically *co-constructed processes*' (Ushioda, 2011b: 21–22; emphasis added). Rather than treating the context as a background variable, such an approach would hold that individual actions are constrained and made possible by context, while also acting to change the context. Recursively, each step we take alters both the context and ourself. Moreover, in contrast to a mechanistic cause-effect approach, such a perspective requires a 'relational (rather than linear) view of these multiple contextual elements' and encourages us to conceptualise motivation 'as an organic process that emerges through the complex system of interrelations' (Ushioda, 2009: 220).

Despite recognising an important need in language learning research for approaches that treat the language learner as 'an active self-reflective agent in interaction with the social context', Taylor (2013: 34–35) also calls for further conceptualisation and empirical research in support of Ushioda's (2009) exposition of a 'person-in-context relational view of motivation'. My experience with this research leads me to suggest that this is an area in which there is great potential for future expansion of the language learning motivation agenda.

Much recent research has taken as its level of focus the individual language learner when investigating the L2 Motivational Self System (e.g. Irie & Brewster, 2013; Kojima-Takahashi, 2013; Lamb, 2011; Papi & Abdollahzadeh, 2012) or drawing on complex systems theory to understand language learning self and motivation (e.g. Finch, 2010; Hiromori, 2014; Mercer, 2011a; Paiva, 2011; Pigott, 2012a; Sade, 2011). As a matter of fact, Schumann (2015) argues in critiquing traditional research on motivation in SLA that complex systems theory can offer valuable new insights precisely because it 'prioritizes *individual* accounts over groups; values variation as strongly as states; ... makes us deal with the way the world actually works ... and leaves us open to the notion of investigation without an expectation of an ultimate answer' (Schumann, 2015: xviii; emphasis added). In congruence with the findings presented in the previous section, focus on individuality is indeed a sound approach that can tell us much about, for instance, the dynamic development of present and future ideas of self and motivation based on unique histories of past experiences, or the interaction of an individual's self with contextual factors. Indeed, previous studies from a complex systems perspective discussed in Chapter 6 clearly uncover fluctuations in students' motivation over time, connected to their learning experiences in EFL classrooms, by taking just such an individual focus.

However, if we are to 'deal with the way the world actually works' (Schumann, 2015: xviii) and attempt to understand the experience of motivation for these individuals in the *classroom* spaces where much additional language learning is conducted, a complex systems view of motivation *also* suggests a focus on what is emergent at the class group level. As Vauras and Volet (2013: 2) argue, in a classroom context 'goals and motivations are further shaped through a group's joint enterprise, as learners' identities and positions within the group evolve along with the characteristics and structure of the group itself'. Throughout Chapters 7–10, the analysis showed that motivation in this classroom was relational and organic as individuals brought their own experiences and interpretations *into* the classroom, co-created new experiences *in* the classroom *with* the other members, and co-fostered perceptions of future possibilities in this space and spaces more temporally removed.

My understandings from the current study suggest that a complex systems theory approach to research and interpreting classroom motivation could provide empirical and theoretical support for Ushioda's (2009) person-in-context relational approach. Such an approach to motivation directs our focus concurrently to both individuals and the way in which they affect and are affected by the learning context. As was apparent throughout the current study, classroom systems develop their own motivational trajectories through the interactions and relations between the members that make up the system and what they bring with them at any point in time. If we want to gain an understanding of language learning motivation in classroom settings, a complex systems theory perspective urges us to look at relations between both the real classroom systems *and* the real people – learners and teachers – who dynamically co-form these social spaces.

12 Conclusion and Iteration

In promoting practitioner action research as a means to foster new understandings and action, McNiff and Whitehead (2011) argue passionately that

> Future social orders begin here and now, where you are. Because of the inherent generative transformational nature of human processes, new practices, influenced by new thinking and forms of knowledge, will develop out of old ones. You can influence your own contexts and your contexts can influence increasingly wider contexts. (McNiff & Whitehead, 2011: 258)

The previous chapter began to bring together implications for such new practices through discussing understandings of classroom foreign language learning motivation theory emergent from the study. Given my perceptions of low levels of engagement and motivation for EFL learning of the non-English major students in this context at the commencement of the study, a further aim of the study was to explore how the introduction of change-action in parallel with regular classroom English lessons might affect learners' motivation. This chapter therefore commences with a discussion of two pedagogical implications that emerge from the study. Following, I reflect on the methodological limitations and strengths of the research process, further discussing implications for future language learning motivation research.

What Do Students Gain from EFL Lessons?

As reflected in the previous chapter, the classroom context had a crucial impact on the self ideas and motivation of the students. Besides the ideal and ought-to L2 selves, Dörnyei's (2009a) tripartite L2 Motivational Self System includes the emergent context in which people undertake their studies as the *learning experience*. Drawing on the L2 Motivational Self System to study the motivation of adolescent learners in Indonesia, Lamb (2012) found that it was this situation-specific learning experience that played the key role in motivation. While his analysis revealed that students understood the utility of English, were interested in other countries and cultures and wanted to see themselves as users of English in the future, he concluded that 'what makes them more likely to invest effort in learning is whether they feel positive about the process of learning' (Lamb, 2012: 1014).

Considering the particular geographical and cultural location of this study, there is a large body of literature detailing Asian learners' preferred approaches to learning. Most of this research can be divided into two distinct groups. On the one hand, there is a body of literature that takes the broad and somewhat essentialised view that the learning styles of Asian students disincline them towards communicative approaches to language learning (Burrows, 2008; Hu, 2005; Kolarik, 2004; Samimy & Kobayashi, 2004; Zhenhui, 2001). This body of literature suggests that for Asian students to engage in communicative language learning these learners would need to make fundamental changes to their beliefs, values and resulting behaviour (Kolarik, 2004: 2). A review of literature describing these supposedly set forms of Asian learning behaviour paints a picture of Asian students as subservient and passive, unwilling to volunteer opinions or engage in activities, and as finding difficulty with autonomous learning situations (Burrows, 2008; Xiao, 2006; Zhenhui, 2001).

On the other hand, a second body of research asserts that, when given the opportunity to choose, many Asian students may prefer communicative approaches (Cheng, 2000; Falout *et al.*, 2008; Kikuchi, 2005; Littlewood, 2001). Indeed, Cheng (2000) argues that rather than the existence of culturally defined, set learning styles for Asian students, learner behaviour is more influenced by situation-specific elements.

As far as the motivation of students was concerned, the findings of my study align strongly with this second body of literature. In contradiction to assertions in the literature about the tendency of Asian students towards passive, disengaged, teacher-reliant learning styles, the analysis reveals that in the task-based lessons my Japanese learners were motivated and engaged. They were *not passive* in their learning. Without direction from me as the teacher, students were able to reflect on their actions in lessons and consciously formed images of a revising self, thus fostering a classroom environment more conducive to communicating (see Chapters 8 and 9). Furthermore, the analysis shows that they were not only very *willing to engage* in the task-based activities, but that they also identified opportunities for language use and interaction as motivating (Chapter 8). As one student observed in Chapter 9, the change to the active, task-based lesson style was 'a breath of fresh air' for many students. Lastly, the analysis of data collected from participants in the build-up to the presentation of the infomercials (Chapter 10) implies that students worked effectively to negotiate roles and collaborate during this project. Across a number of lessons, students *worked autonomously* in their groups and cooperated with other groups to arrive at the outcome of the infomercial.

It has been consistently found that the transition to adolescence, with increasing tendencies to social comparison of ability with peers and a shift to more abstract learning, witnesses a decrease in students' perceptions of competence (Wigfield & Wagner, 2005). However, in alignment with the findings of Ronfeldt and Grossman (2008) in professional education, the task-based classroom spaces allowed students to try on their English-using self in the present, scaffolded environment of the classroom. The focus on tasks enabled them to make realisations about using English meaningfully and purposefully. These learning experiences provided spaces to reflect on and compare actions with other members of the class, and fostered the iterative development of images of a future English-using self, whether in the classroom or in more removed, often professional settings (Chapter 8). Student reflections hinted at the motivating nature of the match between the textbook theme of working at an international technology company and the focus of the college. Bolstered by the possible-self change-actions, one of the primary pedagogical insights from this study is the motivational benefit of EFL curricula that foster experiences of success and assist students in understanding the meaning of their studies as a personal investment for their own, constantly evolving future.

Burrows (2008) has warned that for some Japanese students the move from teacher-centred to more collaborative, communicative learning may prove difficult. Specifically, he cautions that there will be motivational challenges as learners adjust from traditional, passive lesson environments in which there is a clear step-by-step progression in grammar learning to the 'apparent randomness' (Bowen, 2004, para. 11) of the task-based classroom (Burrows, 2008: 17). My own writing from the research journal as well as extracts from students gave voice to the very real incidence of such concerns becoming manifest as students appeared at times to go 'rampant with the freedom' (RJ, 26/4/2011) during the motivational phase-shift of the class group to the new lesson environment (Chapter 9). The results of my study suggest that, rather than continuing to flail in a sea of 'apparent randomness', however, there was co-adaptation between students and myself as we worked together to form a class group acting more effectively in the task-based classroom. Analysis showed these students to be very motivated to finally be using and interacting with the language that they had studied formally week in and week out from the age of 13. Moreover, while adolescence is frequently portrayed as a period of life in which young people become extremely conscious of how they appear to others (Harter, 2003), the task-based lesson environments afforded a space for learners to interact and learn with/about each other as a class group.

However, Burrows' (2008) point is certainly one that requires careful consideration. Indeed, there is an ongoing debate in Japan about the effectiveness and suitability of communicative pedagogy and task-based language teaching for Japanese classrooms. This debate often revolves around the extent of a focus on form in instruction (e.g. Burrows, 2008; Sato, 2010, 2011; Sybing, 2011; Urick, 2011). In the present study, concurrent with the task-based English lessons, learners also had two more traditional, grammar-translation English lessons each week. As one aspect of exploring the suitability of task-based language teaching for Japanese EFL classrooms, a natural next step for research in contexts in which students have independent, differently focused English subjects would be to investigate the motivational effects of such combinations of separate communicative and form-focused or skill-based lessons on particular class groups. By collecting data from one class group across a number of different English subjects, we might be able to ascertain how students make their own links between subjects, and any motivating effects of feedback loops between grammar or skill study and usage.

Intervening in the Possible-selves of Students

At a time of life when they are striving to develop a coherent sense of self and ideas of their future in society beyond school, adolescent students may struggle to find motivation in classroom foreign language learning, particularly when it is part of a set of compulsory subjects for non-language major learners. At such a crucial developmental stage, this study involved the use of activities drawing students' attention to possible selves in the form of an intervention. At the commencement of my study, while I was aware of the conditions for motivation from possible selves proposed by Dörnyei and Ushioda (2011), I was unable to find any examples of intervention programmes based on the L2 Motivational Self System (barring my own study published in Sampson, 2012). As a result, in Chapter 3 I described two interventions conducted in general education settings that provided significant direction in the development of the possible-self change-action activities introduced in the current research. However, the passing years have seen a gradual increase in the number of published possible-self intervention studies with second-language learners. The lion's share of this research focuses on strengthening the ideal L2 self through guided imagery activities (e.g. Chan, 2014; Mackay, 2014; Magid, 2014). In the main, these studies have found moderate to strong benefits for motivation from intervention. For instance, Magid (2014) conducted a study with 31 Chinese international learners majoring in a variety of courses at a British university. He describes his intervention as consisting of four sessions, each of which involved two guided imagery activities, with occasional additional action-planning tasks and a timeline drawing exercise. Data were collected through questionnaires pre- and post-intervention, as well as by means of semi-structured interviews six and 12 weeks after the intervention. Magid (2014: 343) stresses three main findings from his analysis: (i) there was a significant increase in the strength of the participants' ideal L2 self; (ii) participants noted a strong relationship between an increase in their motivation and increased confidence in their English; and (iii) 80% of participants claimed to put more time and effort into their English study above and beyond regular classes after taking part in the intervention.

Based on the analysis, I contend that through the change-action introduced in the current study the class group as a whole also displayed increasingly positive motivational trajectories and forms of behaviour that contributed to an environment more conducive to learning. While Ellis (2012: 286) notes a paucity of research establishing that the ability of learners to recognise the role a second language may play in their lives (possible selves) does lead to better *learning* per se, the results of this study do suggest that a possible-self intervention can have positive influences on *motivation*. Students naturally wrote about L2 self ideas in the course of their English lessons, but the introduced possible-self activities allowed them a space to reflect on and share understandings about the role of English study, and added detail, plausibility and a sense of relevance to the possible-selves of learners (see Chapter 8).

As noted previously, other intervention studies gradually appearing in this field have primarily focused on vision as the key to allowing students to build possible-self images. Extending these findings, a critical implication from the present intervention is the potential for positive motivational outcomes through using activities that introduce 'informative noise' *across* a class group. Learners need to feel that what they are doing has personal relevance for their life (Taylor, 2013), and one way of increasing such relevance may be through providing information about a possible future life domain. Indeed, research by Ueki and Takeuchi (2013) found that language learners' access to information regarding future possibilities with an additional language played an extremely important role in their development of ideal selves. Based on their results, these authors concluded that 'providing information related to what L2 learners want to be (the ideal L2 self) mediates what they feel they are able to become (self-efficacy)' (Ueki & Takeuchi, 2013: 39). Moreover, in a study with undergraduate Japanese engineering students, Johnson (2013: 202) found that, in comparison to those in the first year, second-year learners had more motivation towards studying English, precisely because they had a clearer understanding of the future professional relevance of English.

In my study, a variety of activities fostered such a recognition of the relevance of student action in the present towards building their possible future. For example, drawing a possible-self tree helped students to reflect on their ideas of future potential and to make connections between their current endeavours and a future self. The peer role-model sessions and my own presentation of past language learning endeavours challenged learners' beliefs about English study and the plausibility of a future English-using self.

Another activity explicitly encouraged students to consider the expectations regarding English of teachers, managers at technology companies and their families. Individual reflections were then shared across the class group in a mingling activity, allowing students to compare understandings. I finally showed the actual results of past research (*Koseneigo kenkyuuiinkai*, 2008) concerning the expectations of kosen teachers, university academics and managers at technology companies. In such ways, the change-action activities introduced 'informative noise' that upset the status quo, encouraging students to reorganise their understandings. In most cases this was also not merely an individual process – the activities pushed learners to share understandings across the class group. Such classroom spaces that provided opportunities for realisations were widely regarded by students as motivating (see Chapter 8).

In fact, past research into the development of motivation through possible selves supports these findings. As noted in Chapter 3, possible selves are said to be more motivating when there is a congruency between the ideal self and the ought-to self (Dörnyei & Ushioda, 2011). One of the possible-self interventions from a general education setting that guided my study, Oyserman *et al.* (2006), found a critical role for the classroom in the development of such congruency. As these researchers concluded from their study, 'structured group activities evoked academically focused possible-selves [and] made clear that academic possible-selves were held by peers (and therefore something that "we" aspire to)' (Oyserman *et al.*, 2006: 200). In a similar fashion, I argue that my intervention fostered congruency by conducting sessions together in a class group existing naturally in the setting, locating sessions in both the regular homeroom classroom and the English classroom of this group, and through providing opportunities to challenge current conceptions individually and interdependently. Through these processes, students together developed a shared sense of the relevance of a possible-self using English in the future. Unfortunately, as I noted in Chapter 7, no data were collected overtly as to students' ideas of what their peers were expecting of them, or indeed how these ideas perhaps changed over the course of the year. This does, though, suggest a valuable direction for future research situated in the foreign language classroom (see Murphey *et al.*, 2014 for one interesting possibility for harnessing the potential of students to idealise classmates).

Sounding a note of caution, Pigott (2012c) has argued that conceptualisations of language learning motivation drawing on the L2 Motivational Self System might not be appropriate for adolescents as they are still in the process of developing their future-self images. True, adolescence is a transitory life stage during which students are moving away from familial influence to that of the peer group – a time of making and sorting identities and roles (Harter, 2003). However, rather than writing adolescents out of the L2 Motivational Self System picture, ample research into the development of self and identity reveals that adolescence is an optimum time for trying on new selves (Oyserman & Fryberg, 2006). In line with the findings of research by Mornane (2009), the students in this study were quite willing and capable of reflection on and expression of their experience of the classroom, motivation and (future) selves. Instead of expecting possible selves to be static entities – developed or not developed – my research suggests the positive possibilities (for students, teachers and researchers) of exploring possible selves as works in progress *with* such adolescents.

However, I must urge two cautions to any wholehearted endorsement of educational interventions based on the findings of my study: First, the form of the class group that emerged was a coalescence of multiple factors. I do not presume to suppose that the motivational trajectory of individuals or the whole-class group can be traced purely and linearly back to the possible-self activities that were introduced, or that this motivation was constant. Complex systems theory encourages us to recognise that there are limits to our ability to understand truly complex phenomena, as we cannot know all of the influences on members or the system as a whole (Richardson & Cilliers, 2001). While we can draw on our past experiences or trends from research in similar settings when envisaging the potential benefits of change-action, we certainly cannot make *definite* predictions of the effectiveness of introduced change.

Secondly, the ethicality of externally motivating students through 'motivational interventions' has been criticised by Pigott (2012c). Regarding the L2 Motivational Self System, much theoretical and research literature (e.g. Chan, 2014; Mackay, 2014; Magid, 2014) and pedagogical material (e.g. Dörnyei & Kubanyiova, 2013; Hadfield & Dörnyei, 2013) has focused first and foremost on the interventive development of learners' images of an ideal L2 self. As Pigott (2012c: 428) rightly asks, however: 'Is it ethical to motivate someone to spend thousands of hours of their life studying something they may not need? What is the difference between motivating and manipulating? What are teachers' own motivations for motivating students?' While not raising ethical issues, one participant did observe at the end of the study:

> It's pointless to try to forcibly transfer motivation; I think it's something that changes by your own effort from beginning with an interest. (Aoi, LJ Reflection 2, 9/2/2012)

Ultimately, in agreement with Phelps (2002: 201), I understand that in an educational intervention it is important for students to be introduced to, and allowed to explore, issues and what they themselves perceive as challenges: 'as a teacher, I cannot hope to solve all problems for all students, but I can create an environment rich with potential.'

The results of this study imply that by encouraging students to attend to their ideas of possible futures and providing information we might allow them to *choose* to respond, discover and push into their *own* 'adjacent possible'

(Kauffman, 2008). Furthermore, through encouraging students to interact and exchange ideas regarding their possible selves, this intervention has shown that in classroom settings we might also allow learners to develop understandings together. This study suggests, therefore, the intriguing potential for further research exploring how both teachers and students can work together in educational interventions to co-create the *class group's* 'adjacent possible'.

Reflecting on Action Research

After my initial review of the literature (Chapters 2 and 3), I decided that an action research design would most effectively allow exploration of the effects of deliberate change-action on my students' motivation and self-ideas. In addition, basing my study on underpinnings from complex systems theory, I further asserted that there are complementarities between action research and such a philosophy (Chapter 4). Such congruence has also been previously proposed in the literature (e.g. Cohen *et al.*, 2011; Larsen-Freeman & Cameron, 2008b; Phelps & Graham, 2010). Applying action research in the context of this study, I found the process to offer certain benefits, yet also became all too aware of some major drawbacks.

First, my study shows the adaptive form of the action research cycles to be particularly useful for the dynamic exploration of classroom motivation. Four of the action research cycles employed introspective participant journals as a primary means of collecting data. One of the benefits of using learner and researcher journals was the way in which they allowed participants to give voice to their lived experience of motivation. A further benefit was that, through collecting such rich data from all members of the class group at regular intervals meaningful to participants, I was able to discern certain patterns that developed over time across the whole-class group. As the introduction of change-action, data collection and analysis proceeded in relatively short, self-contained cycles, the action research process allowed me to address questions that arose from these data in a timely fashion by introducing new change-action. This responsiveness to input from the received data afforded the further deepening of understandings of my students' motivation, and also encouraged me to introduce change-action that addressed my perceptions of the students' needs. As I was focusing on this one class group for the year that we were together, the cycles to a certain degree safeguarded against the potential of coming to the end of the research period and finding insipid data that did not foster my understandings, and activities that had not provided any benefit to the participants.

This said, the temporal nature of the action research cycles did lead to certain gaps in the data. For example, my analysis often led to questions about the meaning of what students had written. I was interested in enquiring with them as to what particular aspects of some activities they had found motivating, or gaining more of an understanding of motivational fluctuations connected to different parts of a lesson. In a related fashion, the data collected near the end of the study as well as my reading led me to notice the shared nature of motivation. Although at times it was clear *who* was influencing this motivation and *how*, at other times the source and quality of these influences was not apparent from the gathered data. The cyclical nature of the action research process prompted me to only collect the learning journals at four points during the year. This limited collection meant that by the time I was able to read and analyse the journals, the activities and experiences students wrote about had in most cases been conducted quite some time in the past. It was not reasonable to ask students at such a temporally removed point about their perceptions. One possible solution would have been to collect journals every week, but in my context I still most likely would not have had time to analyse them to a sufficient degree with my teaching load.

A second issue for consideration regards the overt introduction of change-action. Taylor's (2013) research with adolescent EFL learners in Romania found that these young people overwhelmingly expressed a wish for their teachers to take more of an interest in their lives. Such findings are echoed in a study from the United States (Kaylor & Flores, 2007) into a possible-self programme designed to increase the academic motivation of high school learners. One of the primary outcomes of the research was that students consistently reported the interaction with a supportive adult as motivating. As one participant in their study related, 'What I enjoyed most was expressing my goals to someone who thinks that they can happen' (Kaylor & Flores, 2007: 85). At times students overtly mentioned the ways in which they perceived change-action activities communicating such support (see Chapter 8). The very act of introducing change-action conveyed to students my own interest as their teacher in their understandings and their developing futures beyond the classroom.

My experiences also led me to recognise the value of the reciprocal and interactive nature of change-action. Change-action activities asked students to individually consider their past experiences, current perceptions and projections for the future. Many of these activities then continued by encouraging learners to compare their responses with others in the class. The study gathered data from individual students, but I also reintroduced the analysis of these data to the classroom system in the form of half-yearly questionnaires. Students had time to reflect on their own learning journals, and a final reflective activity encouraged groups to discuss their experiences over the year. Such activities shared information across the class system, allowing students to further consider how their own perceptions were reflected (or not) in the perceptions of their classmates. Much educational research merely stops at the description stage, 'taking' energy from the system and 'giving' little directly back. By introducing activities in which experiences and perspectives can be shared and compared across a class group, we can also 'offer' energy to the system. Such an action might assist participants in becoming aware and active in their own learning and motivational trajectories and the influencing of their fellow class members.

A final recognition concerns a number of challenges related to the contextualised implementation of action research (see also Chapter 5). For example, particularly during the first half of the year of study, I became frustrated trying to implement change-action when the concrete here-and-now of the college situation allowed little flexibility. Moreover, as the study progressed I became increasingly aware of the need to examine in more depth the dynamics and diversity of students' perceptions by looking further at data from previous action research cycles. However, the time constraints placed on me as a practising teacher did not allow the kind of holistic analysis and deep insights into my classroom in which I was interested. During the course of the action research, I simply did not have time to go back and review my analysis as a whole.

In dealing with qualitative data such as those in this study, analysts select which events and data to include and bring their own understandings to the interpretation of these data (Cohen *et al.*, 2011; Dörnyei, 2007). Due to developments in my thinking brought about by the experiences I was having as a teacher-researcher with the students, and interactions with the literature (especially regarding complex systems theory), I wanted to go back and look at the data as a whole. However, during the action research cycles the constraints of the context meant that I could not act on this development in my thinking. With my teaching load, I became frustrated that I simply did not have time to go through the data again at points in between action research cycles.

In fact, a major problem discussed in connection with action research conducted in educational settings is the time and pressure that it adds to the lives of those practising as teachers in classrooms (e.g. Allwright, 2005; Dörnyei, 2007). Allwright (2005: 354–355) notes an impression that action research is 'parasitic' and could lead to 'burnout', being so demanding on teachers' time that it would only realistically be feasible in a case where teachers were undertaking a teacher development course. With regard to data analysis, my experience came close to that of Zuber-Skerritt (1996: 17), who has commented that those conducting action research alongside regular work might struggle to make processes sufficiently economical yet enable 'a small-scale investigation by a practitioner to lead to genuinely new insights'.

As a result of these realisations, I reformulated my understanding of the action research process to include revisiting the data set in its entirety after the completion of data collection. The change in my thinking was along the lines of Radford's (2007) arguments regarding the combination of practitioner action research and complex systems theory:

Complexity theory, insofar as it sees the practitioner as one factor among a multiplicity, a majority of which are likely to be outside his or her control, tends to offer a more realistic perspective on the limits of the teachers' control and responsibility. This is not to say that practitioners cannot formally seek to understand their classrooms through observation and engagement, indeed they should, but the link between research and action is much more tenuous than the action research approach suggests. ... Practitioner researchers need to be analysts and critical interpreters of practice in a way that helps them to understand and explain what is happening, but the approach is more likely to be historical, exploratory, interactive and reflectively analytical rather than directly interventionist or controlling. (Radford, 2007: 276)

There are two points from Radford's (2007) writing that I feel it important to address. First, what Radford seems to be proposing for practitioners is something closer to exploratory practice (e.g. Allwright, 2005). The observation of existing, ongoing processes in classrooms can afford valuable understandings of action and learning in these spaces. Nevertheless, I still believe that there are additional insights that can be obtained through the targeted introduction of change-action in action research. As Larsen-Freeman and Cameron (2008b: 207) contend, the act of 'deliberately introduc[ing] "noise" into the system' allows 'investigation of the system's response to a perturbation [which] contributes to a deeper understanding of system dynamics'. Secondly, however, as Radford (2007: 276) urges, my conceptualisation of analysis in action research altered to be more 'historical ... and reflectively analytical' as the study went on. My study was clearly interventionist in nature. I had analysed data during the research cycles and introduced new change-action based on my understandings at those points. This change-action then altered the trajectory of the research and the possibilities for the class group. However, my own understandings had developed through interaction with the students and the data over the year. Rather than asserting that the change-action linearly *produced* certain effects and considering similar effects to be predictable in the future in this (or other) class groups, the process of revisiting the data set as a whole assisted me in becoming aware of the ways in which control was decentralised as learners made their own adaptations. It was a more historical approach to analysis that fostered these understandings.

Representing Research as Voiced Experience

Alongside my professional inquisitiveness, it was a recognition that much previous research in this context failed to investigate the motivational idiosyncrasies of dynamic, real classrooms with real people that led to a longitudinal approach to the present research. Ortega and Iberri-Shea (2005: 27) have argued that such longitudinal research is vital to the development of understandings about SLA for the simple reason that 'many questions concerning second-language learning are fundamentally questions of time and timing'. Yet, if we are to draw on a complexity philosophy that conceptualises the researcher as part of the research system, the 'questions of time and timing' to which Ortega and Iberri-Shea refer apply equally to the researcher. As Miyahara (2015: 177) puzzles: 'it is somewhat surprising that not many researchers make transparent their journeys as learners, teachers or researchers. Rarely do we find information about them in their writings, yet we are expected to read, contemplate and discuss their research.'

I have argued from the very beginning of this book that research outcomes need to be understood in the context of the processes through which they emerged. In particular, Part 1 of the book shines light on the evolving nature and role of the researcher conducting longitudinal research in a specific context from an insider, emic point of view. The narrative reveals my decision making as I struggled with the research process in-context, my conflicts as I worked to understand the data at certain points in time during the study. It moreover illuminates how these temporally situated insights influenced the further trajectory of the research and the eventual evolution of my thinking represented as research 'findings'. While I present my understandings in these pages, they are the emergent result of experiences over the course of the research.

In addition to 'making transparent' (Miyahara, 2015: 177) the co-adaptive nature of the researcher with the research and the researched, I have sought to develop a more phenomenological representation of the lived experience of motivation through allowing the perceptions of participants to be 'heard'. The research clearly shows that adolescent voices have much to tell those willing to listen about the emergent nature of classroom language learning motivation and self. From the commencement of the study, the students in this class group wrote eloquently about their ideas of a best-possible future self using English, and their reflections on past EFL learning experiences, further development of possible-self ideas, aspects of self brought in from outside the classroom, and interactions within the classroom that affected their motivation. Indeed, one is reminded of the body of literature that asserts that Asian learners are unwilling to offer opinions. In strong contradiction, the use of multiple student voices allowed the study to flesh out adolescent Japanese learners in a way that shows them to be thoughtful and articulate, and might lend much to a more situated understanding of the L2 Motivational Self System.

Finally, despite a gradual increase in the contextualised exploration of teacher understandings of language learning motivation (e.g. Banegas, 2013; Cowie & Sakui, 2011), there still remains a lack of research that explores teachers' roles in the development of classroom motivation from the perspectives of all members in a class group. This absence of teacher voice in the published record appears to be a widespread problem, with Aboshiha (2013: 219) noting that 'teacher knowledge remains majorly unrecorded, with few teachers participating in the codification of their understandings based on practical insights, or pushing forward their own research agendas, or creating new knowledge – despite the recognized gap'. Moreover, there is still a tendency to separate teacher understandings from student understandings. Past research (and the experience of most members of classrooms) has revealed the strong influence of teacher behaviour on student motivation, engagement and self-representations (Assor *et al.*, 2002; Reeve *et al.*, 1999; Taylor, 2013). Through an approach that includes the teacher, a representation of motivation emerged in the current study that hints at the dynamics and effects of my own (teacher/researcher) actions and motivation as interacting with the actions and motivation of the other (student) members of the class group (see also Sampson, in press, 2016). My study suggests possibilities for future classroom research agendas that include representations of the voiced experience of how *all* members of classroom spaces understand their own actions, the actions of others, and the influences of these other-actions on their own (future) forms of behaviour.

Future Directions

Based on the analysis in my study, I believe complex systems theory offers exciting possibilities for exploring and conceptualising motivation in the foreign language classroom. One area that looks to be particularly fascinating is with regard to the co-adaptive roles of students and teachers in the dynamics of classroom motivation to learn. In the present study, there was a range of data that found students reflecting in parallel about their experiences of the same activities or events in the classroom. My research journal also reveals my own perceptions of these events and interactions. While not implemented in the current study, an additional strategy would be to include the micro-perspective allowed by video-recording the classroom. Video-recording would provide a more permanent and detailed account of action in the classroom as learners interact with other learners and the teacher, and profitable use could be made of discourse analysis to triangulate student and teacher perceptions. By specifically collecting such data longitudinally from different participants and perspectives in the same class group, it might be possible to garner insights into the co-forming and dynamic nature of motivation and the classroom context.

To look at things from a slightly different angle, let us consider *teacher motivation* in the classroom for a moment. Past research from both general education (Dinham & Scott, 2000; Martin, 2006; Pelletier *et al.*, 2002) and language teaching (Doyle & Kim, 1999; Erkaya, 2013; Hettiarachchi, 2013;

Kassabgy *et al.*, 2001; Pennington, 1995), has found intrinsic teaching motivation to stem from the feedback that a teacher's efforts are contributing to individual student growth. For instance, Martin's (2006) study found specific forms of student behaviour that directly linked with motivation in teachers. Perceptions that students were focused on developing their skills and abilities correlated with teachers' enjoyment of teaching, while perceptions of student planning and effort most highly correlated with teachers' confidence in teaching (Martin, 2006: 83). Similar findings were forthcoming in a study by Pelletier *et al.* (2002). What is of significant interest for the future study of classroom language *learning* motivation is that their findings suggest an iterative process by which 'a teacher's beliefs about a student's motivational orientation sets in motion interpersonal behaviours towards the student, which in turn, may eventually cause the student's behaviour to confirm the teacher's initial beliefs' (Pelletier *et al.*, 2002: 194). While these studies employed quantitative means, longitudinal qualitative exploration may uncover more of the co-adaptive processes by which both student and teacher motivational trajectories ebb and flow in particular class groups over time, and indeed how student and teacher forms of behaviour encourage those in interaction to act in certain motivating or demotivating ways through co-adaptation (I have begun just such a tentative exploration in Sampson, 2016).

The complex systems properties of self-organisation and emergence also encourage expanded investigation of the co-forming nature of motivation in the classroom. In Chapter 9 I described the way in which I understood participants writing of self-organising motivation to foster a class environment more conducive to communication. While I stopped at a description of the qualities of this self-organisation, Lewis (2005) proposes a series of stages by which self-organisation may proceed. Although some proponents of complex systems theory would resist such a bounded and apparently linear understanding of the development of self-organisation, Hiver's (2015) study of the evolution of language teacher immunity offers one example of how these stages might be profitably used in the analysis of a developmental process. Chapter 10 examined motivational emergence in the class group via a process similar to Dörnyei's (2014) 'retrodictive qualitative modelling'. One way of understanding such emergence during the course of classroom projects that seems to offer intriguing potential is the idea of 'directed motivational currents' (Dörnyei *et al.*, 2015b; Muir & Dörnyei, 2013). Despite these researchers proposing directed motivational currents as essentially individual periods of intense motivation, my analysis suggests that within classroom contexts they may be shared across members as a kind of self-reinforcing motivation.

The ways in which I interpreted student reflections in the current study provided various hints which led me to conceptualise the co-adaptive and co-formed nature of classroom motivation. However, more refined data collection tools might allow increasingly detailed insights into the development of this motivation. I would like to bring this section to a close by examining two recent attempts at data collection based on complex systems approaches. Firstly, Waninge *et al.* (2014) explore in-lesson fluctuations in classroom motivation. These researchers combined classroom observation with a scale on which participants recorded their motivational level from 0 to 100 at five-minute intervals during lessons. The study revealed very different patterns of student motivation across lessons, despite the students experiencing the same learning spaces. Of key importance for the future implementation of similar methods to study motivational dynamics in lessons, short interviews with each student directly after each lesson and the observation notes were shown to be essential to understanding the contextual and temporal influences on motivational fluctuations. In another recent development, Mercer (2015) has introduced the approach of social network analysis to SLA research, offering exciting possibilities in relation to the shared nature of motivation. In this method, questionnaires are used to foster understandings of the intensity, directionality and multiplicity of relationships between members of a social group. These data may then be applied to visually conceptualise a network structure or architecture. As Mercer (2015) notes, such an approach might

> ... prompt us to reflect on the nature of teacher and learner motivation by switching our attention from solely looking at the internal processes of individuals, to instead looking at social motivation and how groups and individuals cooperate and generate collective forms of social motivation. (Mercer, 2015: 79)

These forms of research provide concrete methods that will add further substantial insights to the development of motivation. In considering their use in future research situated in the classroom, however, from my perspective as a teacher-researcher their implementation is not without challenges. For instance, Waninge *et al.* (2014) claim that participants recording their motivational levels every five minutes did not disrupt lessons. In their study, the researchers used a soft chime to announce that five minutes had passed and helped all those present in the classroom to become accustomed to the sound through a pilot lesson. Imagining some of the classroom language learning activities in the current study, however, I do not see how such an action could do anything but disrupt the lesson and indeed students' sense of motivation. When students were in the midst of a discussion, or participating in an information-gap activity mingling with other students, if they then had to stop, record their motivation on a scale, and recommence the activity, would this not have a negative impact on their communication and concentration, and their motivation connected to the activity? Mercer's (2015) proposal of the use of social network analysis certainly offers potential to add detail to the importance of relationships in small groups as well as across the whole-class group as influences on the ebb and flow of motivation. Yet my study suggests the need for repeatedly collecting such data from participants at least every lesson, as well as potentially video-recording lessons to gain an insight into in-the-moment interactions and influences. Such approaches would need considerable adaptation to be implemented by classroom practitioners without detriment to regular curriculum processes. Nevertheless, I am confident that the continued refinement of these and other research tools will enhance our ability to gain a relatively natural, non-intrusive understanding of the complex motivational trajectories of individuals in classroom settings as well as that of class groups as a whole.

Iteration

Through this exploration of language learning motivation in one class group, the student participants, I, the teacher/researcher/writer, and you, the reader, have changed and will continue to change as the systems of which we are part interact with the thinking brought about by this research process. This undertaking has altered my ways of thinking and conceptions to this point, and has also affected my notions of future possibility. These notions will, in turn, affect my present actions such that there is dynamic iteration of the person/teacher/researcher I was, am, and may be.

Although I have already drawn on the following extract in a previous chapter, I wish now for one of the student participants from the current study to have the last word. He sums up my thoughts about this research process with clarity:

> At first my image was hazy. I hadn't thought about that kind of myself [*jibun*] before. By becoming conscious of that kind of thing, I was able to turn my eyes to the future. Even now the image is still hazy, and I don't really know about the future. But now, there is a me who is doing his best to make an image. I can really feel that even just through that, it's different from the me before. (Taku, LJ Reflection 2, 9/2/2012)

Appendix A: Overview of English Course

The textbook for the course was *Widgets* (Benevides & Valvona, 2008). The story-based theme of the textbook involves students training at a fictitious international technology company, using English to communicate about the development of new products and technology. Students were randomly organised into groups of four to 'work' collaboratively in this imagined occupational setting, with groups mixed at four points in the year. My course used five stages of this narrative, in which students: (1) were involved in an orientation to the company and their co-workers; (2) worked in groups to individually develop original product proposals; (3) judged in groups the merits of products developed by other groups, justifying their choice of one product to 'go into production' through a poster presentation; (4) created and conducted a survey in groups to improve the design of a product; and (5) created video-skits of advertisements to 'sell' the products.

Appendix B: Learning Journal Instructions

Learning Journal

- During your studies this year please keep a learning journal – a kind of diary about your English lessons and some homeroom periods.
- I'd like you to **reflect about what we did in class** – think back, and write a very short entry about (for example):
  - something you learned/
  - something you enjoyed/
  - something that made you think about yourself/
  - something that was motivating/
  - something you want to try next lesson …
- Sometimes I might ask you to write about a **specific topic or activity** from class, but otherwise it's your choice what you write about.
- It should be **short** – one paragraph at most. You will have **five minutes** at the end of each lesson to write **in Japanese**.
- Please **bring this journal to class every week**.
- **Example:**

> 12/12/2012
> In today's class we did an activity about dreams for the future. We had to write about our own dream. Next, we asked other students about their dreams. It was really interesting to know about other students' dreams and hopes – they had so many different ideas! Because I heard other students' ideas, I could think more about my own dream…

Appendix C: Outline of Sessions in Action Research Cycles

Period	Cycle	Type[1]	Activity
April 2011	1	HR	Own, others' predictions about future/BPES[2] activity
		EL	PEEL[3] activity/Course rationale
		EL	International company: introductions
		EL	International company: about products/making teams
GOLDEN WEEK HOLIDAYS (10-day school break)			
May 2011	2	EL	International company: opinions about products
		HR	Role-model presentation: overseas work experience
		EL	International company: problems to solutions
		EL	International company: suggestions/three product ideas
MID-TERM EXAM PERIOD (10 days no lessons)			
June 2011	3	EL	International company: product proposal
		EL	International company: new teams/English skills
		EL	International company: pros, cons/discussing
		EL	International company: opinions/narrowing products
July 2011		EL	International company: poster-presentation preparation
		EL	International company: poster-presentation preparation
		EL	International company: poster presentations
		HR	Summer holiday skill-building activity
August/ September 2011		SUMMER HOLIDAYS (six-week lesson break)	
		SEMESTER 1 FINAL EXAM PERIOD (10 days no lessons)	
	3	HR	Summer skill-building reflection
	4	EL	Video (English at technology company)/goal-setting
		EL	International company: gathering information

Appendix C: Outline of Sessions in Action Research Cycles

October 2011	3	HR	LJ Reflection/questionnaire
	4	EL	Telephoning/information gap/product information
		HR	Stress management and image training
		EL	International company: suggesting improvements
		EL	International company: making a product manual
COLLEGE FESTIVAL/NATIONAL HOLIDAY (10 days no lessons)			
November 2011	4	HR	About school festival motivation
		EL	International company: making a survey
EXAM PERIOD (10 days no lessons)			
November		EL	International company: surveying
December 2011	5	EL	International company: data analysis/market report
		HR	Possible-self tree part 1
		EL	Goal review/International company: new products
		HR	Possible-self tree part 2
		EL	International company: infomercial situations
		EL	International company: infomercial script
WINTER HOLIDAYS (two weeks no lessons)			
January 2012	5	HR	Expectations of others
		EL	International company: infomercial preparation/companies
		EL	International company: infomercial preparation
INTERVIEW ENTRANCE EXAM PERIOD (one week no lessons)			
February 2012	5	HR	Role-model student speech: Canada study programme
		EL	International company: student infomercial videos
		HR	Reflection activity

Notes: [1]Homeroom (HR) or English lesson (EL). [2]Best possible English self activity. [3]Past experiences of English lessons activity.

Appendix D: Change-action in Cycle 1

My Future Activity

A. **My Future** Please imagine and write about your future: 5 years later · 15 years later:
1: What kind of job are you doing?
2: How are you using English?
3: How is your general life (family · where you are living · hobbies etc.)?

		5 years later	15 years later
1	Job		
2	English		
3	General life		

B. **Interview** Please *ask other students* to *imagine about your future.*
※ Be sure to ask students from other engineering departments ※

		5 years later	15 years later
1	Job		
2	English		
3	General life		

Best Possible English Self Activity

- Please write about your **ideal life in the future after studying English**. Imagine yourself in the future, after everything has gone as well as it possibly could with studying English. You have worked hard and succeeded in all your goals for studying English. This is your Best Possible English Self.
- Think about:
  - What are you doing every day? What can you do (with English)?
  - How is your English ability helping you? How are you using English every day?
  - Who can you communicate with?
  - What kind of job are you doing?
  - Where are you living?

(You may not have thought about yourself in this way before, but research shows that doing this has a strong positive effect.)

Past Experience of English Lessons Activity

- How did you experience your English lessons at junior-high school? Please write about your perceptions of your studying in junior-high school English lessons.
- Think about (for example):
  - What was a normal lesson like? What were you doing? What were other students doing? What was the teacher doing?
  - How did you feel in English lessons?
  - Why were you studying English?
- After you write your ideas, compare them with other students: Talk to three other students. What is the same (draw a O)? What is different (draw a X)?

Appendix E: Change-action in Cycle 3

Teacher-researcher's Example of a Japanese Study Strategy

I made a short presentation to the students about my own learning experiences with the Japanese language, and the way in which I had used writing in a diary as one strategy to improve my Japanese ability.

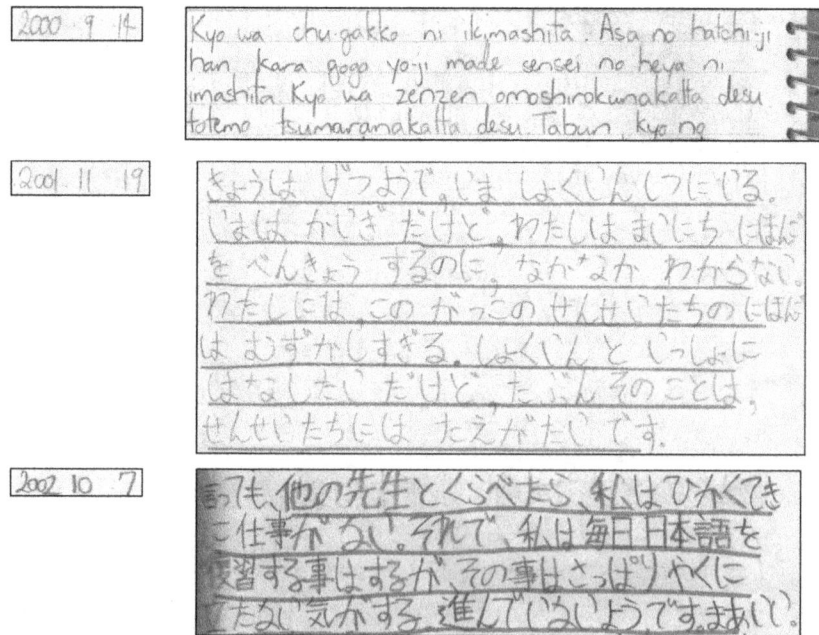

Instructions and List of English Learning Strategies Brainstormed by Student Group

1. **English learning strategies** What can you do to improve? In your group, discuss different ideas about how to improve one English skill. Write the ideas in the box below.

Reading	Writing
Speaking	Listening

2. **Other ideas** Ask other students how to improve English skills. Write their ideas in the remaining boxes.

Reading
Change base-language of computer to English.
Read a book I've already read in Japanese in English.
Read books in English in the order: children's level, elementary-school level, junior-high school level, adult level.
Read picture books.
Think about the meaning of English signs.
Read aloud.
Read some story I already know in English (e.g. traditional Japanese folktales).
Anyway, read lots and lots.
Read a foreign magazine relating to my hobby.

Try reading without caring about the meaning of every single word.
Play a [videogame] role-playing game in English.

Writing

Write the class diary in English (get a response in English from the teacher).
Use grammar I've learnt in the grammar lessons to write my own sentences.
Write my blog in English.
Do Twitter in English.
Write about my everyday life.
Make a vocabulary book.
Make a foreign pen-friend, write email in English.
Write about my everyday life using words I've studied.
Write a diary in English.

Speaking

While I'm doing various things at home, say what I'm doing aloud in English.
Sing English songs at karaoke.
Use Skype to talk with foreigners (make a friend).
Speak about my day in English for one minute every day before sleeping.
Talk with someone from overseas (e.g. Mr Sampson).
Go overseas.
At school, talk about what I'm doing in English with a friend.
Try speaking using what I've learnt in General English lessons.
Go to Kyoto!

Listening

Listen to English CDs (while looking at the lyrics).
Watch my favourite movie in English.
Watch a foreign movie listening to English and reading English subtitles.
Listen to Mr. Sampson's English.
Listen to English radio.
Watch 'NHK News 7' in English (changing the voice channel from Japanese to English).
While studying, read English words aloud.
Watch the same movie [in English] many times.
Watch the same series of movies [e.g. Harry Potter] in English.
Use a smart-phone application to listen to Japanese news in English.

Summer Skill-building Activity Instructions

(1) Look at the list of English learning strategies. Draw a circle (O) next to any you think it would be possible for you to do immediately.
(2) From those with a circle, choose one that you are actually going to try doing over the summer holiday break (colour in that circle ●).
(3) Why did you choose this? What kind of result do you expect? Is there anything that you think might hinder you in doing this thing? Write your ideas in the box below:

(4) Write your reflection about having done this activity over the summer holiday break in the box below. Was it useful? Do you think you will be able to continue? What do you think you could do to make the strategy you used even more effective?

Semester 1 Learning Journal Reflection Activity

- Please reread your Learning Journal. For you, was there anything in homeroom periods, English lessons, or some other experience close to you that connected to your motivation to study English? Please write about it. (If there was something that reduced your motivation, write about that also.)

Mid-Year Questionnaire Instructions and Results

You have been writing your ideas and reflections in your learning journal about 'English activities' and 'activities for thinking about English study' done during these English lessons and homeroom periods. Below are the most prevalent themes from this class's learning journals. Please read the statements and check the box that is applicable for your perceptions. If you have any comments, please write them in the space below each statement. Thank you!

	Agree strongly	Agree	Agree somewhat	Disagree somewhat	Disagree	Disagree strongly
When I'm doing English activities and I succeed, my motivation goes up.	17 (42.5%)	19 (47.5%)	4 (10%)	0	0	0
When I'm doing English activities I can interact with other students, so my motivation goes up.	9 (22.5%)	17 (42.5%)	10 (25%)	4 (10%)	0	0
I have an image of 'myself using English in the future'.	5 (12.5%)	5 (12.5%)	10 (25%)	9 (22.5%)	10 (25%)	1 (2.5%)
When I'm doing English activities, I have thought that there is a gap between 'myself now' and 'myself using English in the future'.	7 (17.5%)	12 (30%)	10 (25%)	4 (10%)	6 (15%)	1 (2.5%)
I am thinking concretely of what I can do to become 'myself using English in the future'.	3 (7.5%)	14 (35%)	8 (20%)	7 (17.5%)	4 (10%)	4 (10%)
When I'm doing English activities, I look at other students and think, 'I ought to study more'.	15 (37.5%)	16 (40%)	4 (10%)	4 (10%)	1 (2.5%)	0
When I'm doing English activities, I look at other students and think, 'I want to study more'.	4 (10%)	13 (32.5%)	13 (32.5%)	8 (20%)	2 (5%)	0
When I hear other people (students/teachers) talking about studying English, I think, 'I ought to study more'.	13 (32.5%)	12 (30%)	11 (27.5%)	4 (10%)	0	0

When I hear other people (students/teachers) talking about studying English, I think, 'I want to study more'.	7 (17.5%)	7 (17.5%)	16 (40%)	7 (17.5%)	3 (7.5%)	0
Through English activities my image of 'myself using English in the future' has become more concrete.	2 (5%)	8 (20%)	12 (30%)	13 (32.5%)	5 (12.5%)	0
My own 'motivation to study English' changes day by day.	10 (25%)	11 (27.5%)	10 (25%)	8 (20%)	0	1 (2.5%)

Appendix F: Change-action in Cycle 4

Two Minutes into the Future English-Self Image Training Activity (adapted from Arnold *et al.*, 2007)

(1) Close your eyes.
(2) Relax ... Concentrate on your breathing ... Slowly breathe in ... and out ... in ... out ...
(3) Imagine you are looking a long way away ... And, a long way away, there is the shape of a person ...
(4) Going closer, you realise that the person is you a number of years later ... You are with some friends the same age, and you're speaking with everyone in English ... Enthusiastically, you're speaking about something in English, and your friends are really listening to what you're saying ...
(5) Then one of your friends asks a question about the topic on which you are talking, and you understand the English of your friend perfectly and answer ...
(6) For a second you think, 'communicating with everyone in English, being able to have interesting conversations is really fun ...'
(7) After a while, you split up from your friends, and walk towards a large building ... This is where you are working ... You go inside, walk to your office, and sit down at your desk ...
(8) After a little time passes, a co-worker comes and hands you a research paper the two of you are writing ... The two of you read the content you have written in English, and discuss in English what parts you think need fixing ... And while you are discussing, you type the corrections into your computer in English ...

(9) For a second you think, 'this work is really fun and worthwhile …' And you think, 'it's so interesting to talk with all these co-workers from different countries in English …'
(10) Keep this feeling … And at the timing that's right for you, keeping this feeling, open your eyes and come back to this room …
(11) Now, quickly, without talking to anyone, put your *feeling* now into a phrase, and write it down.

Appendix G: Change-action in Cycle 5

Possible-self Tree Activity (adapted from Hock *et al.*, 2006)

Possible-self Tree Session 1
(1) Write as many words or phrases as you can that are suitable to express your hopes in the three areas below:
Hopes for yourself   *Hopes as an English learner*   *Hopes as a worker*
(2) Write as many words or phrases as you can that are suitable to express your fears in the three areas:
Fears about yourself   *Fears as an English learner*   *Fears as a worker*
(3) Write what things you are doing now, what abilities or aspects of personality you have now that are helping to realise your hopes:
(4) Write what things you are doing now, what abilities or aspects of personality you have now that hinder your hopes and promote your fears:

Appendix G: Change-action in Cycle 5   201

Possible-self Tree Session 2

- Let's create a 'Possible-self tree'
    - First, draw the trunk – this is yourself.
    - Draw three branches – let's make these the areas of your hopes.
    - Draw twigs growing healthily out of the branches – these are the expressions of your hopes.
    - Draw poison, lightning and termites – these are the expressions of your fears.
    - Draw healthy roots in the soil – these are yourself that is supporting your hopes.
    - Draw rotting roots in the soil – these are yourself that is hindering your hopes.

Teacher's Possible-self Tree

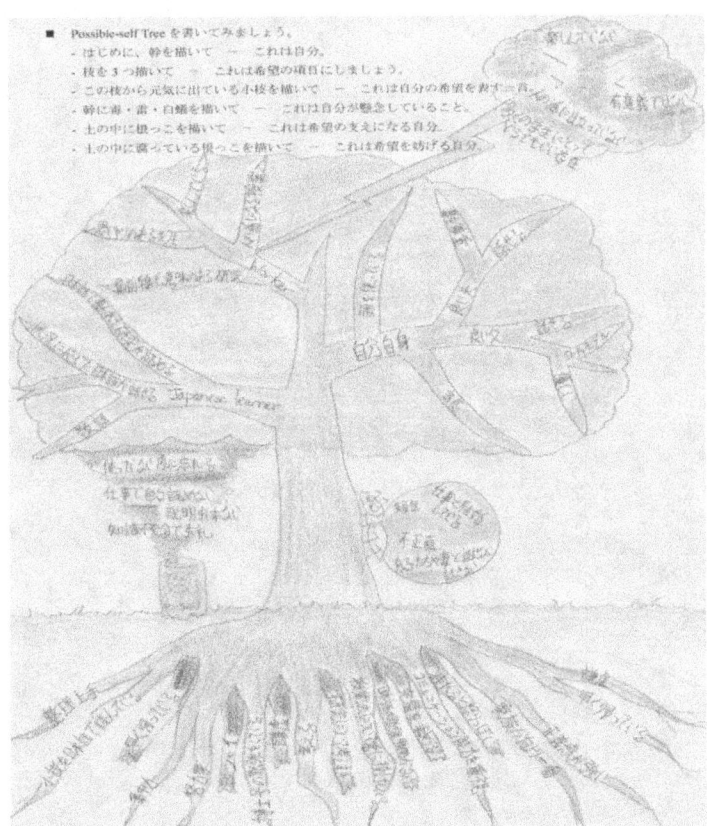

Expectations Activity

- You may have various predictions or expectations about your own future, for example, 'such-and-such English ability is necessary', 'there might be an occasion to do such-and-such using English' or 'as a graduate of kosen I want to be active in such-and-such a field'. However, in the table below, <u>don't write your own ideas</u>, but instead write what you think other people are expecting of you.

	English	*Kosen graduate*
(1) Teachers		
(2) Companies		
(3) Family		

Semester 2 Learning Journal Reflection Activity

- Please write your answers to the questions in sections A–E regarding what you have thought about English or English study this year in these English lessons or homeroom periods. Please follow steps 1–4.
  (1) Please think about A, B and C by yourself, and write by yourself.
  (2) Next, present your answers to C in a group.
  (3) Please write your answers to D and E as a group.
  (4) Choose a student from your group to present the group's answers to D and E.

A	Over this year, how has your English motivation changed? (text, diagram, text + diagram)
B	Over this year, was there anything in homeroom periods, English lessons, or some other experience close to you that connected to your English motivation? (If there was something that reduced your motivation, write about that also.)
C	Over this year, how has your idea of an 'English-using self' changed?
D	Write three points of advice to students in this class in order that they can become their future ideal 'English-using self'.
E	Write three points of advice to 1st-grade students that will enter this college in the next academic year about studying English.

End-year Questionnaire and Results (English)

You wrote your ideas and reflections in your learning journal about 'English activities' and 'activities for thinking about English study' done during these English lessons and homeroom periods. Below are the most prevalent themes from this class's learning journals. Please read the statements and check the box that is applicable for your perceptions. If you have any comments, please write them in the space below each statement. Thank you!

	Agree strongly	Agree	Agree somewhat	Disagree somewhat	Disagree	Disagree strongly
When I'm doing English activities and I succeed doing a difficult task, my motivation goes up.	10 (25.5%)	11 (27.5%)	10 (25.5%)	7 (17.5%)	2 (5%)	0
When I'm doing English activities I can interact with other students, so my motivation goes up.	8 (20%)	22 (55%)	10 (25%)	0	0	0
I have an image of 'myself using English in the future'.	5 (12.5%)	7 (17.5%)	18 (45%)	4 (10%)	6 (15%)	0
My motivation goes up when I study being conscious of the image of 'myself using English in the future'.	6 (15%)	11 (27.5%)	13 (32.5%)	8 (20%)	2 (5%)	0
When I'm doing English activities, I have thought that there is a gap between 'myself now' and 'myself using English in the future'.	13 (32.5%)	14 (35%)	9 (22.5%)	3 (7.5%)	0	1 (2.5%)
I am thinking concretely of what I can do to become 'myself using English in the future'.	3 (7.5%)	12 (30%)	13 (32.5%)	7 (17.5%)	3 (7.5%)	2 (5%)
Through English activities my image of 'myself using English in the future' has become more concrete.	5 (12.5%)	13 (32.5%)	16 (40%)	6 (15%)	0	0
When I'm doing English activities, I look at other students and think, 'I ought to study more'.	19 (47.5%)	14 (35%)	7 (17.5%)	0	0	0

When I'm doing English activities, I look at other students and think, 'I want to study more'.	7 (17.5%)	12 (30%)	13 (32.5%)	6 (15%)	2 (5%)	0
When I hear other people (students / teachers) talking about studying English, I think, 'I ought to study more'.	19 (47.5%)	16 (40%)	4 (10%)	1 (2.5%)	0	0
When I hear other people (students / teachers) talking about studying English, I think, 'I want to study more'.	8 (20%)	13 (32.5%)	10 (25%)	6 (15%)	3 (7.5%)	0
When I'm studying English, my motivation goes up when I feel 'this study has a connection to myself now'.	10 (25%)	14 (35%)	16 (40%)	0	0	0
When I think about getting rid of fears for my future, my motivation goes up.	5 (12.5%)	11 (27.5%)	17 (42.5%)	5 (12.5%)	1 (2.5%)	1 (2.5%)
When my emotions are stirred by an activity, my motivation goes up.	8 (20%)	18 (45%)	6 (15%)	8 (20%)	0	0
My own 'motivation to study English' changes day by day.	16 (40%)	13 (32.5%)	11 (27.5%)	0	0	0
My own 'motivation to study English' is influenced by the motivation of other people (students, teachers) on that day.	7 (17.5%)	14 (35%)	11 (27.5%)	6 (15%)	1 (2.5%)	1 (2.5%)

Appendix H: Outline of Final Infomercial Project

Week	Date	Activity
1	8/12/2011	Teacher divided students into new groups of four. Students took part in a brief self-introduction activity. Students participated in a listening comprehension activity while watching the textbook DVD which introduced the final assignment – making an infomercial. Teacher distributed one student-designed product proposal sheet per group; students then discussed to write details about the product and come up with ways to improve it.
2	15/12/2011	Students watched an example infomercial presentation made by other students. Students watched an infomercial from the textbook DVD, filling in missing words from a script. Teacher explained some possible patterns for the infomercial. Teacher showed and explained examples of some different problem situations for a product he designed. Student groups discussed together to brainstorm some different possible problem situations for their group product.
3	22/12/2011	Teacher showed example of infomercial story for his product. Student groups discussed to choose best situation(s) to show their product. Students groups discussed to write two stories for their infomercial: one situation without their product with a bad ending; one situation with their product with a good ending. Teacher took a poll for how to present infomercials – as a skit in front of the whole class, as a skit in front of one other group at a time, or as a video. Majority chose to make a video. Student groups began to write an English script for their infomercial.
4	12/1/2012	Student groups continued to write the English script for their infomercial. Teacher assisted by suggesting infomercial ideas and checked the English script. Student groups began to make any props they would need for their infomercial.

5	24/1/2012	Student groups worked on finishing the English script, making props or recording their infomercial.
6	2/2/2012	Student groups submitted their infomercial video on a USB memory stick to the teacher. Teacher distributed peer-evaluation sheets to each student. Class group watched the infomercials on a large screen through a projector, with the room darkened like a movie theatre. After viewing all videos, teacher collected peer-evaluation sheets from students.

Glossary

Co-adaptation: A process of mutual causality through which two or more interconnected systems influence each other over time. Change in one system fosters change in other, connected systems, which also feeds back to co-influence the original system.

Complex systems theory: A theory dealing with the study of systems that are complex – open systems in which there are large, interconnecting networks of interacting and co-influencing components with decentralised control from which complex collective forms of behaviour and adaptation or learning emerge over time. This collective behaviour of the whole iteratively feeds back to the behaviour of components at lower levels, as well as interacting with other, interconnected systems.

Demotivation: Particular influences that contribute to a reduction of existing motivation towards an action, either ongoing or planned.

Emergence: The gradual evolution of a complex system through its interactions to display a certain form of behaviour or structure as a whole. Emergence involves the production of new, *novel* properties of the whole that would have been difficult to predict and are not able to be reduced to the properties of the agents in the system (de Wolf & Holvoet, 2005).

English as a Foreign Language (EFL): The study of English in a context in which English is not the first language of the environment. Consequently, Japanese learners of English studying in Japan are classified as EFL learners.

Fearing self: A representation or image of a self in a certain domain that we do not want to become at a time in the future – for example, a student's idea about a self not being able to competently use an additional language during a presentation in the future classroom.

Ideal self: A representation or image of a self that one would ideally like to become at a self-defined time in the future in a certain domain – for example, a student's idea about a 'best' possible self using an additional language competently to interact with other users of that language.

Learning experience (as part of the L2 Motivational Self System): Motives generated through the learning environment, such as the influence of the teacher, curriculum, lesson style. Ideas of the present, actual self are located temporally in the current learning experience.

Motivation: Relating to the direction and magnitude of human behaviour, that is: *why* people choose to do something, *how long* they choose to do some activity, and *how hard* they try to pursue the activity (Dörnyei & Ushioda, 2011). It is 'a cumulative arousal, or want, that we are aware of' (Dörnyei, 2009b: 209). In this sense, motivation in the classroom entails the volition to act and develop one's capacities through the content and activities presented

Ought-to self: A representation or image of a self that one feels obliged or expected to become at a time in the future in a certain domain. It is largely socially constructed – for example, our perceived expectations from family members about what we 'should' become in the additional language domain.

Phase-shift: Sharp alterations in the state and future possibilities of a system as a whole due to the accretion of change at different levels.

Possible self: An individual's conceptions of future selves. Possible selves are proposed to link self-conception and motivation by giving concrete form, imagery and direction to individuals' aspirations and fears (Markus & Nurius, 1986).

Revising classroom self: Proximal ideas of a self acting in the future classroom, such as an idea of oneself using English in the next lesson.

Self-organisation: The gradual evolution of a system through its interactions to form patterns that are more functionally capable of responding to the environment. These processes occur without any predetermined plan or central governing agent that controls behaviour.

State space: A metaphor for visualising all of the possible states in which a system could be at any point in time. Within this space there are usually certain states or areas which might be relatively more stable 'attractor states' or unstable 'repeller states' over particular timescales.

Transportable identity: Identities held through perceived attachment to certain groups or types of people. Although potentially based in certain situational contexts, these identities may also be 'carried' with an individual into different contexts.

References

Aboshiha, P. (2013) 'Native speaker' English language teachers: Disengaged from the changing international landscape of their profession. In E. Ushioda (ed.) *International Perspectives on Motivation: Language Learning and Professional Challenges* (pp. 216–232). Basingstoke: Palgrave Macmillan.

Agawa, T., Abe, E., Ishizuka, M., Ueda, M., Okuda, S., Carreira-Matsuzaki, J., Sano, F. and Shimizu, S. (2011) Preliminary study of demotivating factors in Japanese university English learning. *The Language Teacher* 35 (1), 11–16.

Aguilar, J. (2013) The institutional and beyond: On the identity displays of foreign language teachers. In D.J. Rivers and S.A. Houghton (eds) *Social Identities and Multiple Selves in Foreign Language Education* (pp. 13–32). London: Bloomsbury Academic.

Alhadeff-Jones, M. (2008) Three generations of complexity theories: Nuances and ambiguities. *Educational Philosophy and Theory* 40 (1), 66–82.

Allwright, D. (2005) Developing principles for practitioner research: The case of exploratory practice. *Modern Language Journal* 89 (3), 353–366.

Al-Shehri, A.S. (2009) Motivation and vision: The relation between the ideal L2 self, imagination and visual style. In Z. Dörnyei and E. Ushioda (eds) *Motivation, Language Identity and the L2 Self* (pp. 164–171). Bristol: Multilingual Matters.

Apple, M.T., Falout, J. and Hill, G. (2013) Exploring classroom-based constructs of EFL motivation for science and engineering students in Japan. In M.T. Apple, D. Da Silva and T. Fellner (eds) *Language Motivation in Japan* (pp. 54–74). Bristol: Multilingual Matters.

Arnold, J., Puchta, H. and Rinvolucri, M. (2007) *Imagine That! – Mental Imagery in the EFL Classroom*. Cambridge: Cambridge University Press.

Arthur, B. (1989) Competing technologies, increasing returns, and lock-in by historical events. *Economic Journal* 99, 116–131.

Aspinall, R.W. (2003) Japanese nationalism and the reform of English language teaching. In R. Goodman and D. Phillips (eds) *Can the Japanese Change their Education System?* (pp. 103–118). Oxford: Symposium Books.

Assor, A., Kaplan, H. and Roth, G. (2002) Choice is good, but relevance is excellent: Autonomy enhancing and suppressing teacher behaviours predicting students' engagement in schoolwork. *British Journal of Educational Psychology* 72 (2), 261–278.

Backhaus, P. (2007) *Linguistic Landscapes: A Comparative Study of Urban Multilingualism in Tokyo*. Clevedon: Multilingual Matters.

Bandura, A. (1986) *Social Foundations of Thought and Action: A Social Cognitive Theory*. Englewood Cliffs, NJ: Prentice-Hall.

Banegas, D.L. (2013) The integration of content and language as a driving force in the EFL lesson. In E. Ushioda (ed.) *International Perspectives on Motivation: Language Learning and Professional Challenges* (pp. 82–97). Basingstoke: Palgrave Macmillan.

Benevides, M. (2010) Designing a themed task-based syllabus. *The Language Teacher* 34 (4), 21–23.

Benevides, M. and Valvona, C. (2008) *Widgets: A Task-Based Course in Practical English*. Hong Kong: Pearson Longman Asia ELT.

Biesta, G. (2006) *Beyond Learning: Democratic Education for a Human Future*. Boulder, CO: Paradigm Publishers.

Bowen, T. (2004) Teaching approaches: Task-based learning. See http://www.onestopenglish.com/support/methodology/teaching-approaches/teaching-approaches-task-based-learning/146502.article (accessed 5 January 2014).

Boyatzis, R.E. and Akrivou, K. (2006) The ideal self as the driver of intentional change. *Journal of Management Development* 25 (7), 624–642.

Bronfenbrenner, U. (1979) *The Ecology of Human Development*. Cambridge, MA: Harvard University Press.

Brophy, J. (1998) *Motivating Students to Learn*. Boston, MA: McGraw Hill.

Bukowski, W.M., Bergevin, T. and Miners, R. (2011) Social development. In A. Slater and G. Bremner (eds) *An Introduction to Developmental Psychology* (pp. 551–583). Glasgow: BPS Blackwell.

Burns, A. (2005) Action research: An evolving paradigm? *Language Teaching* 38 (2), 57–74.

Burns, A. (2010) *Doing Action Research in English Language Teaching*. New York: Routledge.

Burns, A. (2011) Action research in the field of second language teaching and learning. In E. Hinkel (ed.) *Handbook of Research in Second Language Teaching and Learning* (Vol. 2, pp. 237–253). New York: Routledge.

Burns, A. and Knox, J.S. (2011) Classrooms as complex adaptive systems: A relational model. *TESL-EJ* 15 (1), 1–25.

Burrows, C. (2008) Socio-cultural barriers facing TBL in Japan. *The Language Teacher* 32 (8), 15–19.

Butler, G.Y. and Iino, M. (2005) Current Japanese reforms in English language education: The 2003 'Action Plan'. *Language Policy* 4 (1), 25–45.

Byrne, D. (1998) *Complexity Theory and the Social Sciences: An Introduction*. Abingdon: Routledge.

Byrne, D. and Callaghan, G. (2014) *Complexity Theory and the Social Sciences: The State of the Art*. Abingdon: Routledge.

Cahour, B. (2013) Emotions: Characteristics, emergence and circulation in interactional learning. In M. Baker, J. Andriessen and S. Jarvela (eds) *Affective Learning Together: Social and Emotional Dimensions of Collaborative Learning* (pp. 52–70). Abingdon: Routledge.

Carpenter, C., Falout, J., Fukuda, T., Trovela, M. and Murphey, T. (2009) Helping students repack for remotivation and agency. Paper presented at the JALT2008, Tokyo, November.

Chan, L. (2014) Effects of an imagery training strategy on Chinese university students' possible second language selves and learning experiences. In K. Csizer and M. Magid (eds) *The Impact of Self-Concept on Language Learning* (pp. 357–376). Bristol: Multilingual Matters.

Chan, L., Dornyei, Z. and Henry, A. (2015) Learner archetypes and signature dynamics in the language classroom: A retrodictive qualitative modelling approach to studying L2 motivation. In Z. Dornyei, P.D. MacIntyre and A. Henry (eds) *Motivational Dynamics in Language Learning* (pp. 238–259). Bristol: Multilingual Matters.

Cheng, X.T. (2000) Asian students' reticence revisited. *System* 28, 435–446.

Chik, A. and Breidbach, S. (2011) Identity, motivation and autonomy: A tale of two cities. In G. Murray, X. Gao and T. Lamb (eds) *Identity, Motivation and Autonomy in Language Learning* (pp. 145–159). Bristol: Multilingual Matters.

Cilliers, P. (1998) *Complexity and Postmodernism: Understanding Complex Systems*. Abingdon: Routledge.

Cohen, L., Manion, L. and Morrison, K. (2011) *Research Methods in Education* (7th edn). Abingdon: Routledge.

Corbin, J. and Strauss, A. (2008) *Basics of Qualitative Research* (3rd edn). Thousand Oaks, CA: Sage.

Costa Ribas, F. (2012) The motivation of EFL public school teachers: What can self-theories tell us? *Horizontes de Linguística Aplicada* 11 (2), 13–38.

Cowie, N. and Sakui, K. (2011) Crucial but neglected: English as a foreign language teachers' perspectives on learner motivation. In G. Murray, X. Gao and T. Lamb (eds) *Identity, Motivation and Autonomy in Language Learning* (pp. 212–228). Bristol: Multilingual Matters.

Csizér, K. and Kormos, J. (2009) Learning experiences, selves and motivated learning behaviour: A comparative analysis of structural models for Hungarian secondary and university learners of English. In Z. Dörnyei and E. Ushioda (eds) *Motivation, Language Identity and the L2 Self* (pp. 98–119). Bristol: Multilingual Matters.

Csizér, K. and Lukács, G. (2010) The comparative analysis of motivation, attitudes and selves: The case of English and German in Hungary. *System* 38, 1–13.

Damon, W. and Hart, D. (1988) *Self-Understanding in Childhood and Adolescence*. Cambridge: Cambridge University Press.

Davis, B. and Sumara, D. (2005) Challenging images of knowing: Complexity science and educational research. *International Journal of Qualitative Studies in Education* 18 (3), 305–321.

Davis, B. and Sumara, D. (2006) *Complexity and Education: Inquiries into Learning, Teaching, and Research*. Mahwah, NJ: Lawrence Erlbaum.

Davis, B. and Sumara, D. (2010) 'If things were simple...': Complexity in education. *Journal of Evaluation in Clinical Practice* 16 (4), 856–860.

de Bot, K. (2015) Rates of change: Timescales in second language development. In Z. Dornyei, P.D. MacIntyre and A. Henry (eds) *Motivational Dynamics in Language Learning* (pp. 29–37). Bristol: Multilingual Matters.

de Bot, K. and Larsen-Freeman, D. (2011) Researching second language development from a dynamic systems theory perspective. In M. Verspoor, K. de Bot and W. Lowie (eds) *A Dynamic Approach to Second Language Development* (pp. 5–23). Amsterdam: John Benjamins.

de Bot, K., Lowie, W. and Verspoor, M. (2007) A dynamic systems theory approach to second language acquisition. *Bilingualism: Language and Cognition* 10 (1), 7–21.

Destin, M. and Oyserman, D. (2009) From assets to school outcomes: How finances shape children's perceived possibilities and intentions. *Psychological Science* 20 (4), 414–418.

de Wolf, T. and Holvoet, T. (2005) Emergence versus self-organization: Different concepts but promising when combined. In S.A. Brueckner, G. Di Marzo Serugendo, A. Karageorgos and R. Nagpal (eds) *Engineering Self-Organising Systems: Methodologies and Applications* (pp. 1–15). Berlin: Springer.

Dick, B. (2000) Approaching an action research thesis: An overview. See http://www.aral.com.au/resources/phd.html (last accessed 13 March 2016).

Dinham, S. and Scott, C. (2000) Moving into the third, outer domain of teacher satisfaction. *Journal of Educational Administration* 38, 379–396.

Dörnyei, Z. (2001) *Motivational Strategies in the Language Classroom*. Cambridge: Cambridge University Press.

Dörnyei, Z. (2005) *The Psychology of the Language Learner: Individual Differences in Second Language Acquisition*. Mahwah, NJ: Lawrence Erlbaum.

Dörnyei, Z. (2007) *Research Methods in Applied Linguistics*. Oxford: Oxford University Press.

Dörnyei, Z. (2009a) The L2 motivational self system. In Z. Dörnyei and E. Ushioda (eds) *Motivation, Language Identity and the L2 Self* (pp. 9–42). Bristol: Multilingual Matters.

Dörnyei, Z. (2009b) *The Psychology of Second Language Acquisition*. Oxford: Oxford University Press.
Dörnyei, Z. (2014) Researching complex dynamic systems: 'Retrodictive qualitative modelling' in the language classroom. *Language Teaching* 47 (1), 80–91.
Dörnyei, Z. and Chan, L. (2013) Motivation and vision: An analysis of future L2 self images, sensory styles, and imagery capacity across two target languages. *Language Learning* 63 (3), 437–462.
Dörnyei, Z. and Kubanyiova, M. (2013) *Motivating Learners, Motivating Teachers: Building Vision in the Language Classroom*. Cambridge: Cambridge University Press.
Dörnyei, Z. and Murphey, T. (2003) *Group Dynamics in the Language Classroom*. Cambridge: Cambridge University Press.
Dörnyei, Z. and Ushioda, E. (2011) *Teaching and Researching Motivation* (2nd edn). Harlow: Pearson Education.
Dörnyei, Z., Csizer, K. and Nemeth, N. (2006) *Motivation, Language Attitudes and Globalisation: A Hungarian Perspective*. Clevedon: Multilingual Matters.
Dörnyei, Z., MacIntyre, P.D. and Henry, A. (eds) (2015a) *Motivational Dynamics in Language Learning*. Bristol: Multilingual Matters.
Dörnyei, Z., Ibrahim, Z. and Muir, C. (2015b) 'Directed motivational currents': Regulating complex dynamic systems through motivational surges. In Z. Dörnyei, P.D. MacIntyre and A. Henry (eds) *Motivational Dynamics in Language Learning* (pp. 95–105). Bristol: Multilingual Matters.
Doyle, T. and Kim, Y.M. (1999) Teacher motivation and satisfaction in the United States and Korea. *MEXTESOL Journal* 23 (2), 35–48.
Dweck, C.S., Higgins, E.T. and Grant-Pillow, H. (2003) Self-systems give unique meaning to self variables. In M.R. Leary and J.P. Tangney (eds) *Handbook of Self and Identity* (pp. 239–252). New York: Guilford Press.
Edge, J. and Richards, K. (1998) May I see your warrant, please? Justifying outcomes in qualitative research. *Applied Linguistics* 19 (3), 334–356.
Ellis, N.C. and Larsen-Freeman, D. (eds) (2009) *Language as a Complex Adaptive System*. Chichester: Wiley-Blackwell.
Ellis, R. (2012) Editorial. *Language Teaching Research* 16 (3), 285–287.
Eoyang, G.H. (2004) The practitioner's landscape. *E:CO* 6 (1–2), 55–60.
Erikson, M.G. (2007) The meaning of the future: Toward a more specific definition of possible selves. *Review of General Psychology* 11 (4), 348–358.
Erkaya, O.R. (2013) Factors that motivate Turkish EFL teachers. *International Journal of Research Studies in Language Learning* 2 (2), 49–61.
Falout, J. and Maruyama, M. (2004) A comparative study of proficiency and learner demotivation. *The Language Teacher* 28 (8), 3–9.
Falout, J., Murphey, T., Elwood, J. and Hood, M. (2008) Learner voices: Reflections on secondary education. *The Language Teacher* 32 (10), 18–19.
Falout, J., Fukada, Y., Murphey, T. and Fukuda, T. (2013) What's working in Japan? Present communities of imagining. In M.T. Apple, D. Da Silva and T. Fellner (eds) *Language Learning Motivation in Japan* (pp. 245–267). Bristol: Multilingual Matters.
Finch, A. (2010) Critical incidents and language learning: Sensitivity to initial conditions. *System* 38 (3), 422–431.
Five Graces Group (2009) Language is a complex adaptive system: Position paper. *Language Learning* 59 (Suppl. 1), 1–26.
Gardner, R.C. (1985) *Social Psychology and Second Language Learning: The Role of Attitudes and Motivation*. London: Edward Arnold.
Gardner, R.C. (2001) Integrative motivation and second language acquisition. In Z. Dörnyei and R. Schmidt (eds) *Motivation and Second Language Acquisition* (pp. 1–20). Honolulu: University of Hawaii Press.

Gardner, R.C. and Lambert, W.E. (1959) Motivational variables in second language acquisition. *Canadian Journal of Psychology* 13, 266–272.

Gardner, R.C. and Lambert, W.E. (1972) *Attitudes and Motivation in Second Language Learning*. Rowley, MA: Newbury House.

Gladwell, M. (2000) *The Tipping Point: How Little Things Can Make a Big Difference*. Boston, MA: Little, Brown and Company.

Gorsuch, G. (2001) Japanese teachers' perceptions of communicative, audiolingual and yakudoku activities: The plan versus the reality. *Educational Policy Analysis Archives* 9 (10), 1–27. See http://epaa.asu.edu/ojs/article/viewFile/339/465 (last accessed 13 March 2016).

Gottlieb, N. (2005) *Language and Society in Japan*. Cambridge: Cambridge University Press.

Gould, D., Damarjian, N. and Greenleaf, C. (2002) Imagery training for peak performance. In J.L. Van Raalte and B.W. Brewer (eds) *Exploring Sport and Exercise Psychology* (2nd edn, pp. 49–74). Washington, DC: American Psychological Association.

Graddol, D. (2006) *English Next: Why Global English May Mean the End of 'English as a Foreign Language'*. London: British Council.

Green, M.C. and Donahue, J.K. (2009) Simulated worlds: Transportation into narratives. In K. Markman, W.M.P. Klein and J.A. Suhr (eds) *Handbook of Imagination and Mental Simulation* (pp. 241–254). New York: Psychology Press.

Guastello, S.J. and Liebovitch, L.S. (2009) Introduction to nonlinear dynamics and complexity. In S.J. Guastello, M. Koopmans and D. Pincus (eds) *Chaos and Complexity in Psychology* (pp. 1–40). New York: Cambridge University Press.

Hadfield, J. and Dörnyei, Z. (2013) *Motivating Learning*. Harlow: Longman.

Haggis, T. (2008) 'Knowledge must be contextual': Some possible implications of complexity and dynamic systems theories for educational research. *Educational Philosophy and Theory* 40 (1), 158–176.

Hardman, M. (2010) Is complexity theory useful in describing classroom learning? Paper presented at the European Conference on Educational Research, Helsinki, August.

Harter, S. (2003) The development of self-representations during childhood and adolescence. In M.R. Leary and J.P. Tangney (eds) *Handbook of Self and Identity* (pp. 610–642). New York: Guilford Press.

Hasegawa, A. (2004) Student demotivation in the foreign language classroom. *Takushoku Language Studies* 107, 119–136.

Henry, A. (2015) The dynamics of possible selves. In Z. Dörnyei, P.D. MacIntyre and A. Henry (eds) *Motivational Dynamics in Language Learning* (pp. 83–94). Bristol: Multilingual Matters.

Herr, K. and Anderson, G.L. (2005) *The Action Research Dissertation*. Thousand Oaks, CA: Sage.

Hetherington, L. (2013) Complexity thinking and methodology: The potential of 'complex case study' for educational research. *Complicity: An International Journal of Complexity and Education* 10 (1/2), 71–85.

Hettiarachchi, S. (2013) ESL teacher motivation in Sri Lankan public schools. *Journal of Language Teaching and Research* 4 (1), 1–11.

Higgins, E.T. (1987) Self-discrepancy: A theory relating self and affect. *Psychological Review* 94 (3), 319–340.

Higgins, E.T. (1996) Ideals, oughts, and regulatory focus: Affect and motivation from distinct pains and pleasures. In P.M. Gollwitzer and J.A. Bargh (eds) *The Psychology of Action: Linking Cognition and Motivation to Behaviour* (pp. 91–114). New York: Guilford Press.

Higgins, E.T., Friedman, R.S., Harlow, R.E., Chen Idson, L., Ayduk, O.L. and Taylor, A. (2001) Achievement orientations from subjective histories of success: Promotion pride versus prevention pride. *European Journal of Social Psychology* 31, 3–23.

Hiromori, T. (2003) What enhances language learners' motivation? High school English learners' motivation from the perspective of self-determination theory. *JALT Journal* 25 (2), 173–186.

Hiromori, T. (2014) Individual differences in patterns of motivation and conditions that increase motivation in L2 acquisition: A dynamic systems theory perspective. *JACET Journal* 58, 21–37.

Hiver, P. (2015) Once burned, twice shy: The dynamic development of system immunity in teachers. In Z. Dörnyei, P.D. MacIntyre and A. Henry (eds) *Motivational Dynamics in Language Learning* (pp. 214–237). Bristol: Multilingual Matters.

Hock, M.F., Deshler, D.D. and Schumaker, J.B. (2006) Enhancing student motivation through the pursuit of possible selves. In C. Dunkel and J. Kerpelman (eds) *Possible Selves: Theory, Research and Applications* (pp. 205–221). New York: Nova Science.

Horn, J. (2008) Human research and complexity theory. *Educational Philosophy and Theory* 40 (1), 130–143.

Hoyle, R.H. and Sherrill, M.R. (2006) Future orientation in the self-system: Possible selves, self-regulation, and behavior. *Journal of Personality* 74 (6), 1673–1696.

Hu, G.W. (2005) Contextual influences on instructional practices: A Chinese case for an ecological approach to ELT. *TESOL Quarterly* 39 (4), 635–660.

Huang, H., Hsu, C. and Chen, S. (2015) Identification with social role obligations, possible selves, and L2 motivation in foreign language learning. *System* 51, 28–38.

Humphries, S. (2011) The challenges of communicative pedagogy in kosens. *Research Reports of the Council of College English Teachers* 30, 93–102.

Ibarra, H. (1999) Provisional selves: Experimenting with image and identity in professional adaptation. *Administrative Science Quarterly* 44, 764–791.

Idson, L.C., Liberman, N. and Higgins, E.T. (2000) Distinguishing gains from non-losses and losses from non-gains: A regulatory focus perspective on hedonic intensity. *Journal of Experimental Social Psychology* 36 (3), 252–274.

Irie, K. and Brewster, D.R. (2013) One curriculum, three stories: Ideal L2 self and L2-self-discrepancy profiles. In M.T. Apple, D. Da Silva and T. Fellner (eds) *Language Learning Motivation in Japan* (pp. 110–128). Bristol: Multilingual Matters.

Jang, H. (2008) Supporting students' motivation, engagement, and learning during an uninteresting activity. *Journal of Educational Psychology* 100 (4), 798–811.

Jarvis, S. (2001) Research in TESOL: Sunset or a new dawn? *TESOL Research Interest Section Newsletter* 8 (2), 1–7.

Johnson, M.P. (2013) A longitudinal perspective on EFL learning motivation in Japanese engineering students. In M.T. Apple, D. Da Silva and T. Fellner (eds) *Language Learning Motivation in Japan* (pp. 189–205). Bristol: Multilingual Matters.

Jones, L. and Stuth, G. (1997) The uses of mental imagery in athletics: An overview. *Applied and Preventive Psychology* 6, 101–115.

Juarrero, A. (2002) *Dynamics in Action: Intentional Behavior as a Complex System* (1st MIT Press paperback edn). Cambridge, MA: MIT Press.

Kassabgy, O., Boraie, D. and Schmidt, R. (2001) Values, rewards, and job satisfaction in ESL/EFL. In Z. Dörnyei and R. Schmidt (eds) *Motivation and Second Language Acquisition* (pp. 213–237). Honolulu: Second Language Teaching and Curriculum Center, University of Hawai'i.

Kauffman, S. (2008) *Reinventing the Sacred*. New York: Basic Books.

Kaylor, M. and Flores, M.M. (2007) Increasing academic motivation in culturally and linguistically diverse students from low socioeconomic backgrounds. *Journal of Advanced Academics* 19 (1), 66–89.

Keating, D.L. (1990) Adolescent thinking. In S. Feldman and G. Elliot (eds) *At the Threshold: The Developing Adolescent* (pp. 54–89). Cambridge, MA: Harvard University Press.

Kemmelmeier, M. and Oyserman, D. (2001a) The ups and downs of thinking about a successful other: Self-construals and the consequences of social comparisons. *European Journal of Social Psychology* 31, 311–320.

Kemmelmeier, M. and Oyserman, D. (2001b) Gendered influence of downward social comparisons on current and possible selves. *Journal of Social Issues* 57, 129–148.

Kiesner, J., Cadinu, M., Poulin, F. and Bucci, M. (2002) Group identification in early adolescence: Its relation with peer adjustment and its moderator effect on peer influence. *Child Development* 73 (1), 196–208.

Kikuchi, K. (2005) Student and teacher perceptions of learning needs: A cross analysis. *Shiken: JALT Testing & Evaluation SIG Newsletter* 9 (2), 8–20.

Kikuchi, K. (2009) Listening to our learners' voices: What demotivates Japanese high school students? *Language Teaching Research* 13 (4), 453–471.

Kikuchi, K. (2013) Demotivators in the Japanese EFL context. In M.T. Apple, D. Da Silva and T. Fellner (eds) *Language Learning Motivation in Japan* (pp. 206–224). Bristol: Multilingual Matters.

Kikuchi, K. and Browne, C. (2009) English educational policy for high schools in Japan: Ideals vs. reality. *RELC Journal* 40 (2), 172–191.

Kikuchi, K. and Sakai, H. (2009) Japanese learners' demotivation to study English: A survey study. *JALT Journal* 31 (2), 183–204.

Kim, T. (2009) The sociocultural interface between ideal self and ought-to self: A case study of two Korean students' ESL motivation. In Z. Dörnyei and E. Ushioda (eds) *Motivation, Language Identity and the L2 Self* (pp. 274–294). Bristol: Multilingual Matters.

Kimura, Y., Nakata, Y. and Okumura, T. (2001) Language learning motivation of EFL learners in Japan: A cross-sectional analysis of various learning milieus. *JALT Journal* 23 (1), 47–65.

Knox, M. (2006) Gender and possible selves. In C. Dunkel and J. Kerpelman (eds) *Possible Selves: Theory, Research and Applications* (pp. 61–77). New York: Nova Science.

Kohn, A. (1993) *Punished by Rewards: The Trouble with Gold Stars, Incentive Plans, A's, Praise and Other Bribes*. Boston, MA: Houghton Mifflin.

Kojima-Takahashi, C. (2013) Ideal L2 self and university English learners: An interview study. *The Language Teacher* 37 (6), 3–8.

Kolarik, K. (2004, September) Loosening the grip on the communicative ideal – a cultural perspective. Paper presented at the 17th English Australia Educational Conference, Adelaide.

Kormos, J. and Csizér, K. (2008) Age-related differences in the motivation of learning English as a foreign language: Attitudes, selves, and motivated learning behaviour. *Language Learning* 58, 327–355.

Koseneigokyouikunikansuruchousakenkyuuiinkai [Research Committee for the Survey into English Education at Kosen] (2001) *Koutou-senmon gakkouni okeru eigokyoikuno genjouto kadai [Realities and Challenges for English Education in Kosen]*. Motosu: Council of College English Teachers.

Koseneigokyouikunikansuruchousakenkyuuiinkai [Research Committee for the Survey into English Education at Kosen] (2008) *Koutou-senmon gakkouni okeru eigokyouikuno genjouto kadai (2) [Realities and Challenges for English Education in Kosen (2)]*. Motosu: Council of College English Teachers.

Kubanyiova, M. (2009) Possible selves in language teacher development. In Z. Dörnyei and E. Ushioda (eds) *Motivation, Language Identity and the L2 Self* (pp. 314–332). Bristol: Multilingual Matters.

Kubota, R. (2011) Immigration, diversity and language education in Japan: Toward a global approach to teaching English. In P. Seargeant (ed.) *English in Japan in the Era of Globalization* (pp. 101–122). Basingstoke: Palgrave Macmillan.

Kubota, R. and McKay, S. (2009) Globalization and language learning in rural Japan: The role of English in the local linguistic ecology. *TESOL Quarterly* 43 (4), 593–619.

Kuhn, L. (2007) Why utilize complexity principles in social inquiry? *World Futures* 63, 156–175.

Kuhn, L. (2008) Complexity and educational research: A critical reflection. *Educational Philosophy and Theory* 40 (1), 177–189.

Kunishige, T., Takahashi, A. and Harada, N. (2011) An analysis of the students' motivation for studying English at Tokuyama College of Technology. *Research Reports of the Council of College English Teachers* 30, 15–24.

Lamb, M. (2011) Future selves, motivation and autonomy in long-term EFL learning trajectories. In G. Murray, X. Gao and T. Lamb (eds) *Identity, Motivation and Autonomy in Language Learning* (pp. 177–194). Bristol: Multilingual Matters.

Lamb, M. (2012) A self system perspective on young adolescents' motivation to learn English in urban and rural settings. *Language Learning* 62 (4), 997–1023.

Larsen-Freeman, D. (1997) Chaos/complexity science and second language acquisition. *Applied Linguistics* 18 (2), 141–165.

Larsen-Freeman, D. and Cameron, L. (2008a) *Complex Systems and Applied Linguistics*. Oxford: Oxford University Press.

Larsen-Freeman, D. and Cameron, L. (2008b) Research methodology on language development from a complex systems perspective. *Modern Language Journal* 92 (ii), 200–213.

Lasagabaster, D., Doiz, A. and Sierra, J.M. (2014) Introduction. In D. Lasagabaster, A. Doiz and J.M. Sierra (eds) *Motivation and Foreign Language Learning: From Theory to Practice* (pp. 1–5). Amsterdam: John Benjamins.

Leary, M.R. and Tangney, J.P. (2003) The self as an organising construct in the behavioural and social sciences. In M.R. Leary and J.P. Tangney (eds) *Handbook of Self and Identity* (pp. 3–14). New York: Guilford Press.

Lee, A.Y., Aaker, J.L. and Gardner, W.L. (2000) The pleasures and pains of distinct self-construals: The role of interdependence in regulatory focus. *Journal of Personality and Social Psychology* 78 (6), 1112–1134.

Lee, S.J. and Oyserman, D. (2007) Reaching for the future: The education-focused possible selves of low-income mothers. *New Directions for Adult and Continuing Education* 114, 39–49.

Lemke, J.L. (2000) Across the scales of time: Artifacts, activities, and meanings in ecosocial systems. *Mind, Culture, and Activity* 7 (4), 273–290.

Levine, J.M. and Moreland, R.L. (1998) Small groups. In D.T. Gilbert, S.T. Fiske and G. Lindzey (eds) *Handbook of Social Psychology* (Vol. 2, 4th edn, pp. 415–469). Boston, MA: McGraw-Hill.

Lewin, K. (1948) *Resolving Social Conflicts: Selected Papers on Group Dynamics*. New York: Harper & Row.

Lewis, M.D. (2005) Bridging emotion theory and neurobiology through dynamic systems modeling. *Behavioral and Brain Sciences* 28, 169–194.

Lincoln, Y. and Guba, E. (1985) *Naturalistic Inquiry*. Thousand Oaks, CA: Sage.

Lincoln, Y.S. and Guba, E.G. (2005) Paradigmatic controversies, contradictions, and emerging confluences. In N.K. Denzin and Y.S. Lincoln (eds) *Handbook of Qualitative Research* (3rd edn, pp. 191–215). Thousand Oaks, CA: Sage.

Littlewood, W. (2001) Students' attitudes to classroom English learning: A cross-cultural study. *Language Teaching Research* 5 (1), 3–28.

Lytle, S. (2000) Teacher research in the contact zone. In D.P. Pearson (ed.) *Handbook of Reading Research* (Vol. 3, pp. 691–718). Mahwah, NJ: Lawrence Erlbaum.

MacIntyre, P.D., Mackinnon, S.P. and Clement, R. (2009) Toward the development of a scale to assess possible selves as a source of language learning motivation. In Z. Dörnyei and E. Ushioda (eds) *Motivation, Language Identity and the L2 Self* (pp. 193–214). Bristol: Multilingual Matters.

Mackay, J. (2014) Applications and implications of the L2 motivational self system in a Catalan EFL context. In K. Csizer and M. Magid (eds) *The Impact of Self-Concept on Language Learning* (pp. 377–400). Bristol: Multilingual Matters.

Magid, M. (2014) A motivational programme for learners of English: An application of the L2 motivational self system. In K. Csizer and M. Magid (eds) *The Impact of Self-Concept on Language Learning* (pp. 333–356). Bristol: Multilingual Matters.

Malcolm, D. (2013) Motivational challenges for Gulf Arab students studying medicine in English. In E. Ushioda (ed.) *International Perspectives on Motivation: Language Learning and Professional Challenges* (pp. 98–116). Basingstoke: Palgrave Macmillan.

Markus, H.R. (2006) Foreword. In C. Dunkel and J. Kerpelman (eds) *Possible Selves: Theory, Research and Applications* (pp. xi–xiv). New York: Nova Science.

Markus, H.R. and Nurius, P. (1986) Possible selves. *American Psychologist* 41 (9), 954–969.

Markus, H.R. and Ruvolo, A.P. (1989) Possible selves: Personalised representations of goals. In L.A. Pervin (ed.) *Goal Concepts in Personality and Social Psychology* (pp. 211–241). Hillsdale, NJ: Lawrence Erlbaum.

Martin, A.J. (2006) The relationship between teachers' perceptions of student motivation and engagement and teachers' enjoyment of and confidence in teaching. *Asia-Pacific Journal of Teacher Education* 34 (1), 73–93.

Mason, M. (2008) What is complexity theory and what are its implications for educational change? *Educational Philosophy and Theory* 40 (1), 35–49.

Masters, J. (1995) The history of action research. *Action Research Electronic Reader*. Sydney: University of Sydney. See http://www.iopp.ru/pub/21sept06_M2.doc (last accessed 13 March 2016).

McAdams, D.P. (2008) Personal narratives and the life story. In O.P. John, R.W. Robins and L.A. Pervin (eds) *Handbook of Personality: Theory and Research* (3rd edn, pp. 242–262). New York: Guilford Press.

McNiff, J. and Whitehead, J. (2011) *All You Need to Know about Action Research* (2nd edn). London: Sage.

McVeigh, B.J. (2002) *Japanese Higher Education as Myth*. New York: M.E. Sharpe.

Mercer, S. (2011a) Understanding learner agency as a complex dynamic system. *System* 39, 427–436.

Mercer, S. (2011b) *Towards an Understanding of Language Learner Self-Concept*. Heidelberg: Springer.

Mercer, S. (2015) Social network analysis and complex dynamic systems. In Z. Dörnyei, P.D. MacIntyre and A. Henry (eds) *Motivational Dynamics in Language Learning* (pp. 73–82). Bristol: Multilingual Matters.

MEXT (2002) Developing a strategic plan to cultivate 'Japanese with English abilities'. See http://www.mext.go.jp/b_menu/hakusho/html/hpac200201/hpac200201_2_015.html (last accessed 13 March 2016).

MEXT (2003) Action plan to cultivate 'Japanese with English abilities'. See http://www.mext.go.jp/english/topics/03072801.htm (last accessed 13 March 2016).

Miller, R.B. and Brickman, S.J. (2004) A model of future-oriented motivation and self-regulation. *Educational Psychology Review* 16 (1), 9–33.

Mitchell, M. (2009) *Complexity – A Guided Tour*. Oxford: Oxford University Press.

Miura, T. (2010) A retrospective survey of L2 learning motivational changes. *JALT Journal* 32 (1), 29–53.

Miyahara, M. (2015) *Emerging Self-Identities and Emotion in Foreign Language Learning: A Narrative-Oriented Approach*. Bristol: Multilingual Matters.

Mizuno, Y. (2008) Keidanrento 'eigogatsukaeru' nihonjin [Japan Business Federation and Japanese 'who can use English']. *Eigo Kyouiku* [*The English Teachers' Magazine*] 57, 65–67.

Morin, E. (2006) Restricted complexity, general complexity. Paper presented at the Colloquium 'Intelligence de la complexité: épistémologie et pragmatique', Cerisy-La-Salle, France, 26 June (trans. C. Gershenson). See http://cogprints.org/5217/1/Morin.pdf (last accessed 13 March 2016).

Mornane, A. (2009) Adolescent students' views of factors influencing their learning. *International Journal of Learning* 16 (5), 221–230.

Morrison, K. (2006) Complexity theory and education. Paper presented at the Asia-Pacific Educational Research Association International Conference, Hong Kong, November.

Muir, C. and Dörnyei, Z. (2013) Directed motivational currents: Using vision to create effective motivational pathways. *Studies in Second Language Learning and Teaching* 3 (3), 357–375.

Murphey, T. and Arao, H. (2001) Reported belief changes through near peer role modeling. *TESL-EJ* 5 (3). See http://tesl-ej.org/ej19/a1.html

Murphey, T., Falout, J., Fukada, Y. and Fukada, T. (2012) Group dynamics: Collaborative agency in present communities of imagination. In S. Mercer, S. Ryan and M. Williams (eds) *Psychology for Language Learning: Insights from Research, Theory and Practice* (pp. 220–238). Basingstoke: Palgrave Macmillan.

Murphey, T., Falout, J., Fukada, T. and Fukada, Y. (2014) Socio-dynamic motivating through idealising classmates. *System* 45, 242–253.

Newton, P. and Burgess, D. (2008) Exploring types of educational action research: Implications for research validity. *International Journal of Qualitative Methods* 7 (4), 18–30.

Nitta, R. (2013) Understanding motivational evolution in the EFL classroom: A longitudinal study from a dynamic systems perspective. In M.T. Apple, D. Da Silva and T. Fellner (eds) *Language Learning Motivation in Japan* (pp. 268–290). Bristol: Multilingual Matters.

Noffke, S. (1997) Professional, personal, and political dimensions of action research. *Review of Research in Education* 2, 305–343.

Norman, C. and Aron, A. (2003) Aspects of possible self that predict motivation to achieve or avoid it. *Journal of Experimental Social Psychology* 39, 500–507.

Nowak, A., Vallacher, R.R. and Zochowski, M. (2005) The emergence of personality: Dynamic foundations of individual variation. *Developmental Review* 25, 351–385.

Nunan, D. (2004) *Task-Based Language Teaching*. Cambridge: Cambridge University Press.

Nunan, D. and Bailey, K.M. (2009) *Exploring Second Language Classroom Research: A Comprehensive Guide*. Boston, MA: Heinle.

Ohata, K. and Fukao, A. (2014) L2 learners' conceptions of academic reading and themselves as academic readers. *System* 42, 81–92.

Op't Eynde, P. and Turner, J.E. (2006) Focusing on the complexity of emotion-motivation issues in academic learning: A dynamical component systems approach. *Educational Psychology Review* 18, 361–376.

Ortega, L. and Iberri-Shea, G. (2005) Longitudinal research in second language acquisition: Recent trends and future directions. *Annual Review of Applied Linguistics* 25, 26–45.

Osberg, D., Biesta, G. and Cilliers, P. (2008) From representation to emergence: Complexity's challenge to the epistemology of schooling. *Educational Philosophy and Theory* 40 (1), 213–227.

Otani, H. (2001) Seeking definite motivations for kosen students to study English. *Research Reports of Kita-Kyuushuu Kosen* 34, 199–208.

Oyserman, D. and Fryberg, S. (2006) The possible selves of diverse adolescents: Content and function across gender, race and national origin. In C. Dunkel and J. Kerpelman (eds) *Possible Selves: Theory, Research and Applications* (pp. 17–39). New York: Nova Science.

Oyserman, D. and James, L. (2009) Possible selves: From content to process. In K. Markman, W.M.P. Klein and J.A. Suhr (eds) *Handbook of Imagination and Mental Simulation* (pp. 373–394). New York: Psychology Press.

Oyserman, D. and James, L. (2011) Possible identities. In S.J. Schwartz, K. Luycyx and V.L. Vignoles (eds) *Handbook of Identity Theory and Research* (Vol. 1, pp. 117–145). New York: Springer.

Oyserman, D. and Markus, H.R. (1990) Possible selves and delinquency. *Journal of Personality and Social Psychology* 59 (1), 112–125.

Oyserman, D., Terry, K. and Bybee, D. (2002) A possible selves intervention to enhance school involvement. *Journal of Adolescence* 25, 313–326.

Oyserman, D., Bybee, D., Terry, K. and Hart-Johnson, T. (2004) Possible selves as roadmaps. *Journal of Research in Personality* 38, 130–149.

Oyserman, D., Bybee, D. and Terry, K. (2006) Possible selves and academic outcomes: How and when possible selves impel action. *Journal of Personality and Social Psychology* 91 (1), 188–204.

Page, S.E. (2011) *Diversity and Complexity*. Princeton, NJ: Princeton University Press.

Paiva, V.L.M.O. (2011) Identity, motivation and autonomy in second language acquisition from the perspective of complex adaptive systems. In G. Murray, X. Gao and T. Lamb (eds) *Identity, Motivation and Autonomy in Language Learning* (pp. 57–72). Bristol: Multilingual Matters.

Papi, M. and Abdollahzadeh, E. (2012) Teacher motivational practice, student motivation, and possible L2 selves: An examination in the Iranian EFL context. *Language Learning* 62 (2), 571–594.

Pelletier, L.G., Séguin-Lévesque, C. and Legault, L. (2002) Pressure from above and pressure from below as determinants of teachers' motivation and teaching behaviors. *Journal of Educational Psychology* 94 (1), 186–196.

Pennington, M.C. (1995) Work satisfaction, motivation and commitment in teaching English as a second language. Unpublished manuscript, University of Luton. ERIC Document ED 404850.

Phelan, S.E. (2001) What is complexity science, really? *Emergence* 3 (1), 120–136.

Phelps, R. (2002) Mapping the complexity of computer learning: Journeying beyond teaching for competency to facilitating computer capability. Unpublished doctoral dissertation, Southern Cross University, Australia.

Phelps, R. and Hase, S. (2002) Complexity and action research: Exploring the theoretical and methodological connection. *Educational Action Research* 10 (3), 507–524.

Phelps, R. and Graham, A. (2010) Exploring the complementarities between complexity and action research: The story of Technology Together. *Cambridge Journal of Education* 40 (2), 183–197.

Pigott, J.D. (2011) Self and motivation in compulsory English classes in Japan. In A. Stewart (ed.) *JALT2010 Conference Proceedings* (pp. 540–550). Tokyo: JALT.

Pigott, J.D. (2012a) Motivation and complex systems theory: An exploratory view of the motivation of four Japanese university students. *OnCUE Journal* 6 (2), 27–47.

Pigott, J.D. (2012b) A call for a multifaceted approach to language learning motivation research: Combining complexity, humanistic, and critical perspectives. *Studies in Second Language Learning and Teaching* 2 (3), 349–366.

Pigott, J.D. (2012c) It's for your own (country's) good: The struggle to be a motivated English learner in Japan. In A. Stewart and N. Sonda (eds) *JALT2011 Conference Proceedings* (pp. 426–433). Tokyo: JALT.

Pizzolato, J.E. (2006) Achieving college student possible selves: Navigating the space between commitment and achievement of long-term identity goals. *Cultural Diversity and Ethnic Minority Psychology* 12 (1), 57–69.

Plimmer, G. and Schmidt, A. (2007) Possible selves and career transition: It's who you want to be, not what you want to do. *New Directions for Adult and Continuing Education* 114, 61–74.

Porto, M. (2007) Learning diaries in the English as a foreign language classroom: A tool for accessing learners' perceptions of lessons and developing learner autonomy and reflection. *Foreign Language Annals* 40 (4), 672–696.

Radford, M. (2007) Action research and the challenge of complexity. *Cambridge Journal of Education* 37 (2), 263–278.

Radford, M. (2008) Prediction, control and the challenge to complexity. *Oxford Review of Education* 34 (5), 505–520.

Rapley, D.J. (2010) Learning to speak English: Japanese junior high school student views. *The Language Teacher* 34 (6), 33–40.
Reason, P. and Bradbury, H. (2006) Introduction: Inquiry and participation in search of a world worthy of human aspiration. In P. Reason and H. Bradbury (eds) *The Handbook of Action Research* (Concise Paperback edn, pp. 1–14). London: Sage.
Reeve, J. and Jang, H. (2006) What teachers say and do to support students' autonomy during a learning activity. *Journal of Educational Psychology* 98 (1), 209–218.
Reeve, J., Bolt, E. and Cai, Y. (1999) Autonomy supportive teachers: How they teach and motivate students. *Journal of Educational Psychology* 91 (3), 537–548.
Reeve, J., Jang, H., Hardre, P. and Omura, M. (2002) Providing a rationale in an autonomy-supportive way as a strategy to motivate others during an uninteresting activity. *Motivation and Emotion* 26 (3), 183–207.
Renninger, K.A., Bachrach, J.E. and Posey, S.K.E. (2008) Learner interest and achievement motivation. In M.L. Maehr, S.A. Karabenick and T.C. Urdan (eds) *Advances in Motivation and Achievement 15: Social Psychological Perspectives* (pp. 461–491). Bingley: Emerald.
Richards, K. (2006) 'Being the teacher': Identity and classroom conversation. *Applied Linguistics* 27 (1), 51–77.
Richardson, K. and Cilliers, P. (2001) Special editors' introduction: What is complexity science? A view from different directions. *Emergence* 3 (1), 5–23.
Ronfeldt, M. and Grossman, P. (2008) Becoming a professional: Experimenting with possible selves in professional preparation. *Teacher Education Quarterly* (Summer), 41–60.
Ruvolo, A.P. and Markus, H.R. (1992) Possible selves and performance: The power of self-relevant imagery. *Social Cognition* 10 (1), 95–124.
Ryan, G.W. and Bernard, H.R. (2003) Techniques to identify themes. *Field Methods* 15 (1), 85–109.
Ryan, R.M. and Deci, E.L. (2002) Overview of self-determination theory: An organismic dialectical perspective. In E.L. Deci and R.M. Ryan (eds) *Handbook of Self-Determination Research* (pp. 3–33). Rochester: University of Rochester Press.
Ryan, S. (2009a) Self and identity in L2 motivation in Japan: The ideal L2 self and Japanese learners of English. In Z. Dörnyei and E. Ushioda (eds) *Motivation, Language Identity and the L2 Self* (pp. 120–143). Bristol: Multilingual Matters.
Ryan, S. (2009b) Ambivalence and commitment, liberation and challenge: Investigating the attitudes of young Japanese people towards the learning of English. *Journal of Multilingual and Multicultural Development* 30 (5), 405–420.
Ryan, S. and Mercer, S. (2011) Natural talent, natural acquisition and abroad: Learner attributions of agency in language learning. In G. Murray, X. Gao and T. Lamb (eds) *Identity, Motivation and Autonomy in Language Learning* (pp. 160–176). Bristol: Multilingual Matters.
Sa, J. (2002) Diary writing: An interpretative research method of teaching and learning. *Educational Research and Evaluation* 8 (2), 149–168.
Sade, L.A. (2009) Identidade e Aprendizagem de Ingles sob a Otica do Caos e dos Sistemas Complexos [Identity and apprenticeship of English under the lens of chaos and complex systems]. Unpublished doctoral dissertation, Universidade Federal de Minas Gerais, Brazil.
Sade, L.A. (2011) Emerging selves, language learning and motivation through the lens of chaos. In G. Murray, X. Gao and M. Lamb (eds) *Identity, Motivation and Autonomy in Language Learning* (pp. 42–56). Bristol: Multilingual Matters.
Sakai, H. and Kikuchi, K. (2009) An analysis of demotivators in the EFL classroom. *System* 37, 57–69.
Samimy, K.K. and Kobayashi, C. (2004) Toward the development of intercultural communicative competence: Theoretical and pedagogical implications for Japanese English teachers. *JALT Journal* 26 (2), 245–261.

Sampson, R.J. (2010) Student-negotiated lesson style. *RELC Journal* 41 (3), 283–299.
Sampson, R.J. (2012) The language-learning self, self-enhancement activities, and self perceptual change. *Language Teaching Research* 16 (3), 313–331.
Sampson, R.J. (2016) Same classroom, different stories: Motivational outcomes and the non-linear context of action. Manuscript in preparation.
Sampson, R.J. (in press) EFL teacher motivation in-situ: Co-adaptive processes, openness and relational motivation over interacting timescales. *Studies in Second Language Learning and Teaching*.
Sato, R. (2010) Reconsidering the effectiveness and suitability of PPP and TBLT in the Japanese EFL classroom. *JALT Journal* 32 (2), 189–200.
Sato, R. (2011) The author responds: A reply to responses to 'Reconsidering the effectiveness and suitability of PPP and TBLT in the Japanese classroom'. *JALT Journal* 33 (1), 72–76.
Schumann, J.H. (2015) Foreword. In Z. Dörnyei, P.D. MacIntyre and A. Henry (eds) *Motivational Dynamics in Language Learning* (pp. xv–xix). Bristol: Multilingual Matters.
Schunk, D.H. and Pajares, F. (2007) Competence perceptions and academic functioning. In A.J. Elliot and C.S. Dweck (eds) *Handbook of Competence and Motivation* (pp. 85–104). New York: Guilford Press.
Seargeant, P. (2009) *The Idea of English in Japan*. Bristol: Multilingual Matters.
Seargeant, P. (2011a) Introduction: English in Japan in the era of globalization. In P. Seargeant (ed.) *English in Japan in the Era of Globalization* (pp. 1–12). Basingstoke: Palgrave Macmillan.
Seargeant, P. (2011b) The symbolic meaning of visual English in the social landscape of Japan. In P. Seargeant (ed.) *English in Japan in the Era of Globalization* (pp. 187–204). Basingstoke: Palgrave Macmillan.
Shah, J. and Higgins, E.T. (1997) Expectancy x value effects: Regulatory focus as a determinant of magnitude and direction. *Journal of Personality and Social Psychology* 73, 447–458.
Shah, J., Higgins, E.T. and Friedman, R.S. (1998) Performance incentives and means: How regulatory focus influences goal attainment. *Journal of Personality and Social Psychology* 74 (2), 285–293.
Sheldon, K.M. and Lyubomirsky, S. (2006) How to increase and sustain positive emotion: The effects of expressing gratitude and visualizing best possible selves. *Journal of Positive Psychology* 1 (2), 73–82.
Somekh, B. (1995) The contribution of action research to development in social endeavours: A position paper on action research methodology. *British Educational Research Journal* 21 (3), 339–355.
Stanlaw, J. (2004) *Japanese English: Language and Culture Contact*. Hong Kong: Hong Kong University Press.
Swain, M., Kinnear, P. and Steinman, L. (2011) *Sociocultural Theory in Second Language Education: An Introduction through Narratives* (1st edn). Bristol: Multilingual Matters.
Sybing, R. (2011) A response to criticism of TBLT in Japan's language classrooms. *JALT Journal* 33 (1), 67–69.
Taguchi, T., Magid, M. and Papi, M. (2009) The L2 motivational self system among Japanese, Chinese and Iranian learners of English: A comparative study. In Z. Dörnyei and E. Ushioda (eds) *Motivation, Language Identity and the L2 Self* (pp. 66–97). Bristol: Multilingual Matters.
Takahashi, K. (2013) *Language Learning, Gender and Desire*. Bristol: Multilingual Matters.
Tanaka, H. (2009) Enhancing intrinsic motivation at three levels: The effects of motivational strategies. *JALT Journal* 31 (2), 227–250.
Tanaka, H. and Hiromori, T. (2007) The effects of educational intervention that enhances intrinsic motivation of L2 students. *JALT Journal* 29 (1), 59–80.
Taylor, F. (2013) *Self and Identity in Adolescent Foreign Language Learning*. Bristol: Multilingual Matters.

Taylor, S.E., Pham, L.B., Rivkin, I.D. and Armor, D.A. (1998) Harnessing the imagination: Mental simulation, self-regulation, and coping. *American Psychologist* 53 (4), 429–439.

Thelen, E. and Smith, L.B. (1994) *A Dynamic Systems Approach to the Development of Cognition and Action*. Cambridge, MA: MIT Press.

Ueki, M. and Takeuchi, O. (2013) Exploring the concept of the ideal L2 self in an Asian EFL context: The case of Japanese university students. *Journal of Asian TEFL* 10, 25–45.

Unemori, P., Omoregie, H. and Markus, H.R. (2004) Self-portraits: Possible selves in European-American, Chilean, Japanese and Japanese-American cultural contexts. *Self and Identity* 3, 321–338.

Urdan, T. and Turner, J.C. (2007) Competence motivation in the classroom. In A.J. Elliot and C.S. Dweck (eds) *Handbook of Competence and Motivation* (pp. 297–317). New York: Guilford Press.

Urick, S.T. (2011) On methodology in Japanese secondary English classrooms. *JALT Journal* 33 (1), 70–71.

Ushioda, E. (2001) Language learning at university: Exploring the role of motivational thinking. In Z. Dörnyei and R. Schmidt (eds) *Motivation and Second Language Acquisition* (pp. 93–125). Honolulu: University of Hawai'i Press.

Ushioda, E. (2009) A person-in-context relational view of emergent motivation, self and identity. In Z. Dörnyei and E. Ushioda (eds) *Motivation, Language Identity and the L2 Self* (pp. 215–228). Bristol: Multilingual Matters.

Ushioda, E. (2011a) Context matters: A brief commentary on the papers by Housen *et al.* and Munoz. *International Review of Applied Linguistics in Language Teaching* 49 (2), 187–189.

Ushioda, E. (2011b) Motivating learners to speak as themselves. In G. Murray, X. Gao and T. Lamb (eds) *Identity, Motivation and Autonomy in Language Learning* (pp. 11–24). Bristol: Multilingual Matters.

Ushioda, E. (2013a) Motivation and ELT: Looking ahead to the future. In E. Ushioda (ed.) *International Perspectives on Motivation: Language Learning and Professional Challenges* (pp. 233–239). Basingstoke: Palgrave Macmillan.

Ushioda, E. (2013b) Motivation and ELT: Global issues and local concerns. In E. Ushioda (ed.) *International Perspectives on Motivation: Language Learning and Professional Challenges* (pp. 1–17). Basingstoke: Palgrave Macmillan.

Ushioda, E. (2015) Context and complex dynamic systems theory. In Z. Dornyei, P.D. MacIntyre and A. Henry (eds) *Motivational Dynamics in Language Learning* (pp. 47–54). Bristol: Multilingual Matters.

Ushioda, E. and Dörnyei, Z. (2009) Motivation, language identities and the L2 self: A theoretical overview. In Z. Dörnyei and E. Ushioda (eds) *Motivation, Language Identity and the L2 Self* (pp. 1–8). Bristol: Multilingual Matters.

Vallacher, R.R. and Nowak, A. (2009) The dynamics of human experience: Fundamentals of dynamic social psychology. In S.J. Guastello, M. Koopmans and D. Pincus (eds) *Chaos and Complexity in Psychology* (pp. 370–401). New York: Cambridge University Press.

van Geert, P. (2008) The dynamic systems approach in the study of L1 and L2 acquisition: An introduction. *Modern Language Journal* 92 (ii), 179–199.

van Lier, L. (2004) *The Ecology and Semiotics of Language Learning: A Sociocultural Perspective*. Boston, MA: Kluwer Academic.

Vauras, M. and Volet, S. (2013) The study of interpersonal regulation in learning and its challenge to the research methodology. In S. Volet and M. Vauras (eds) *Interpersonal Regulation of Learning and Motivation: Methodological Advances* (pp. 1–13). Abingdon: Routledge.

Verspoor, M.H., de Bot, K. and Lowie, W. (eds) (2011) *A Dynamic Approach to Second Language Development: Methods and Techniques*. Amsterdam: John Benjamins.

Waninge, F., Dörnyei, Z. and de Bot, K. (2014) Motivational dynamics in language learning: Change, stability and context. *Modern Language Journal* 98 (3), 704–723.

Weaver, W. (1948) Science and complexity. *American Scientist* 36, 536–544.

Wentzel, K.R. (2005) Peer relationships, motivation, and academic performance at school. In A.J. Elliot and C.S. Dweck (eds) *Handbook of Competence and Motivation* (pp. 279–296). New York: Guilford Press.

Wetherell, M., Taylor, S. and Yates, S. (2001) *Discourse as Data*. London: Sage.

Wigfield, A. and Wagner, A.L. (2005) Competence, motivation, and identity development during adolescence. In A.J. Elliot and C.S. Dweck (eds) *Handbook of Competence and Motivation* (pp. 222–239). New York: Guildford Press.

Willis, D. and Willis, J. (2007) *Doing Task-Based Teaching*. Oxford: Oxford University Press.

Xiao, L. (2006) Bridging the gap between teaching styles and learning styles: A cross-cultural perspective. *TESL-EJ* 10 (3), 1–15.

Yamagami, M. and Tollefson, J.W. (2011) Elite discourses of globalization in Japan: The role of English. In P. Seargeant (ed.) *English in Japan in the Era of Globalization* (pp. 15–37). Basingstoke: Palgrave Macmillan.

Yano, Y. (2011) English as an international language and 'Japanese English'. In P. Seargeant (ed.) *English in Japan in the Era of Globalization* (pp. 125–142). Basingstoke: Palgrave Macmillan.

Yashima, T. (2000) Orientations and motivation in foreign language learning: A study of Japanese college students. *JACET Bulletin* 31, 121–133.

Yashima, T. (2002) Willingness to communicate in a second language: The Japanese EFL context. *Modern Language Journal* 86 (i), 54–66.

Yashima, T. (2009) International posture and the ideal L2 self in the Japanese EFL context. In Z. Dörnyei and E. Ushioda (eds) *Motivation, Language Identity and the L2 Self* (pp. 144–163). Bristol: Multilingual Matters.

Yashima, T. and Arano, K. (2015) Understanding EFL learners' motivational dynamics: A three-level model from a dynamic systems and sociocultural perspective. In Z. Dörnyei, P.D. MacIntyre and A. Henry (eds) *Motivational Dynamics in Language Learning* (pp. 95–105). Bristol: Multilingual Matters.

Yoshida, K. (2003) Language education policy in Japan: The problem of espousing objectives versus practice. *Modern Language Journal* 87 (2), 290–292.

Zhenhui, R. (2001) Matching teaching styles with learning styles in East Asian contexts. *Internet TESL Journal* 7 (7). See http://iteslj.org/Techniques/Zhenhui-TeachingStyles.html (last accessed 13 March 2016).

Zimmerman, D.H. (1998) Discoursal identities and social identities. In C. Antaki and S. Widdicombe (eds) *Identities in Talk* (pp. 87–106). London: Sage.

Zuber-Skerritt, O. (1996) Introduction. In O. Zuber-Skerritt (ed.) *New Directions in Action Research* (pp. 3–9). London: Falmer.

Index

action research 37–39, 52–53, 182
  benefits and drawbacks 39, 62–63, 68–70, 177–180
  and complex systems theory 42–45, 179–180
  philosophical foundations 39–40
adolescence 14–16, 19, 21, 29, 31–32, 34, 90–91, 172, 175
affect (and emotion) 27, 29, 62, 81, 90, 93, 96, 101, 107, 110, 112, 117, 121, 125, 132, 143–144, 146, 152–153, 159, 161, 166–168
agency 8, 57, 95, 117, 125
agents (in complex systems theory) 73–78, 85, 112, 116, 138, 141, 145, 151–153
attractor states 44, 76, 104–105

Burns, Anne 8, 38–40, 44–45, 100

Cilliers, Paul 41–42, 74–75, 77, 79, 85, 105, 176
classroom interactions 16, 56, 62, 64, 67, 78–79, 89, 95, 111–117, 125, 130, 133–134, 140, 147, 149, 150–151, 153, 164–169, 181, 183, 185
co-adaptation 6, 41, 44–45, 75, 78, 82, 104–105, 123–126, 131–132, 134, 136, 140, 151–152, 166–167, 172, 182–183
competence 21–23, 58–59, 63–64, 76, 95–96, 98–99, 108–109, 114, 121–122, 128, 145, 172
complex systems (theory) 6, 73
  and education 6–7, 77–79, 80–82, 83–85
  philosophical foundations 40–42
  properties 73–77
  and research 7–8, 41–45, 78–79, 80–82, 85, 102, 142, 169, 179–180, 182–185
  see also agents, attractor states, co-adaptation, emergence, non-linearity, openness, phase-shifts, repeller states, self-organisation, state space, timescales
comprehension (in lessons) 22, 54, 56–57, 101, 107, 110–111, 114, 135–136, 140
context 7–9, 28, 31, 52, 74, 81, 83–85, 100–102, 125, 137–138, 142, 145, 151–152, 162, 168
control parameters 105, 108, 113, 118

Davis, Brent 8, 42–45, 74, 78, 84–85, 103, 112, 116–117, 139–140, 147, 153
De Bot, Kees 44, 108, 164
demotivation 2, 15–16, 21–22, 24, 54, 87, 183
distributed control 74, 153
diversity 62–63, 74, 80, 112, 119, 150, 153, 179
Dörnyei, Zoltan 1, 5, 8, 13, 15, 26–32, 35, 44, 50, 63–64, 82, 91, 98, 114, 120–121, 142, 151–153, 161–162, 183
  L2 motivational self system 28–32, 63, 102–103, 104–106, 162–163, 168–169, 175–176

emergence 77, 141–145, 150–153, 183
expectations 2, 13, 18, 27–28, 31, 33, 65, 84, 90, 94, 96–100, 115, 121–122, 161–162, 175

Falout, Joseph 15, 22, 24, 82, 171
family influence 31, 65, 94, 99–100
fearing self (also feared self) 32, 67, 109–110, 114–115, 121–122, 161, 166
feedback 21, 75, 116, 119, 128–131, 134, 166, 183

globalization 3, 17, 23, 87, 96–97, 158, 163

Higgins, E. Tory 27–28, 32
Hiromori, Tomohito 21–22, 108, 169

ideal self 27–32, 34–35, 56–57, 63, 67, 86–89, 94, 97, 103, 108–109, 114, 117, 120–121, 159–161, 163–164, 174, 176
initial conditions (in complex systems theory) 44, 76
interactions (in complex systems theory) 6–7, 41–43, 74–77, 84–85, 102–103, 105, 129, 141–142, 145

kosen 2, 18–19, 24, 31, 47, 160
Kikuchi, Keita 15–16, 23–24, 87, 91, 171

L2 learning experience (in L2 motivational self system) 28–35, 104–105, 162–163, 166, 169, 170, 172
language education in Japan 1–3, 14–15, 16, 22–25, 87, 97, 99, 101, 161, 171–173
language use 4, 87–89, 92–93, 96, 98–99, 105–111, 115–116, 136, 146–147, 160–161, 163, 166, 170–172
  and success 3–4, 21–23, 59, 93, 107–109, 111–112, 118, 128, 147, 172
Larsen-Freeman, Dianne 6, 9, 42–43, 50, 74–75, 78–79, 103–105, 130, 151–152, 180
longitudinal research 43, 46, 69, 80, 123, 163, 181–183

Markus, Hazel Rose 27–30, 32, 146
Mercer, Sarah 93, 95, 158, 184
motivation (definition) 1, 13, 104
Murphey, Tim 118, 149, 152–153, 175

non-linearity (in complex systems theory) 74–76, 80–81, 91, 103, 119–120, 138–140, 168, 180

occupation (and English use) 18–20, 54–55, 87–88, 99, 109–110, 114, 118–122, 158–159, 172
openness 74–75, 83–85, 102–103, 146
ought-to self 27–29, 31–32, 97–98, 103, 114–115, 121, 160–162, 175

Oyserman, Daphna 29–35, 37, 94, 158, 175–176

participant journals 49–50, 117–118, 122, 177–178, 187
past experience 4, 7, 15, 24, 54, 80, 82, 86–87, 98, 107–108, 119, 125, 127–128, 132, 160, 163, 174
peer group 5, 31, 35, 63, 89–91, 94, 97–98, 100, 112, 115, 118–119, 133, 149, 153, 172–174
personality 81, 89–91, 117
phase-shifts (in complex systems theory) 76–77, 126–127, 131, 133, 167, 172
Pigott, Julian 81, 97, 151, 161–162, 175–176
plausibility (of future self) 30, 56, 59, 94, 113–114, 146, 159, 174
possible self theory 27–28, 29–30, 33
present-self future-self gap 28–30, 56–57, 59–60, 109, 120

redundancy 74, 112, 119, 153
relevance (of study) 13, 16–19, 34, 54, 91, 93–94, 118–119, 175
repeller states 76, 104–105, 109, 121
researcher positioning in research process 8–9, 47–48, 180–182
revising classroom self 110–111, 115–116, 122–123, 127, 133–135, 140, 159, 163, 168
Ryan, Steven 20, 26, 95, 160

self 5, 16, 19, 27–28, 30, 90–91, 93, 99, 104–106, 109–110, 123, 125, 157–164, 169, 173
  self discrepancy theory 28–30, 32
self-organisation 75–78, 133, 137–140, 183
self-reflection 5, 29–30, 47, 62, 67–68, 108, 118, 122, 134, 140, 163, 167, 175–176
social comparisons 32, 67, 97, 107, 113–114, 118–119, 136, 140, 163, 166, 172
state space 44, 76, 104–106, 123–125
strategies 30–31, 34, 57–58, 61, 140, 192–193, 195
Sumara, Dennis 8, 42–45, 74, 78, 84–85, 103, 112, 116–117, 139–140, 147, 153

task-based learning 45, 55, 105, 125, 127, 141, 171–173
teacher/researcher identity 39–40, 52, 54–55, 57, 64, 69, 95–96, 128–130, 179
timescales (in complex systems theory) 7, 9, 75–76, 81, 123, 129–131, 133, 142, 166
transitions 5, 16, 21, 126–127, 131–133, 137, 158–159, 167–168, 172
transportable identities 89–91, 93–96, 132, 166–167

Ushioda, Ema 8–9, 13, 26, 29–32, 44, 63, 81, 89, 99, 111, 114, 168–169

vision (and image/imagery) 2–3, 20–21, 27, 29–35, 54–55, 57, 59–63, 66, 87–88, 94, 97, 109, 114, 117, 120–123, 133–134, 152, 158–163, 173–176, 198

Yashima, Tomoko 17, 19–20, 80–81, 118

For Product Safety Concerns and Information please contact our EU Authorised Representative:

Easy Access System Europe

Mustamäe tee 50

10621 Tallinn

Estonia

gpsr.requests@easproject.com